The Service of Beauty

ISBN: 1-4392-5220-3
ISBN-13: 9781439252208
Library of Congress Control Number: 2009907677

To order additional copies, please contact us.
BookSurge
www.booksurge.com
1-866-308-6235
orders@booksurge.com

The Service of Beauty

Discovering Art and Ethics in Jewish Worship

Andrew Vogel Ettin

2009

Dedication

For Carole

and our dears: Emily, Anna and Susannah

Bread and Roses

Table of Contents

Acknowledgements

I appreciate the years of encouragement and the lessons learned from my congregation, Temple Israel, in Salisbury, NC and the other congregations that I have been closely associated with: Temple Emanuel (Winston-Salem), Congregation Emanuel (Statesville) and the Blumenthal Home for the Aged.

I am profoundly grateful for the inspiration and encouragement of the rabbis who have been my teachers, mentors, colleagues and friends in Aleph: Alliance for Jewish Renewal, especially Marcia Prager, Shaya Isenberg, Shefa Gold, Louis Sutker and Pamela Frydman Baugh, and Hazzan Jack Kessler. At the deepest level this book stems from the challenging, illuminating and beautiful teachings of our spiritual guide, Reb Zalman Schachter-Shalomi sh'lita.

Among my Wake Forest University colleagues, Ulrike Wiethaus merits special appreciation as a fellow wayfarer along mystical paths.

I am deeply appreciative of Rebecca Valla for her insight and her wisdom about spirituality and beauty.

My wife, Carole Maxwell Stuart, has been my companion on this journey and many others. Her gifts are beyond words. One that deserves specific mention is her photograph of the pomegranate blossom flowering in the Alhambra that adorns the cover.

July 31, 2009-10 Av 5769
Ending the week of the Sabbath of Comfort, *Shabbat Nachamu-Shabbat V'etchanan* on which we read the Ten Commandments and *Sh'ma Yisrael*

Chapter 1
Serious Enjoyment

Food for thought

Light and color, fragrance, sound, movement, taste and texture: our senses are part of our experience of living, and if we are made in the divine image, they must also be part of our experience of spirit, of what some of us call (for want of a precise word) God. Our senses connect us with both beauty and spirituality. We can feel that connection in the presence of the austere simplicity of a single candle casting flickering shadows against a white wall or the vast magnificence of a luminous Pacific sunset. In company with the aesthetic feeling comes an ethical sensibility, a sort of piety that wants to preserve and protect and remember that beauty, recognizing it as having intrinsic value that goes beyond its own place and moment. Through this piety we may intuit a complex of moral obligations. Such ethical beauty animates the deep core of religious rituals, and in this book we will explore its presence in the rituals of Judaism.

The Service of Beauty often refers to works of art, music and literature, many of which are not religious in any obvious way. Although this is a book about religious expression, many of our most profoundly spiritual experiences come to us outside of explicitly religious situations. Before I became a rabbi I was a professor of literature, as I still am; but before I was either of those, I was raised in a secular Jewish home to love reading and the arts. In our apartment there was a large framed photograph of my mother's Russian-born and largely self-educated grandfather, for whom I was named when I was born a month after his death. Dapperly dressed and hatted, he stands on a city street with a large book tucked under his arm. It was Emil Ludwig's biography of Michelangelo. In the household in which I grew up, nobody had gone to college; they had not traveled beyond their little section of America; they neither owned nor played any musical instrument; they attended no synagogue; they worked hard for long hours, and they had no two-day weekends. But the apartment was filled with well-worn books for reading, not show. The New York Philharmonic and the Metropolitan Opera performed regularly in our three-room flat, thanks to the radio. Caruso, whose recordings had made my great-grandfather cry, sang for us through our record player. In our living room that seemed not much bigger than a balcony, Pablo Casals played the cello and Maria Tallchief danced ballet when we got a television. With access to a bus and a great city nearby, I saw for myself wonderful paintings and sculpture, splendid buildings, modern dance and ballet. In time, I too performed on stage in minor ways.

But there is a more profound reason for approaching Jewish religious practices from the perspectives of the arts. Artists, like mystics—or "the lunatic, the lover and the poet" in Shakespeare's terms, for the mystic is some of all three—communicate in boundary-bridging ways. They do so from their own time and place and through their specific vocabulary, the language that comes from their art form or their religion. Whistler and Gauguin each understood Asian art in their personal terms; Paul Simon and Ladysmith Black Mambazo joined in a musical conversation that brought together their separate harmonic and linguistic cultures in mutual understanding; thus too, Yo-Yo Ma and the Silk Road Project, Nigel Kennedy and the Kroke Band. In earlier centuries, Jewish, Muslim Sufi, and Christian mystics explored techniques and insights together, nourishing their own religious ideas from a spiritual storehouse to which they all had their own keys and entrances, and in which they sometimes met, conversed and shared. Some of us attempt to carry forth that tradition by learning with and from one another today, both as scholars and as people who care about spiritual insight.

In the following pages you will find explorations of the artistry and ethical illuminations that come through Jewish worship in daily living, in holiday celebrations and in daily prayers. Experiences, suggestions, and some personal moments of awakening are offered along with information as incentives for your inner journey. Even if the information is not always news to you, meeting it in a different setting might be eye-opening, like seeing a familiar landscape from an unfamiliar perspective; we derive a new way of perceiving what we thought we knew well enough to take for granted.

If, regardless of our theology or lack of one, we get spiritual pleasure and ethical coherence, in addition to beauty, from a Beethoven quartet or a Japanese garden or a van Gogh painting, we can also find artistry and ethics in a religious ritual or a prayer when the person doing them is not simply "going through the motions." It doesn't have to be a ritual or prayer from whatever we consider our own tradition, for beauty and integrity might be as important as the religious content of the words and actions. They can be essential to one another much as the heart, brain and skeleton are essential to each other.

Knowing how this work started out might help you see where we are going. A few years ago a Christian campus minister asked that I lead a Passover seder for high school and college students in the performing arts degree programs at the prestigious North Carolina School of the Arts. Actually, he asked if I would "lead us in a seder meal," but I knew what he meant. Christians inexperienced with seders often refer to it by the term "seder meal," perhaps not realizing that although the meal is part of the seder, the seder is not the meal. Sometimes they don't know that there is a meal in the seder, something more substantial than the nibbling of ritual foods like matzah, horseradish and parsley. No wonder they are puzzled by Jewish practices! They will be even more puzzled when they begin to fathom what is entailed in producing the annual seder meal itself, let alone negotiating the liturgy that is the "seder" or order of the evening as expounded in the *Haggadah shel Pesach*, the Haggadah or Narrative of Passover.

Naturally I said yes first and then began to figure out how we would be able to do this. Because of the campus calendar, the event needed to be scheduled unusually for an evening in the midst of the holiday rather than on the first or second night and rather late, after rehearsals for these students, who would have eaten dinner already at the much earlier commissary time. The high school students would need to get special permission to stay out beyond their curfew. After a bit of education and negotiation, and along with some luck, daring, and hard labor, albeit not equal to what the Hebrew slaves endured in Egypt, something like a light seder meal was put together by the good-hearted minister, a couple of Jewish students, and some other volunteering helpers.

Every seder, if it is a living experience, will be shaped somewhat by the people present. I had led many campus seders but never one at this school. Looking around the U-shaped arrangement of tables at a group of young people (and some older ministers) completely new to me, I asked everyone to say who they were. The gathering included instrumentalists, ballet and modern dancers, singers, actors, scenic and costume designers and filmmakers; a few of them, albeit definitely a minority, were also Jews, for whom this at least was not a once-in-their-life adventure. I began to think freshly about the occasion in the light of those who were gathered there.

One of the core teachings of the seder, spelled out in the Haggadah, is that in every generation we must imagine that we ourselves experience the exodus. We say explicitly that we observe Pesach because "this is what God did for me when I was a slave in Egypt," not for some "them" back in ancient times. How would I connect this ritual to the central experiences of their lives, even to the arts and crafts that would be at the heart of their lives if they were favored and disciplined enough to attain their dreams? For if I could not do this, it would be little more than a superficial taste of an interesting ritual observed by a quaint culture but best appreciated from the inside.

That evening we set the table as prettily as we could. Someone brought flowers; I had a colorful blue ceramic seder plate with brightly painted floral decorations and gold lettering, and a modern silver goblet for the wine blessings. The three ceremonial pieces of matzah were slipped into a white satin embroidered cloth. The Haggadah itself, the Passover narrative and liturgy borrowed from the local Reform synagogue, was a modern edition printed on good paper in multiple colors, illustrated with full-page reproductions of colorful, bold Leonard Baskin prints; it provided readable English translations and commentaries cleansed of archaisms and included musical scores for the table songs. Liturgy is of course an art form, a ritual performance that has the potential to be expressively beautiful. Working through this one in the company of artists and theater technicians around the table, I recognized the Haggadah as the libretto for an annual production involving the various arts and crafts that these students were practicing for their life's work, not unlike the school's annual production of *The Nutcracker*, plus some others like cooking that are not included in their formal program but require talent, taste and hard effort.

These students knew how to work hard for long hours; they knew aches, exhaustion and injuries, along with devotion, power and exultation. They knew that success was uncertain, heartbreaks inevitable. Sometimes rewards came, even if the rewards were only in the doing; and sometimes (as for the Hebrew slaves of the Passover narrative) the expenditures of effort and abilities were sadly ungratifying, at least to them, at every level that counted. Directors, conductors, choreographers, coaches and teachers could be tough, demanding overseers, driven by vision and results while often indifferent to the human expenses.

The students knew something beyond that: they labored in the service of beauty. The teacher, the mirror or recording, the audience and the image in the mind or sound in the ear will help a dancer work toward a beautiful line of his body or a violinist shape a beautiful tone that comes close to her expressive ideal. That does take work, but even more important than the effort is the performer's conviction that it is worth doing because beauty is worth expressing. At the end of their life their entire career might live on for them through the memory of one radiant moment when they got something precious exactly right and knew it. And they would not really care that it happened at a small-town matinee with seventy people in the audience and not a critic in town.

In the process of their efforts, they each change something of themselves and redefine themselves. Instead of someone who plays the piano, the performer becomes a pianist; instead of someone who acts, the performer becomes an actor; the person who paints scenery becomes a painter or a scenic designer. In perhaps all-too-rare moments, someone who prays may become a pray-er, or, indeed, a prayer. Some like to read the Hebrew of Psalm 69, verse 14, *ani t'filati l'kha* (which seems to mean simply "I pray to You") as really saying, "I am my prayer to You." Imagine moving from saying prayers to becoming one with the prayer, as fully as a great actor "becomes" the person she or he is portraying! Learning to pray and becoming accustomed to it does not necessarily lead to that union between the action and the actor. Some people "get it" as if this were organic to them, even as some people know instinctively that an art or instrument is the right one for them. Others benefit from knowledge and experience that moves us closer to the fusion of "the words of my mouth and the meditation of my heart" (*Ps. 19: 15*).

That is beauty embodied, and this too is deep within artistic and religious expression. Like Keats's Grecian urn, an artist lives at the connection between beauty and truth. Religious ritual, music and language as well need to dwell in those realms. If religious expression is merely serviceable and not beautiful, it will not speak profoundly to the heart and mind, to the physicality that holds our souls; nor will it express divinity that makes itself known to us at least as much through vernal daffodils and autumnal sunsets and the face and body and voice of our own beloved as through ideas or doctrines.

Beauty is not necessarily prettiness but rather, apt perfection. The two qualities are sometimes in conflict with one another. Telling a painter that her work is "pretty" is usually not complimentary unless the artist is a child or someone striving only to be decorative. The classical pianist Imogen Cooper, who says that her Schubert performances probe "the darker depths" of that composer's troubled inner life, feels "angry" and "a slight sense of failure" when well-intentioned audience members come to her after a concert to exclaim, "That was delightful!" (*BBC Music Magazine,* June 2009, 21). Certainly there are moments in art and prayer where we hope for delight and prettiness. At other times, beauty comes from honesty, conviction and understanding. Often, young performers will offer recitals or produce recordings of works that they can sing or play with technical proficiency and tonal beauty, yet the performances seem soulless and undifferentiated, rather like paintings that could have been done by anyone possessing sufficient technique but no personal style. Nothing distinguishes that maker ("artist" does not seem quite right) from any other. In the case of the musician, the usual causes are that they do not yet have either the stage or the life experience that could prompt them to deeper insights. Without having lived the role or the experience, they have not entered into the singularity of the piece they are performing. The great opera soprano Maria Callas had a voice that not every listener thought was pretty; indeed, even some opera fans could not stand to listen to her; but she inhabited every character that she portrayed, bringing out through her vocal and physical expression detailed nuances of emotion and behavior that other singers with more immediately attractive tones never seemed to notice, and she sustained her attentiveness every moment that she was on stage, whether in a grand ensemble filled with soloists and chorus or a solo recital. That was not prettiness; instead, it exemplified what I have termed "apt perfection." A Callas performance was not pedantic but in the most significant ways it taught the audience.

As I discussed the seder with those students that night, talking of aesthetics and ethics, of doing something beautifully because it mattered, grasping that in some mysterious way it mattered more because of the beauty and that there was some moral value implicit in that, knowing that committedly doing one's best was a profound obligation of integrity and responsibility, this book germinated in my mind. At the level of art and ethics, the canard about Judaism as a religion based "merely" on law ceased even to make sense.

But suppose . . .

"But suppose I don't believe?"

Many years ago the comedian Sam Levinson (I think) told the story of his agnostic father's surprisingly regular synagogue attendance.

"Pop, you tell me that people go to *shul* to talk to God, right? But you also say you don't believe in God. So how come you go to *shul* every day?"

"You know my friend Garfinkel? Garfinkel goes to *shul* every day to talk to God. I go to talk to Garfinkel."

Having conversations: that is one way of thinking about what we do in life. An author talks to readers through a book. Sometimes we talk back, especially if we are critics, whether the author hears us or not. It has been said that in the Torah God talks to us and in prayer we talk to God. Day in, day out, we also talk to one another, which for some people is another way or maybe the only way of talking to God. In some moments we need to communicate information or express opinions; at others, we have to talk out our feelings. Conversations are horizontal as well as vertical, and the horizon is 360 degrees, much as vertical is down as well as up. It takes in people over there as well as right here, and future generations as well as past ones. Sometimes the conversational partner is inside, the inner voice challenging our "Yes" with a "No" or "Yes, but . . . " or "What if . . . ?"

Especially if our prayers originate in a set of words, a liturgy, constructed over many years, we recite passages that have been phrased for us and for a world of other speakers with the confidence of direct, assured address. That becomes our tone of voice and our vocabulary. If we imagine the liturgy to be like a script in a movie or play in which we have one of the leading roles, and we find that the role we are playing has a lot to do with who we really are "offstage," the script leads us to self-expression and maybe even to self-discovery. We know what we want to say to the Someone out there whom we know is listening to us in the moment; even if we confess faults, we can articulate them in suitably general and discrete terms through the words that come from the prayer book, as if we are positive that conversation is always possible. For is it not said in the Talmud (*Bava Metzia 59a*) that the heavenly gates of sincerely expressed need are always open?

However, those who pray regularly, and especially those who lead worship, are aware that there is a nagging problem with this neat formulation, even when we accept it as a religious conviction. It makes the interchange sound too easy and nice, like a congenial afternoon chat over cocoa and cookies or the intense heartfelt sharing of intimate confidences with our closest, best-trusted friend, and coffee or a stronger drink to sustain us. But we know that not all conversations go that way. If we need evidence beyond our own experience, the plays of Beckett, Pinter, Albee, Marsha Norman or August Wilson remind us of what can happen between two people who share the routines of daily living and presumably communicate with one another all the time. Sometimes there are misunderstandings and quarrels. Painful things might have to be said. We converse but disagree. We trade mutual recriminations. Tension builds. Tempers flash.

We talk past one another. Maybe a shrug or a raised eyebrow or a sigh communicates more precisely than words. Silences interrupt; and they may linger. Sometimes those silences are meaningful, pregnant pauses. Sometimes they express mutual placid acceptance. And sometimes we just don't know what to say to one another.

All of this also occurs in the conversations that we engage in when we pray, or we say the words that we associate with prayer. For who is to say that we are really praying when we speak those familiar words? The phrases come out, and in Judaism (like other highly liturgical traditions) they can come unimpeded because tradition has written them for us. People who *davven* (pray) daily or at least occasionally do so in a traditional *shul* are familiar with what some call "speed davvening," as leader and worshippers dash through an accustomed text, barely touching the surface of the words, occasionally raising our voice at the beginning or end of a section to mark our spot. Our minds might be elsewhere—maybe even praying but praying apart from the language we are speaking, not through it. There's no uplink. True, by being there at the appointed time of worship we meet an obligation; we have satisfied what Jewish law (*halakhah*) calls *keva*; and there is merit in that, but it is certainly different from being in the conversation, having the intentional focus termed *kavvanah*. Imagine two people agreeing to have lunch with one another and finding when they are seated at the table that they actually don't have much to talk about and are not really interested in what each other has to say.

This is normal. Naturally, if it happens all the time, we may wonder if there is a point to continuing the lunch dates. But it is unrealistic to expect every conversation to be inspiring, magical, deep, profound, uplifting, eye-opening, even if it is with someone whom we love. People often worry when their attempts at prayer feel superficial or even artificial. If we think about how we converse with those with whom we feel closest, we know that the depth of the relationship cannot be measured solely on the quality of verbal communication. Staying in the conversation is more important.

I grew up hearing my maternal grandmother, Birdie, who lived with us, talking to God. She never went to a synagogue, knew no Hebrew, did not read from or even own a prayerbook, spoke in perfect unaccented native-born English with an occasional bit of Yiddish inserted only at strategic moments, and did not keep regular times for prayer; rather, her praying was spontaneous and might occur at any time of the day or night that she felt the need to open the conversation. In the same way and in the same tones of voice she frequently spoke to her mother and father, both of whom had died before I was born. "Mamenyu, Tatenyu, Gottenyu" were conversationally somewhere near about in the domestic air. Whether God or her parents ever responded to her, I could not say. She certainly gave no indication that she was hearing voices. I am not persuaded that they were reassuring to her but it was clear that expressing herself out loud was necessary. If the conversation seemed to be a monologue rather than a dialogue, the other participant was apparently playing a useful therapeutic role as an un-anxious presence, the essential patient listener. Her exclamations seemed to be unaffected by whether or not any of those prayers was ever answered. At a time when "God is dead" was a fashionable theological phrase, my grandmother's attitude seemed to be, "What is 'dead'?"

But what is prayer, really? The question is not exactly rhetorical, though it has, and should have, many answers. We can at least begin to say what is not a prayer.

Around 1928-29 a Belgian-born Surrealist artist named René Magritte painted a simple-looking canvas: against a flat tan background, a darker brown curved tobacco pipe with a black mouthpiece is the solitary image occupying the center of the work. As many viewers have remarked, it looks as if it could be a tobacconist's store sign. We see the painting and immediately recognize, Aha! It's a pipe. However, below the object the artist has also painted in script, *Ceci n'est pas une pipe*, "This is not a pipe." Our initial response is probably that this is an outrageous bit of absurdist mockery. Of course it's a pipe, as anyone can see. It is nothing other than a pipe, and there is nothing else to see in the painting. Oh, but wait, the <u>painting</u>—At that point we get the artist's idea. No, it is not a pipe but a painting of a pipe. Or an arrangement of pigments that resembles a pipe. Now we start to tally the differences. Despite the highlights painted on the image, this is a flat, two-dimensional representation; it has no inside. Besides, if it were a real pipe, it would be far too large, probably over two feet long. And come to think of it, it is floating in some undifferentiated mocha-hued space that has no whereness to it, no dimension or physical presence and looks like nothing we could name. We have never seen such a thing in our life, a real object suspended unsupported in that sort of color field. Of course it isn't a pipe. How silly of me to think that it was. That is why the painting's real title is *"La trahison des images,"* The Treachery of Images.

We should imagine that every prayerbook bears on the top of each page a running heading that says, "This is not a prayer." We think they are prayers; we usually refer to them as if they were. Actually, there are words on the page that bear a relationship to prayer that is similar to the relationship between Magritte's canvas and a real pipe that one could smoke. The words in the book are two-dimensional, and maybe too big; they also usually occupy some undifferentiated space devoid of what I have called where-ness. They could be the pattern for prayers. For that to happen, we have to make them three-dimensional, give them voices and bodies, put them into the contexts of lives that we know from the inside. A prayer that is not a real prayer ("Words, words, words," to quote *Hamlet*) is not a satisfactory offering, no more than a blemished sacrificial offering in the days of the Temple was acceptable. A prayer that hopes against the fact of things or wishes that a misfortune fall upon someone else rather than oneself ("I hope that ambulance is in front of my neighbor's house and not mine") is a vain, improper prayer (Talmud *Berakhot* 54a). What we think of when we talk about "saying the prayers" is truly a form of lip service. The prophets and sages remind us, however, that the more valued service is that of the heart.

Jewish liturgy developed during times when kings and emperors represented absolute legal authority and protective security. Naturally, our prayers imagined God as "He" (*atah* is a masculine pronoun) and addressed *"Him"* as "king of kings," "Lord, ruler of the universe" and so on. Even *"barukh"* in the opening phrase of countless blessings *"Barukh atah"* (usually translated as "Blessed") comes from the word *berekh*, "knee," probably reflecting the practice of kneeling before a ruler. Some today are exploring other terms and ways of thinking about that vast power that many people call "God" for want of a more accurate name. No single alternative has emerged clearly as preferable, and there is some value in keeping the traditional phrasing in Hebrew while interpreting it more freely in our thoughts and our own daily language.

Therefore Jewish tradition provides countless ways to imagine and speak about this holy essence of life, which we understand is beyond all language and imagery. When Moses, the greatest of all Jewish prophets, asks God's real name, this apparently simple question meets with profound yet obfuscating answers. *"Ehyeh asher ehyeh,"* I-am/will be – what I am/will be, God replies, as if to say: I am Existence and Becoming. That is profound and difficult, yet it seems a clear enough direct statement. But then: Tell the people, "ehyeh sent me to you." And yet again in the very next verse, "You shall say that Y-H-V-H the God of your ancestors, God of Abraham, God of Isaac and God of Jacob sent me to you; this shall be my name forever, the way to remember me for all generations" (*Ex. 3: 14-15*). After these two verses, we know more but understand less about how to name God or what the names might denote.

On Mt. Sinai, when Moses wants to see God's full glory, the divine response is, "No-one can see my face and live." Instead, God hides Moses safely and promises that when God's glory sweeps by, "you shall see my back" (*Ex. 33: 18-23*). This amazing image suggests that we perceive the after-effects of God's presence. Not only can't we see God's "face," meaning that we cannot envision with mortal eyes what God fully is, we can only take in what God does when the action is done. Much as we are unable to live our lives as if we had no free will, for if we did that, we might never get out of bed and make breakfast, much less commit ourselves to a career and personal relationships, so it is only after the fact that we might look back and interpret what has happened as predetermined, *bashert*. Retrospectively, we perceive that what occurred was the apparently inevitable consequence of all the factors that led up to it. We appeared to choose, but the choice was inevitable. Another way of saying this might

15

be, It was in God's hands. The Torah acknowledges that even for our teacher Moses, *Moshe rabbenu*, God transcends our ability to label or imagine God. The best we can do is see the effect of God's work in the world and multiply terms that approximate some attributes of God. One of the morning prayers, known as *Barukh she'amar*, declares, *barukh sh'mo*, that is, "blessed is God's name." We can also read that phrase as saying that "Blessed" is yet another name for God. *No-one can see my face and live:* if we could "take in" the totality of the divine, it would indeed blow our minds. Every circuit in us would overload and self-destruct.

Therefore some limited name or image can be useful. Of course we need not feel confined to a specific one as we pray. Above all, God is *Eyn Sof*, "endless," "limitless." But *Eyn Sof* encompasses even the seemingly boundless universe. It is a deep field of the Unlimited. Truly, about such a dimension of God there seems nothing possible to say except, as the ultimate Hasidic prayer says, *du*, "You." We often use "Adonai" as a respectful substitution for Y-H-V-H, the most specific sacred name in Judaism, represented by the Hebrew letters *yud-hey-vav-hey*. That is the distinctive Hebrew appellation for *eloheynu*, "our god." Sometimes "Yah," a name appearing frequently in the psalms, seems a fitting alternative, while some prefer "Ha-Shem," literally, "The Name." We might choose "God" or other general terms for writing in English but often use simply the breath-like, unpronounceable consonants "Y-H-V-H." Whatever words we use, we cannot find just one that adequately designates the force that keeps the universe going and at the same time is for us a source of comfort, resilience, encouragement and moral clarity. One possible name, imperfect as it is, might be Beauty.

✳ ✳ ✳

"But what if I don't know Hebrew?" Learning a bit of Hebrew, or a lot of it, is not impossible, even for Americans, who often seem reluctant to learn a foreign language even when it is a demonstrably useful one. Admittedly, anything can be said in English—more or less; and therein, as they say, lies the rub. That we lose something in translation is axiomatic. Just try coming up with one English word that substitutes accurately for "lasagne"! That is why I sometimes discuss nuances of a Hebrew word or phrase. I wish it were practical to do so even more. The sounds of a language in our ears, the feel of it in our mouths and on our lips, its linguistic reverberations in roots and cognates—the *ta'am* or taste of it, so to speak—are as significant as the denotations and connotations. I hope you will be able to "hear" these words as well. There is poetry in our prayers. Some of that comes through biblical and later Hebrew poems included in the liturgy; much more of it dwells in the nuanced precision of what appears as prose.

Still, if English is the language in which we express ourselves most directly, clearly, authentically, it is the language in which we ought to be able to say prayers. As you read, you will see that I provide, along with mainly phonetic transliterations of Hebrew, translations as well. Those keep fairly close to the literal original so that you will not be misled about what the Hebrew actually says, but I intend them to seem natural and pertinent to a modern reader of English. If successful, these translations of biblical and liturgical texts should not sound passé after their fifteen minutes of historical time.

❊ ❊ ❊

A Closed Canon but an Open Book

The numerous imposing volumes of the Talmud that shape rabbinic Judaism are the basis of what is often referred to as the Oral Law or (better) Oral Torah, since it was first transmitted orally, though it has existed in written form for centuries. The way that it works suggests a lot about the values of Jewish religious life and thought, built on dialogue, disagreement and elaboration. What we usually call the Torah, meaning the first five biblical books of *Genesis* through *Deuteronomy*, is of course the Written Law. Why do we need an Oral Torah? If the Written Torah is imagined as the constitution intended for the people of Israel living as a nation in their own land, the Oral Torah is like the various codes of law that are the essential legal guides for putting it into effect. Although it discusses details of religious practice, it is far more concerned with pragmatic issues of economic responsibilities, torts, and criminal law, many of which have ethical implications. How do we define the "corner of the field" that must be left for the poor, the widow, the orphan and the non-citizen if this is not merely a worthy ethical exhortation but a legal obligation with economic ramifications for the field owner as well as the beneficiaries? Who is responsible for the damage caused by a sharp splinter protruding from a fence that tears the clothing of a passer-by walking very close to it? When a trial requires witnesses, what constitutes valid testimony?

Traditional teachings hold that the Oral Torah was also given to Moses at Sinai and transmitted verbally since his time to that of the Talmud. "These are the *torot* that Y-H-V-H made between himself and the children of Israel in Mt. Sinai by the hand of Moses." (*Lev. 26:46*). The early rabbinic commentary *Sifra* on this passage does not simply take *torot* to mean "laws" or "teachings" but rather asks and answers, "why is *torot* plural? To teach that two Torahs were given, one written and the other oral." That is a way of saying that it is impossible to imagine the Written Torah standing on its own without such commentary.

To describe the Oral Torah as it is embodied in the Talmud as a dialogue might misleadingly suggest the refined artfulness of Plato's Socratic dialogues. That is neither its goal nor effect. In contrast to Plato's crafty methodology, in which Socrates always knows the right answer in advance and through the dialogue prods his companions to recognize the single truth toward which he is leading them, the Talmud freely includes rejected as well as minority views, the "out-takes" along with alternative readings that, if this were a movie, would be relegated to the disk of extras on the DVD version. These are preserved within the text so that we can understand what interpretations were not accepted and have a repository of options to draw on in changed circumstances. Although some authorities generally take precedence over others, there is no "Socrates" who understands everything, no one true interpretation to which some wise teacher will always guide us.

Instead, as happens in other disciplines, subtle analytic minds disagree with one another, and sometimes are in apparent conflict with themselves; the opinion of a great sage might be rejected in favor of a solution proposed by someone whose name is not even recalled. Forerunners of academics and lawyers, they tell stories, get diverted onto tangents, become snippy with one another, quibble over what look like petty details, challenge one another not because they disagree with an answer but because they have a better way to derive it. At times we are offered two different but valid decisions from which to choose; occasionally the sages simply cave in, declaring an impasse that will be resolved only when the messiah arrives. Though the tractates of the Talmud seem to be arranged by topics, the discursive nature of the text and the tendency to think analogically work against neat systematizing. Citing the opinion of a certain Babylonian sage on a given topic prompts someone to quote a series of diverse, totally unrelated rulings and practices of that sage, prompted merely by the fact that his name has come up. The crucial discussion of Hanukkah's origin occurs in the volume on Shabbat because both are associated with kindling lights. It might remind us a lot of work that we know, not from the edited official minutes of meetings but through the meandering and haggling, wrangling and accommodating that actually take place in time's flow, except that the Talmud's time is a period of centuries and its place embraces both the land of Israel and the land of Babylonia all condensed to simultaneity, a conversation that disregards the potential inconvenience of the participants living in different places and centuries.

If the Greek works of Plato and Aristotle remind us of the geometrically orderly design of Athenian public buildings in which formal speeches and debates ruled by abstract logic might take place, the Jewish one calls to mind meanderings and unpredictable juxtapositions in a marketplace or the shouk and the later shtetl, in which the conversations are characterized by fortuitous encounters, tightly argued disagreements, and deals that are or are not closed. In its own quirky ways, the collective enterprise of the Talmud is a postmodern text, more varied, colorful, ambiguous and intellectually fair to us than Plato's overdetermined dialogues or Aristotle's lectures.

Turning to the Talmud to look for what Western philosophy considers great ideas or profound truths, we will be disappointed. A lot of it deals with really little questions. Pages, for example, are devoted to what kinds of material can be used as wicks for Sabbath lights. Instead of unfolding grand concepts, it seems intended to help train the minds of scholars and judges who will become the authorities on practical legal and religious observance among their community followers. The "rav" (rabbi) or "mar" (master, i.e., a sage) at that point in history was not necessarily expected to be a spiritual counselor or theologian but primarily an expounder of Torah, a transmitter of religious "best practices," and a judge applying Jewish law to all sorts of questions, many of them mundane but immediate such as, "Is this chicken kosher?" or "Who pays damages here?" They had to be prepared to function on their own in communities in which they expected to be the leading authority. They needed not simply to memorize but to know how to analyze issues and think through analogies in anticipation of meeting cases that did not precisely fit the precedents they had studied. For that reason, they often ask, "What is this like?," seeking the simile or analogy that will allow them to move from distracting specifics to the essence of the issue; their conflicts frequently take place over what the underlying principle really is, framed in terms of what the proper metaphor should be.

So the Talmud is rather like a textbook of case law in which the experts wrestle to understand how the law should be applied, and how the ideal law fits with community practice, which of course can also mean understanding what the purpose of the law is. That sometimes gets us into what are big issues to us. Clearly, some of those sages were searching for answers to profound questions. Generally, though, that is not what they are noted for in their own time. But candidly, just as writers of modern law codes expect that they will only be read by people familiar with such material (not those of us who are simply citizens interested in "justice," for example, or "right and wrong"), the compilers of the Talmud imagined that the teachings would be studied by people gaining specialized knowledge and sharpening their minds to apply their information to new situations. They were not writing what is sometimes called Wisdom literature, like *Job* or *Ecclesias-*

tes. Nevertheless, many find in talmudic discourse not only logical rigor but intellectual dance conveying the artful sorts of delights and challenges that others experience while playing chess or bridge, or following the lines of a fugue.

Sometimes the sages' search for the right explanation takes them into the imaginative kind of literature that we call *midrash.* Midrash is not the name of one particular book, though the existence of numerous volumes with that word in the title obscures the fact. It is a type of interpretation, usually of the *Tanakh,* and frequently homiletic, designed to make a point. Midrash might include what today might be called the "back story." For example, from *Genesis* we know only that God told Abraham, at that point still called Abram, to leave the homeland of his father Terah in Haran and travel to Canaan (*Gen. 12*). We might question, why choose Abram? And why did he have to leave home in order to follow God's ways? Midrash gives contexts for interpretation. It also tries to explain apparently irrelevant details that crop up in the spare verbal texture of the *Torah.* Therefore, midrash treats the seemingly extraneous word or variant spelling the way the author of a well-crafted mystery or the careful analyst of poetry would. When Noah is described as "a righteous man in his generation," the midrash commentators pounce on the last phrase, which is just one word in the Hebrew original. Why specify *b'dorotav* when obviously the one in which he was living had to be "his generation"?

Midrashic stories expound on possibilities with dramatic details of their own that are not found in the Torah. Further, midrash infers meanings from otherwise unexplained gaps in the narratives. After the binding of Isaac on Mt. Moriah, the text simply says that Abraham descended to the waiting servants; it does not mention Isaac leaving the mountain, nor does it tell us what happened to him until he reappears more than sixty-five verses and a considerable length of time later when Rebecca comes to be his wife. The midrashic imagination wants to enter into the silent years, filling in a tale that not only gets the story line from one point to another but makes an arc of Isaac's character development by shaping a life of spiritual training for him during that "missing" period.

Midrash often seems fanciful and playful, but it is so in a serious cause, the way art often seems like playfulness with a purpose. The aesthetic imagination at work on the biblical text might also be musical, visual, poetic or theatrical. From these few examples we can understand why modern literary critics think of midrash as antecedent to both critical interpretations and also to much imaginative literature, Milton's *Paradise Lost* being a stellar example of a radical Protestant poetic midrash on the story of Adam and Eve. To our ancient ancestors, the closed biblical text was nonetheless an open book.

Max Kadushin in *The Rabbinic Mind* coined a paradoxical phrase to describe Jewish religion, calling it "normal mysticism." At first this looks like an oxymoron, for a mystic seeks a condition that is anything but normal, to unite with the divine, ideally to become one with whatever the mystic understands as God. The mystic endeavors to reach that state through various esoteric studies and rituals that are particular to each religion and maybe to that practitioner. But Kadushin explains that the characteristic Jewish prayers and blessings assume that we are normally in the direct dialogic presence of God, to whom we regularly speak in terms that Buber described as "I and Thou." Imagine that our religious practice wants us to be ever mindful of the blessings and prayers that daily living make possible. Therefore we avail ourselves repeatedly of the most frequent verbal formula in Jewish prayer, the direct address to God using the second-person familiar pronoun, *barukh atah adonai*, "blessed are you, God." (Hebrew being a grammatically gendered language, this customary phrase is masculine; some now vary it with or substitute the feminine *b'rakha aht*.) This is my grandmother's *gottenyu* translated into Hebrew and regularized into liturgical practice.

Not that esoteric forms of mysticism are missing from Judaism. Rather, Jewish traditions include both arcane and practical teachings about the mystical as well as philosophical insights and of course guidance on daily life. However, Jewish mystical approaches do not offer an alternative path to religion but one possible continuation of the path toward fully living and practicing a religiously aware life. Not <u>instead of</u> but <u>in addition</u>. Significantly, there is no commandment to be a mystic, and among the many blessings that the rabbinic traditions have imparted for us to say on the occasion of all sorts of experiences in life, there is no blessing specifically for having a mystical one. In Judaism, mysticism is not supposed to be an alternate way, an antinomian substitute for regular observance. Rather, it is the "over and above" for people who perceive that further dimensions may exist beyond the written words of the text and the prescribed rituals, which they practice and with which they are already deeply familiar.

Philosophy might be described in similar terms. However, the philosophers' God is a God of perfection, the ideal One. The mystics' God is a God of completeness, the all-embracing Oneness. Jewish mystical tradition is built on the practice of Judaism, a practice that may lead some people to a mystical perception, but not necessarily. The perception develops from the practice, if it comes at all; it is not a substitute for the practice.

Further, the early kabbalistic teachers were exceptionally careful about choosing whom to teach and how much to teach each person. They did not publish but rather they orally instructed selected individuals if and when those people (presumably only men at that time) appeared ready. These acolytes were brought along at an individually appropriate pace. Dissemination of manuscripts and development of printing changed that forever. Still, the principle was a good one. The principle that one was not to study Kabbalah until the age of forty, if one did study it at all, meant that the student was a mature adult with an occupation, knowledge of the ways of the world, a fully developed regular religious practice (including thrice-daily prayers along with observing biblical and rabbinic *mitzvot*) and familiarity with the crucial foundational material common to the religious tradition, such as biblical commentaries, Talmud and midrash. Most likely he also had a family to whom he was responsible, and who grounded him in the practicalities of daily living in a community. The self-aware teachers, choosing and closely guiding people whose abilities they could judge, expressed themselves in metaphors and similes intended for students whom we might describe as poets and imaginative artists working in the field of religious thought, not in diagrams for mechanics to memorize.

The sages were also concerned that younger people might be drawn into the potentially distracting, richly detailed intricacies of kabbalistic and other mystical systems or imaginative worlds, which are poetically described in allegorical or metaphorical terms. That risked diverting them from accepting the responsibilities of a mature adult such as earning a living, becoming part of a religious and secular society, marrying, raising children and meeting the needs of one's family. Such mundane matters could seem irrelevant and even annoying if one is already engrossed at 15 or 16 in trying to understand the arcane processes by which one metaphysical *sefirah* or quality flowing from God relates to another and what that means for the balance of energies in the cosmic order that stretches from the beginning to the end of time. We need only notice how adolescents today immerse themselves in details of fantasy worlds through video games, books and movies.

The *Zohar* in particular (though not alone in this regard) is also filled with sexual imagery, some of it quite explicit. That is often the vocabulary in which it expresses theological allegories and parables. It is common for mystics to use such imagery as they express their yearning to be close enough to cling to the object of their most intense desire. If one longs for that which is unattainable, no matter how tantalizingly near or how improbably far, the terms that one uses are going to be approximately the same whether one's beloved is of flesh and blood or the beloved is the maker of flesh and blood. The language can be baffling, upsetting, or misleadingly literal even to an adult who is sexually experienced already; all the more so for somebody who is not. Taken as written, without the reader knowing more of life directly and an attentive teacher alert to the dangers of overly explicit interpretation, this is a seriously confusing introduction to mysticism and a dangerous introduction to sexuality. One must be firmly grounded in the life and responsibilities of this physical world to be safe with the mystics' speculations about the transcendent spiritual world.

Kadushin's concept can also help us in understanding that particularly odd practice of speaking to God with the word *barukh*, usually translated as "blessed." Deriving from the root *bet-resh-khet*, "knee," *barukh* carries the concept of the deity as the ultimate sovereign, worthy of being bowed to, as in the tradition of bending our knees at the beginnings and endings of some prayers. Also, God is "blessed" by having and bestowing all that there is in the universe. Yet there is a much more profound relationship suggested here if we imagine that through this pronouncement we return blessedness to God. The covenant has reciprocal benefits and obligations; it is a two-way commitment. In ways that we can talk about but perhaps not fully comprehend, somehow God wants us to complete the circuit of giving and receiving. We do this by not being merely passive receptors but grateful givers whose *barukh atah* or *b'rakha aht* is both thanks and reciprocal generosity. It is as if our gratitude replenishes the store of divine munificence. Without meaning to trivialize the relationship with the sacred, we might use the analogy of the attention and applause that energize and inspire the performing artist. A stage performer senses the living presence of the audience that they cannot see beyond the footlights and knows whether "the house" is "alive" or not at that performance. Would God be less aware?

A rationalist thinker like Maimonides will argue fervently against the anthropomorphism of saying that God wants or needs our applause. Acting as if God does, however, cultivates our habit of grateful awareness of experiences and gifts. The rewards seem reciprocal. Going through an airport security check early one recent December 25, I felt sorry for the rude way that a traveler in front of me snapped impatiently at a security agent who was merely doing her job of verifying passengers' identification. As I handed her my boarding pass and driver's license, I thanked the agent for being there on that Christmas morning. Pausing from her work to look me in the eyes, she said emphatically, "Thank you—thank you for saying that." If it is good to thank people who are just doing their job, it must also be good to thank God. Or so it felt.

Chapter 2
Tradition, "Tradition"!

A friend often joins us for Jewish holiday celebrations. When we get to a familiar blessing like the *kiddush*, she is likely to grimace, squint or shake her head because we aren't doing the "right" melody. The right melody, of course, is the one that she learned. Hers is not wrong; but it isn't the only one, and not necessarily the customary one for the festival. Those are also authentic but not in her repertoire.

Anyone leading worship at an unfamiliar congregation for the first time who asks about their tunes or rituals knows to expect the unhelpful answer, "The traditional one" or "The usual one." Judaism is built on tradition, so the word commands authority. Tradition is like the foundations and mechanical infrastructure of a community, the essential groundwork providing a solid underpinning for the whole. Yet it is broader than usually recognized, for Mordechai Kaplan was correct in calling Judaism a civilization. Even "civilization" oversimplifies. If we speak of "Western civilization," are we thinking of *Beowulf* or Mozart, the Athenian republic or European fascism? And does the canon include Maimonides and the *Zohar*? So in Judaism we should speak of "tradition," or "a tradition," or even "traditions," rather than "the tradition," as if there were only one. Further, the community is more than those subterranean elements. Once the foundations are set, they need to be added to so that the structures become livable and the community works. Over time, the many parts require repairs, renovations and additions. These elements also become traditional over time.

The innovations can be good but "it ain't necessarily so." The latest music might not better than something written generations ago, and the accretions of time do not inherently validate themselves just because we have taken them for granted. Here is an analogy. Many of us became accustomed to the look of Michelangelo's Sistine Chapel as it existed for countless years, its surface crackled or broken, its hues muted yet unified through the overlay of dirt and soot and earlier attempts at cleaning. A controversial major restoration project undertaken between 1984 and 1994 gave us the current look of Michelangelo's work, the colors brilliant (detractors of the project called them garish), the figures emergent with new clarity and distinctiveness, though again the opponents would say at the cost of smooth integration that they believe the artist had anticipated would occur over time, and at the loss (they believe) of some of the master's original work. In their current state, the frescoes communicate their scenes lucidly. The quality of light in the paintings has become vivid, indeed, luminous; folds of fabric and shading of musculature now reveal themselves.

When I saw the chapel in its former state, although I was already impressed by what I had been taught of the scope and imagination of Michelangelo's design, I was privately disappointed by the somber, seemingly faded or shadowed tones and the difficulty of discerning the biblical episodes through that muddiness. However, I would not say publicly what my eyes, mind and feelings were registering. Everyone concurred that Michelangelo's Sistine Chapel frescoes were among art's greatest masterpieces, so presumably this was how they were supposed to look. I thought that my disenchantment must reveal my limits, not the work's. Some years later, when the restoration was in progress, the cleaned section emerged with vivid clarity. There was an additional surprise: for the first time I could relate Michelangelo's palette to those of other artists of his era such as Botticelli and Raphael whose works we had seen just outside the chapel.

The controversy has subsided now that the deed is done, although disagreement remains. Was the earlier patina venerable or merely elderly? The paradox is that the "traditional" look of the chapel has given way to a much more youthful appearance that is (most agree) more <u>traditional</u> because it is closer to the original colors. But—opponents will protest—the painter intended those hues to temper with age, like a wine becoming more harmonious and better integrated as it matures.

This is just one instance of the difference between "authenticity" and "tradition." There is a similar one regarding classical Greek statues, especially the magnificent representations of gods and goddesses. For centuries, we have seen them in the natural tones of white marble, and those images are fixed in our minds as the idealized perfection of timeless beauty, as they were for generations of sculptors, painters and writers. Art historians, however, now tell us that such statues were originally painted to look lifelike.[1] People who saw them in their early glory were struck by the realistic yet oversized representations, as if in the presence of deities in perfect human form, with flawless but natural-seeming skin and hair. It is hard for most of us to visualize classical statuary in this way, though it might be more authentic. It was not the image of these sculptures that previous generations of artists had, as representing idealized splendor that was bloodless and pure white as well as timeless, unmarked by the particularities of human coloration, garbed (if at all) in the same alabaster hue. Michelangelo sculpted his enormous "David" in exquisitely persuasive anatomical detail, but it probably never occurred to him to paint the figure in appropriately Mediterranean skin and hair color, nor can we imagine it that way. Artists and writers at least from the Renaissance through the 20th century have reinforced through their own works the almost axiomatic harmony between the classical image and white marble. That, for them, was the tradition, and therefore it became tradition for us.

What we find on closer look is that tradition is broader and more complex than first appearance suggests. Generations of artists were influenced not by the Sistine Chapel paintings as visitors now see them but by the pre-restoration appearance. Tradition is a chain of transmission, not as is sometimes supposed, the "original" or solely authentic way. Arrangements of Bach's work by other composers or skilled orchestrators such as Busoni, Elgar and Stokowski, Liszt's transcriptions of Mozart or Mahler's of Beethoven, reveal the forms of artistic expression later artists recognized and wanted to hear in the compositions by their great predecessors. Trying to do everything in the way it was described in the Bible is going to produce some absurd and now-meaningless anachronisms and clueless befuddlements. Each generation and each practitioner contributes a link or ornament on the chain, rather than merely handing it on, as-is, to the next, and they do this with their own degree of independence.

There is a video recording of the great violinist David Oistrakh performing the Mozart Sinfonia Concertante for two violins with his son and pupil, Igor, who was also a distinguished player. During one extended passage, the camera catches the father and son, side by side, totally in unison, their two bows at precisely the same angle and moving at exactly the same speed, as though both were attached to one arm. It is a touching instance of how precisely the interpretation and method have been transmitted from one generation to the next, father to son, and all the more so because as a teacher the elder Oistrakh was known to foster independence rather than mere imitation. The son seems to have imbued the father's technique of bowing that section as simply right. This is tradition that we might understand as direct transmission, unaltered so far as possible because the teacher reached the heart of truth in the matter. It is orthodox but not as a result of coercive conformity.

A more complex relationship appears in the work of the legendary sitar player Ravi Shankar and his daughter and pupil, Anoushka. In performance the younger artist listens and responds attentively to her father's playing, answering and trading off with him in duets according to well-established raga patterns. However, her phrasing suggests something other than precise imitation; her own recordings also show that she is not purely channeling her father's tutelage but developing her characteristics as a musician in ways that complement the underlying instruction she has received in the principles of Indian music. This is tradition understood as rootedness, from which a branch may grow as it needs, or a new shoot develop as a tree in its own right. It might remind us of the story told of the early 19th century Hassidic rabbi, Noah of Lekhovitz. After he was appointed to replace his late father, he received complaints from their hassidim that he was not following his father's practices. He insisted that he was, claiming, "My father didn't just imitate, and neither do I."

Early in the rabbinic period scholars known as *tannai'im*, "teachers," were skilled in memorizing and transmitting orally communicated rulings and practices of the sages with whom they had studied, and their work became the basis of the Mishnah. Often, they concentrated in certain areas of Jewish law, much as today one attorney might specialize in contract law, another in criminal law, and so on. They were not merely passive in this role; some of them were crucial shapers of interpretations. However, they apparently preferred to represent themselves primarily as handing on what they had been given. Similarly, the great Russian pianist Sviatoslov Richter said in an interview that "I only did what was in the score." Asked whether he contributed anything of himself to a performance, this brilliant interpreter of great music demurred, asserting, "No. Only the text matters, nothing else." He persisted when the questioner insisted that people would enjoy hearing Richter play Schubert but would not enjoy hearing the interviewer play the same work, protesting, "Then you would not be doing what is in the score."[2] Presumably even the *tanna'im* who did more than just quote verbatim would say that they were transmitting "only the text." Later generations, called *amora'im*, "interpreters," were more overtly analytic and transformative, sometimes rather boldly re-making the sense of tannaitic teachings and even Torah law to accommodate a new place and time or their own sensibilities. Yet they also would argue, even if they did so ingenuously, that they just made the text clear. Their elucidations and the attendant disagreements fill out the body of the Talmud, consequently also becoming part of tradition.

There are also countless instances of a local custom, *minchag*, which acquire the status of halakhah and often interact oddly with it. Here are two examples. In a Reform congregation some years ago, a newly hired rabbi with some traditionalist leanings introduced a variation in the synagogue's Torah ritual. The local practice had been simply to lift the scroll from the ark ceremonially, remove its ornaments and mantle, and place it on the reading desk. This rabbi took out the scroll and, accompanied as usual by organ music, carried it formally down the aisle and up again as congregants familiar with the ritual of *hakafah* reached out to touch the Torah mantle with their prayerbooks or fingers and then bring them to their lips. One long-time regular attendee raised in the classic Reform tradition complained privately, "I thought I was going to faint. It was like being in a Catholic church with people kissing the cross." She was not alone. But the rabbi was following a widely observed Jewish practice of giving the whole congregation a physical connection with the *sefer torah*. His "innovation" merely introduced an authentic tradition, albeit one that ran so much against this congregation's *minchag* and the usual Reform attitudes toward rituals at that time that some viewed it as idolatrous and alien. It subsequently became the congregation's standard practice.

The second example is a congregation's more recent development of a *minchag* regarding the way that the *sefer torah* is carried during that *hakafah*. There are variant schools of thought about whether the scroll should be carried against the bearer's left side because it is nearer the heart, or the right side because the right is usually the stronger arm. This synagogue has two sections of seats with a center aisle and an aisle on each side. The practice developed here is that the bearer holds the scroll on the shoulder nearest the congregants. While this makes perfect choreographic sense, as I was leading the congregation at the time that it came about I can attest to how the local custom developed. The side aisles of the sanctuary are narrow; consequently, people carrying the *sefer* on the shoulder away from the seats sometimes banged it into the wall. After two successive bar or bat mitzvah youngsters loudly knocked off the thermostat covering and dented the scroll's sterling silver ornaments while carrying the Torah during their ceremonies, the "proper" method was found by reasonable pragmatism.

35

Within a couple of generations, the origins will be totally forgotten, and congregants will suppose that the rituals should be done just in these ways. Naturally, since they are traditional.

✳ ✳ ✳

Jewish practice and worship have never been as homogeneous as some practitioners would like to claim. It is at least a four-lane highway, not a two-lane rural road with a 20-mile-an-hour speed limit. Today, when we know of different varieties of Orthodox (several hassidic varieties, modern, ultra-Orthodox), Conservative, Reform, Reconstructionist, Renewal, and humanistic expressions of Judaism, "traditional" is the simplest way to designate what most of them accept in common.

Let us use the analogy of a literature class. Some students are curious about technique; they like learning how a Shakespearean sonnet works, for instance, maybe because they themselves are writers or quite the reverse, because recognizing patterns of rhyme and meter suits their need for quantifiable information. With other students, after two minutes of that sort of analysis you can practically hear their eyelids snapping closed, but they might be more interested in the historical context. This one wants to explore the poem's implied philosophical beliefs, another wonders how this text relates to other writings of the period, while somebody else is critiquing the work's social attitudes. They are all part of a conversation about the work. Each, being drawn to a different aspect of it, perceives it differently, and they may have discordant, incompatible ideas even about the same word, yet they have a text in common and broadly accept much about it without disagreement. Their contributions to the discussion become in greater or lesser ways parts of the tradition by which we understand the material and transmit our understanding to the next round of students, another generation of interpreters.

Some of those new perspectives might find their way into the mainstream of acceptance, perhaps in the way that local medieval practices (the bar mitzvah ceremony) did. Other positions might remain on the margins, adhered to by some and perhaps brought toward the center at another time and place in order to answer a current need, much as the kabbalists' Tu b'shevat seder (discussed below) has become a feature in countless mainstream congregations and religious schools that would ordinarily shun any explicit teaching or practice of Kabbalah.

Judaism is dynamic; its vibrancy lies in its capacity to conserve, reform, reconstruct and renew its traditions as well as to devise new ones. As Zalman Schachter-Shalomi teaches, its periodic major renewals can be understood as "paradigm shifts," such as the movement from Temple-centered worship to the synagogue-centered practices of prayer and study, or the currently ongoing revival and expansion of our notions of Jewish spirituality and broadly inclusive spiritual practices drawing upon a wide range of meditative, liturgical and musical resources. Some of those are renewals of older Jewish practices, such as the feminist and spiritually driven rediscovery of immersion in the mikvah (ritual bath) as personally meaningful. Others are newly developed rites, while still others adapt or "convert" elements of non-Jewish systems like yoga for our uses.

Here, two concerns might arise. One of those is to what extent we can incorporate into our own practice, or our congregation's, some of this great imaginative creativity that Judaism is now enjoying. There are so many points of possible resistance that we can anticipate the objections. "The ritual committee will never go for it." "It feels like too much of a stretch." "I tried it, and for every compliment there were three complaints." "I can't play the guitar." Perhaps. All the more reason to be creative yourself about attaining what you need. It is said that when George Balanchine was asked how he made his dances, he replied, "On union time." We work with the resources we have, with the time we have been allotted, the people who belong to our congregation and show up for the service, not the congregation we dream of. On union time, Balanchine made masterpieces. We might be able to achieve something very good on the time we have.

Another is whether these innovations are truly and authentically Jewish. At this point it is helpful to distinguish between truth and facts. Facts are verifiable information. A date or a measurement is a fact. That fish swim in water is a fact. That Bordeaux is a region in France is a fact. The statement that Bordeaux produces the world's greatest red wines is true for some wine drinkers, but it is not a fact because there is no way to verify it. The existence of the planet we call Earth is as close to a fact as anything we know. "God created the Earth" is not a fact, though for many people it is true. A succinct distinction is ascribed to the great Danish physicist Niels Bohr, who said something rather close to this: "The opposite of a trivial truism is a false statement. But the opposite of a profound truth may well be another profound truth." Mordechai Kaplan phrased his observation about truth in this way: "When we speak of our religion as the truth, we forget that 'truth' is an abstract noun derived from the adjective 'true,' and that what may be true for certain people in certain situations is not necessarily true for others in other situations."[3] To perceive someone else's truth, I must either take them at their word ("I accept that is true for you") or set aside my own shaping experiences sufficiently to perceive how the other person comprehends truth. That movement naturally expands my perception of possibilities, which in turn may stimulate me to consider my own truth outside of complacent or passive unexamined acceptance. Looking for facts about Jewish practices across the centuries and continents, we realize that the truth has many hues beyond black and white.

✳ ✳ ✳

Do we have to?

"But"—you might say—"can't we just do it the old familiar way?" Of course. And the best reasons for doing it the old familiar way are two. One of them is that you appreciatively sense the connection with the chain of transmission that got it to you. You stand gratefully in the place of your grandmother or Maimonides or Hillel. The opening of the mishnaic chapter entitled *Pirke Avot* traces the train of tradition, investing the leaders of that day with the authority of the transmittal: "Moses received the Torah at Sinai and transmitted it to Joshua, Joshua to the elders, the elders to the prophets, and the prophets to the men of the great synagogue." As much as this authorizes the later generation to speak and teach, it also honors the past. So it is said in the Talmud that when a teaching is transmitted in this world in the name of sages who have passed on, their lips move in the grave (*Yevamot 97a, Sanhedrin 90b*). That is, they live on when their teachings are quoted and they are recognized as teachers. We sense this powerfully in the arts. Particular phrasing connects you the dancer with your teacher who learned it from a student of Martha Graham, by whom it was created, or you the violinist with your teacher who learned it from Nathan Milstein who learned it from Leopold Auer who learned it from Joseph Joachim who learned it from Brahms who played it for Clara and Robert Schumann, who had been acquaintances of Mendelssohn.

The other is that the direct eloquence of the accustomed words and tunes still communicates with and for you. The 17th century British religious poet and Anglican priest George Herbert recognized this power as he wrote in "Jordan (1)",

> Is there in truth no beauty?
> Is all good structure in a winding stair?

In the companion poem "Jordan (2)" he puts the issue squarely as a compositional issue:

> I sought out quaint words, and trim invention;
> My thoughts began to burnish, sprout, and swell,
> Curling with metaphors a plain intention,
> Decking the sense, as if it were to sell.

We ought to be able to do a traditional ritual in a time-sanctioned way or speak the accustomed words, however our modern minds want to understand them, without falsifying or distorting what we do in order to "sell" it.

Innovation does have great value, especially when neither of the reasons for following the usual path is sufficiently persuasive when they are balanced against the possibly deadening effect of rote repetition or the continuing proclamation of something that we cannot believe or beneficially transmit from the previous generation to the next. However, as countless stage directors and scenic designers have inadvertently proven, ingenuity might not be a good end in itself.

Furthermore, rituals exist in especially sensitive microclimates. Divorced acquaintances of ours who were about to wed one another decided that they would celebrate Thanksgiving by having their teen-age children from their previous marriages join them for a special holiday dinner that could bond them in what would be a new tradition. As the parents hoped to get away from the tainted memories of prior Thanksgivings and enjoyed cooking Chinese food together, they prepared a splendid Chinese banquet. Their plan succeeded in a completely unanticipated way. His children and hers did connect with one another in mutual rage against their parents for ruining the anticipated Thanksgiving feast. They didn't want thousand-flavor chicken and braised bok choy, they wanted platters of turkey and bowls of mashed sweet potatoes.

"Don't be afraid to be boring." That simple but useful piece of advice came from a distinguished artist, the great pianist Claudio Arrau, and has been quoted by another, Andras Schiff. Neither of them is a "boring" musical interpreter. But both recognize that the fear of seeming boring may induce us into distortions and excesses. While trying to invest every moment with special meaning, we call attention to ourselves, either deliberately or not. Even if we don't intend to play the star, we end up doing so for the wrong reasons; we pull the focus away from the purpose we should be serving. This is the trap as well for amateur performers, and the more familiar and obvious the text, the fussier the delivery becomes. At some level that is understandable. The opera singer whose only line in *La Traviata* is *"La cena é pronta,"* "Dinner is served," naturally yearns to turn it into a moment that will be noticed. With inexperience, we work too hard. The performance becomes just that, and it becomes "about" us. In Paul Rudnick's play *I Hate Hamlet*, the star's girlfriend, Dierdre, who plays a lady-in-waiting in *Hamlet*, recounts the director's notes to her following the dress rehearsal:

> He said I was very good, but that when they announce that Ophelia is dead, I shouldn't scream. Or stagger. Or grab your sword and try to stab myself. He said the play wasn't called "The Tragedy of Ophelia's Best Friend."[4]

A tyro Hamlet is just as prone to working through countless subtly different choices of inflections, phrasing and pauses to make the so-familiar "To be or not to be, that is the question" at once memorable, insightful and original, to deliver a reading that will astonish the audience by being fresh yet perfect. What is likely to come out of all that effort, of course, is something eccentric, studied and unnatural; and in that case, woe to the production whose Hamlet is his own director.

As Andras Schiff remarks, "Of course when we are young, we exaggerate. When you are young you must exaggerate. From too much you can reduce. Only with experience can you learn to do nothing." Quoting Arrau, he then observes that "Today people are really afraid to be boring," Mr. Schiff said. "They have to be original. They have to be interesting. God forbid that somebody might not pay attention. The courage to be boring, to do nothing, is very important. The silence is as important as the actual notes."[5] "Don't just do something; stand there" is not merely joking advice. "Less is more," as Robert Browning (and subsequently Mies van der Rohe) wrote. Or, as Hamlet's mother acerbically urges him, "More matter, with less art."

The lesson is that we don't have to squeeze every last possible meaning or drama from a text or ritual in order to make an effect. Doing something attentively with full *kavvanah*, a fully focused purpose, as expressed through our personal engagement in the event may be exactly what is needed, and sufficient to the occasion. A ballet dancer's perfect *plié* at the appropriate moment can be as significant as a brilliant *tour en l'air* and far more impressive than a poorly executed or badly timed one, even as Giotto was said to have demonstrated his artistic prowess to the pope by simply drawing a perfect circle freehand. There are times when "Dinner is served" means just that and nothing more, no matter how lavish the meal itself might be or how many critics and impresarios are in the audience. Over-selling the message won't improve the cuisine, turn the dinner into more of an occasion than it is, or transform a line into an aria. Make the announcement and get off stage. With maturity, we sense where and when to expand or innovate. Doing a ritual with full concentration and commitment can be more beautiful than trying to beautify it with over-elaboration.

This takes us naturally to the role of ritual in the sense of established routine. We frequently think of ritual as a special series of arcane gestures. However, ritual can be as simple as a morning routine. Feeding the cat or letting out the dog, getting the newspaper, starting to heat water for coffee, pouring juice or putting out the daily vitamins—the predictable and customary order in which we do such activities without deliberation has a ritual quality if we feel that something is amiss when we skip one of those steps or do them in the wrong sequence. For some of us, the morning commute is crucial to the process of preparing ourselves for the work-day ahead; it becomes part of our ritual. We might need a cup of coffee at hand before we sit down to work. The ritual might have elements of necessity. Unless we work at home, the process of getting to our job is built into our work day, but what we make of it—think through our schedule or rehearse what we need to say, or listen to the same program on the radio—is up to each of us. We make that into our own ritual. But not everything we do ritualistically has a compelling logic.

A personal example might be useful. Having taught for many years, I would have to force myself to walk into a classroom without a pen and a full cup of hot coffee in addition to the class roster and textbook. What actually happens during the class? I rarely take the roll, though I use the roster to remind me of names. Not usually recording the roll, I seldom use the pen. While I occasionally manage a sip of coffee, more often I pick up the mug, answer a question or think of something else I want to say, and set it down untasted; or I pick it up not with the intention to drink but to give myself a pause for thought in a way that seems more involved than silently staring at my fingers for 15 seconds. Despite knowing that I do not really require them, if I find myself heading to class without the complete complement of my "ritual items," I will turn back and get what I am missing; and if for some reason I can't get coffee or realize as I walk through the doorway that I don't have a pen, I start class feeling a bit distracted by the lack, as if I were unprepared, even though only taking the correct book has anything to do with readiness.

Some of these items and the behavior traits that go with them are relics of once-meaningful activities. The pen and roster sheet certainly go back to the days when taking attendance was part of the daily opening rite of every class; and the coffee mug for negotiating reflective moments is most likely a partial substitute for the pipe that I used to smoke or at least toy with to fill pauses for thought during class. Some other drink or object (eyeglasses, for instance) could serve that purpose just as well, as would mere unaided silence. The class roster is useful, though it could be dispensed with as soon as I learn students' names. Actually, the only essential item is the textbook; and even so, there are major works that I have taught often enough to be able to cite without having the text before me, meaning that there are times when even the essential item could be discretionary. But I still expect to have it with me.

That is how rituals take shape and sustain themselves. The Four Species that are involved in the waving of the lulav is a good example of how tradition persists. *Leviticus 23:40* mandates,

"And you shall take on the first day the fruit of a lovely tree [*p'ri eytz hadar*], branches of palm trees, and boughs of a dense tree [*eytz avot*], and willows of the brook; and you shall rejoice before the Lord your God for seven days." We insist on having the exceptionally expensive *etrog*, and none other, though relatively few have ever seen the *eytz hadar* on which it grows and therefore could not say whether it is in truth a lovely tree; neither would we consider substituting the fruit of a more familiar tree the attractiveness of which we could more readily attest. Even if we go back to the talmudic discussion, the designation of the etrog seems arbitrary, though unchallenged. Indeed, it is taught (*Sukkah 31a*) that if an etrog cannot be found, we cannot use instead "a quince or a pomegranate or anything else." Accept no substitutes, even (the talmudic sages say) of fruit like a quince or pomegranate, both of which resemble the etrog in shape and size; and certainly the pomegranate tree and its blossoms are quite *hadar*, beautiful. The required boughs will be myrtle, another relative rarity outside of Mediterranean climates. More a shrub than a tree, the myrtle is no more dense or thick than many other species that might be more readily attainable, but nothing else will do.

Maybe nothing else will do because over time our sensory memory of these ritual plants has become essential to the festival's total experience. No other plant has quite the appearance of the beautiful little almond-shaped lime-green spades of the myrtle leaf nor the same scent when rubbed, more delicate than bay, more floral than thyme, less pungent than basil. No other fruit has the same aroma as the etrog, similar to a lemon but with a brighter fragrance; we could call it a lemon with a smile. Even though its thick pith and meager interior fruit mean that it has limited culinary uses and is chosen for its looks alone, the etrog's devotees differ greatly in their preferences for shape, size and color; they willingly pay premium prices for their favorite, be it with or without *pitom* (the remnant of the blossom), spherical or elongated shape, smooth or nubby texture, green or yellow rind, or one that is just ripening and changing color.

Another familiar instance is the kindling of lights just before sundown on Friday to inaugurate the sabbath. Even those who use other forms of electricity throughout *shabbat* mark the day by lighting candles. Except when unusual circumstances prevent the use of fire (for instance, in a space shuttle or a hospital room), few people would substitute turning on a couple of light bulbs, though screwing in bulbs on top of electrified "candles" could suffice. Even when permutations occur in the rituals, the original is reflected in the basic structure of the rite. We usually light candles, but of course they have largely superseded the more ancient standard source of light, oil lamps.

The most arcane yet deeply rooted of the traditions are those involving Passover foods. I was once asked to lead a model seder for a large rural church whose education director assured me that she knew the logistical details from previous demonstrations by Rabbi X, who had since left the area. Checking with her a week before, I struggled to regain my voice when she told me that they were expecting a wonderful turnout and had already bought "enough pita for 150 people." Pita? "But I looked at the package carefully and it has no leavening." She had gotten the biblical principle but missed the centuries of interpretation that differentiated between matzah for Pesach and other flour products made without leaven that would be acceptable to eat during the rest of the year. It was a teaching moment, and I could only hope that those attending their Wednesday night church suppers would not mind eating pita for as many weeks as it would take to finish the countless packages that were replaced by a few boxes of matzah, a food seldom enjoyed by anyone who did not grow up in a Jewish household, and sometimes not by them either. But who would do without a taste of matzah on Pesach?

For some Jews, a seder without matzah ball soup is unimaginable; for others, especially some hassidic Jews, a matzah ball lightened by beaten egg whites seems too much like a leavened product to eat on the first or second night of the festival, regardless of whether the particular matzah is indeed fluffy enough to float on the soup, not sink like lead (another tradition of sorts). Whether legumes or rice are acceptable during Pesach is a matter of complex ethnographic distinctions within each community or even each household. So too is the question of whether lamb can be served in any form at the seder. Absolutely not at all? Most certainly yes? Yes, but braised, not roasted? Yes, but not leg of lamb because the shankbone on the seder plate represents the *Pesach* offering? This is not simply a question of doing what is "traditional" but of understanding whose tradition we are following, and to what end.

Another way to think about this idea is to recognize that we have to know a tradition in order to depart effectively from it. Schoenberg, Balanchine, Picasso, Joyce—they know the history and vocabulary of their art form. When they depart from the conventions, they know what they are doing and why. They know where the traditional approach does not satisfy them, which is the point of uniqueness that we usually notice, as well as where it does. When they innovate, they do so with conviction, just as they accept other conventions with conviction.

As the choreographer Twyla Tharp writes, "Before you can think out of the box, you have to start with a box."[6] Occasionally a couple says they want to write their own wedding ceremony.

They imagine something unique that doesn't sound like every other couple's ceremony. Before long they admit that they do not really know the content of "the traditional ceremony." If thoughtfully guided, they may realize that the conventional ritual expresses what is essential and that can be done creatively. But if what they devise for themselves is truly unique, will it seem like a wedding? Will everyone know that what they have witnessed is a marriage ceremony? The traditional ceremony is the box. It could still be a nice box and beautifully wrapped. The so-called tradition can be a dead hand or the breath of life.

Consider one of the spectacular moments in ballet, Marius Petipa's classic choreography for the entrance of The Shades in *La Bayadère*. It is a vision of white tutus and white veils draped over ballerinas' arms. The dancers enter one by one, assume the pose of *arabesque cambré* in profile to the audience, arch their bodies to lift their arms into a lyre-like fifth position *port de bras* and take two steps, making room for the succeeding dancer. Each dancer moves down an inclined ramp from the right until the stage is filled with (traditionally) 32 identically garbed women moving in unison to the same repeated sequence as they split into eight rows of four dancers, all now facing forward. Each repeated element is simple in itself. The effect could be stupefyingly boring but instead, it should be and often is exquisite.

When I have the opportunity to see this ballet, I am conflicted about where I want to sit. Do I want the illusion? That is, do I want to be far enough back to appreciate how the ensemble moves as if it were one great organism breathing harmoniously and inching its way slowly and sinuously in perfect coordination, a miracle brought to life? Or do I want to be as close as possible to focus on the intense effort from every artist in the performance that makes this beauty—the lift of the ribcage, the tremor in the calf, the intensely focused concentration that shows in the eyes and sweat-rimmed forehead as each dancer first carefully senses whether she is securely placed and if her weight is properly distributed on the sloping ramp before she raises herself into the arabesque position, knowing that a bobble will mar the entire effect, and worse, that it is a misstep that will nag at her all night and one that she will have to contend with again mentally and emotionally until she safely negotiates the next performance?

There is beauty in the night sky whether it is seen plain by wondering earth-eyes or differently through the intense focus of a telescopic lens. What we want to see in the dance or in any authentic expression of art, fine craftsmanship or a religious ritual is the human being alive to the full potential for meaningful expression and communication in the moment. Are we happy with the service leader's smoothly polished performance taking us apparently effortlessly to the end of the liturgy or would we rather follow a riskier, less certain exploratory journey that might offer discoveries along with one or two anxiety-provoking wobbles? Whether we are conscious of the creative effort or beguiled by seeming effortlessness, either can be beautiful.

✳ ✳ ✳

Musical Variations

In 1819 an Austrian music publisher and composer named Anton Diabelli wrote a little waltz that he sent to numerous prominent composers, asking each to compose a variation that Diabelli would publish in a single volume, the sale of which would presumably be boosted by the appearance of works by (for instance) Schubert and the new prodigy, Liszt. Eventually, about fifty turned in something for the enterprise. One who did not because his original opinion of Diabelli's waltz was sheer contempt began playing around with the work and got intrigued enough to produce thirty-three variations himself. Beethoven's subsequently published set of the Diabelli variations stands as one of the keyboard masterpieces of all time. One simple theme, many variations, each distinctive, whether by fifty different compositional hands or by just one.

Jewish music's fine nuances are too often lost in the undifferentiated sameness of melodic familiarity. We sing the tunes we know best, and the ones we know best are likely to be the ones most easily learned. However, traditionally, the times of daily prayer and each of the special days have all been characterized by their own particular musical modal qualities. In addition, musical scales have differed across the world, broadly differentiating Ashkenazic, Sephardic and Mizrahi (Eastern) melodic characteristics, with some communities developing their own distinctions. Variety in Jewish music is much like variety in Jewish food: there is much more to it than would be imagined by those for whom the staples of Eastern European Jewish cuisine (some of it borrowed from Polish, German, Austrian and Romanian cooking) defines "Jewish." Today, the range is probably broader than at any other time in Jewish history, thanks to recordings and travel. We have access to the older expressive and often ornate cantorial styles, rhythmic traditional hassidic tunes and *niggunim* (melodies generally sung on repeated syllables rather than words) or new ones such as the songs of Shlomo Carlebach, Italian Renaissance settings by Salomone Rossi or 19th and 20th century European compositions by classically trained composers like Sulzer and Lewandowsky or Ernst Bloch and Steve Reich, Sephardic ballads from all around the Mediterranean, traditional and contemporary klezmer, folk-and-pop influenced religious songs such as Debbie Friedman's, as well as Shefa Gold's modern chants composed for liturgical use from biblical and siddur texts.

We can build a prayer service from an eclectic mix, as usually happens, or find our voice in inner religious life through one particular style.

Morning, afternoon and evening prayers, even when the texts remain the same, acquire their own temperaments from the *nusach* or characteristic tonality associated with them; so too do the prayers and songs associated with Shabbat, the festivals, the Days of Awe and differentiated from the services of standard times. On the *Yomim Tovim* the melody used for the reading of the Torah differs from the customary one used during the rest of the year; the simple shift from one nusach to another evokes for the experienced synagogue-goer the nuanced texture of a particular time, very much in the way that a home filled with aromas of cooking may announce Thanksgiving, Hanukkah, or Pesach even before we walk into the kitchen. One whiff, or one musical cadence, is all that it takes for almost instantaneous time travel, not just in our heads but in our senses and internal network of emotions. Maybe it would be more accurate to call this mood travel. Certain other passages in the Torah have distinctive tunes associated with them, as do the five *megillot* (*Lamentations, Ecclesiastes, Esther, Song of Songs, Ruth*) designated for Tisha b'Av, Sukkot, Purim, Passover and Shavuot. Shabbat, Passover and Hanukkah have their own vast characteristic musical repertoires.

Music's resonances come through especially strongly at the shiva minyan. Imagine being in a house of mourning, where the family and friends of the deceased are assembled in fresh grief. In this setting the joyful, often lilting tunes of Shabbat feel totally inappropriate. Those, however, are the ones most familiar (indeed, often the only ones familiar) to Jews whose backgrounds do not encompass traditional *nusach*. Not knowing the distinctive daily morning, afternoon (*mincha*), or evening melodies, they may be reluctant to join in reciting even the most familiar texts if those sound alien and unfamiliar to them in new musical garb. Having learned the text through singing it for many years in its customary shabbat melody, they might not even recognize that they know the words in a different setting. One ends up with people who have assembled to make possible a religious service in which they do not feel able to participate if the music is strange to them; but choosing the familiar tunes produces a discordantly joyful-sounding service. What to do? If we are able to develop more common awareness of these nuances of musical modes, we also attune ourselves to nuances of emotional moods. If not, we may need to seek ways in the moment of need so that we can teach and lead, maybe taking over and bending a melody to a more appropriate shape.

This has been the essence of the art of the *hazzan*, the cantor. A *hazzan* who has received investiture or ordination is, like the rabbi, a member of the clergy. Since Jewish musical expression is primarily vocal, the cantor has transmitted this element of the liturgy. Only in the last two centuries have instruments such as the organ or piano found a place in the synagogue through Reform congregations, with the guitar appearing in the mid-twentieth century and percussion added more recently, especially in Renewal-influenced services. Some cantors have been legendary for their glorious, well trained voices of operatic quality and their capacity to stir deep emotions in their listeners. The cantor's main cultural role, however, is as specialist in the details of the liturgy and its appropriate musical expression. Jewish liturgical music, like opera, relies on recitatives as much as arias. More so than the rabbi, who is mainly a teacher-scholar and Jewish legal authority but not necessarily charged with being the principal leader of religious services, the *hazzan* needs to know the proper liturgical and melodic variations, the *nusach*, for every section of every service, including the Torah and other biblical readings as well as the variants for all times of day and holidays, to be deeply acquainted with the Hebrew language and music theory in order to compose or extemporize appropriately. Necessarily, the ideal *hazzan* also has an authoritative grasp of Jewish liturgy and ritual observances and is able to convey their essences through melodic expression. For this reason, we refrain from the slippery tendency to use the title of cantor for a congregation's customary vocal soloist, reserving it for those men and women who truly have the traditional Judaic learning as well as musical ability.

The style of praying aloud that we call *davvenen* is very much like the sung recitatives that we find in many operas, in which the characters converse in melodic patterns that are not like songs but musical speech. A religious service in which *davvenen* is the norm, especially when the *hazzan* can establish the appropriate *nusach*, will seem completely different from the same service when the participants speak the text instead, most often by reciting it in unison. Music raises the emotional and spiritual level of the ceremony above the solely rational level of normal spoken communication. It signifies that we are purposefully doing something with a different part of our brain than the one that we normally engage. It also eases the transition to the explicitly sung portions of the liturgy. They seem less like performance pieces inserted into a spoken drama and more like the natural intensification of emotion and spiritual transcendence. Because this is not normal speech, some people find it awkward, at least at first, and others resist it entirely. Still others have the reverse response, feeling that this is the natural and right way of prayer, such that doing so in merely spoken discourse is stiff and flat, "preachy" rather than lyrical and that it is more unnatural for people to read prayers like speeches said in unison. When you try both, you will discover something about your own prayer.

Chapter 3
Embodied Faith

If we are hosting a dinner party, we may set out our finest crystal wine glasses, choosing the shape appropriate to bring out the qualities of the wine we are serving and to honor our guests with the best that we are able to offer, even though we know that it is possible to drink any beverage from a paper cup. However, using a beautiful ceremonial goblet (a *kiddush cup*) for the wine blessing at a festive religious occasion is not done to enhance the taste of the ceremonial wine, which is usually impervious to any enhancement. Rather, we use a special vessel to honor the holiday or ceremony. We could use an ordinary glass, or even paper or plastic, but prefer not to. Showing up at a wedding wearing jeans and a t-shirt is not illegal but neither does it honor the event and its celebrants.

Similarly, brief moments of liturgical practice—lighting a candle, singing a line of a blessing—may be done merely pro forma, satisfying the requirement of doing the action without bringing genuine presence and commitment to it, and they are often done in that way even by people who deeply believe in the observance. The *keva* or fulfillment of the act can be sufficient without *kavvanah*, focused intention. Few of us, after all, are so integrated spiritually and bodily that we are always as fully immersed in our practices as a dolphin in water. But we may strive for that more focused expression, like a pianist appreciating that turning one perfectly nuanced phrase in a bar of a Chopin impromptu is a satisfying feat of artistry that lingers pleasurably in the mind.

If our understanding of Judaism is shaped by thinking of it as "law," we might forget that Judaism advocates a practice called *hiddur mitzvah*, which has nothing to do with legalism. The word *hiddur* comes from the verb *hadar*, which primarily means to make beautiful. It is the sort of beautification, however, that is not mere adornment because the word also means to show honor, respect or reverence. Fulfilling a commandment in a beautiful way might seem at first like a strange pair of imperatives, but it makes sense if we compare it with the dancer who tries to make a beautiful arabesque even in class, not just on stage, or if we have seen a military honor guard carrying out the ritualized steps of its duties with precise elegance no matter whether they have an audience or not.

This also pertains to our treatment of ritual items. We do not worship objects, but Jewish practice encourages a tactile physical relationship with anything for which we say a blessing. We say a blessing for bread while holding it, and then taste it before eating anything else or even speaking. Putting on or removing a tallit, most of us bring the neckpiece to our lips; we kiss tefillin in taking them from their case and putting them away after use, and when passing through a doorway we might touch our fingers to the mezuzah and then bring them to our lips, as we do with a Torah scroll when it is carried. Someone given the honor of reciting the blessing for the reading from the scroll touches the edge of a prayerbook or the tallit fringes to the margin of the scroll and then to his or her lips, then holds onto the wooden roller handles while giving the blessing. If a prayerbook or other Hebrew religious text falls, we kiss it respectfully when we pick it up. Through our hands and lips, we also extend our hearts.

The biblical descriptions of the tabernacle and the first Temple in Jerusalem may just sit on the page when we encounter them as historical records, but if we think of them as accounts of images and rites of living people, their physicality becomes overwhelming. Incense elaborately concocted of eleven ingredients mingled with the aroma of roasting sacrificial animals; the Levites on the steps chanted the psalms in a variety of melodies, rhythms and modes; a menorah of hammered gold branched into blossom-shaped cups filled with finest olive oil, burned daily.

Some reading these descriptions, seized with inappropriately nostalgic awe for a kingdom lost in ancient times, yearn to rebuild a grand temple and reinstitute its priesthood with the accompanying pageantry and even sacrifices, though presumably without our ancestors' internecine power struggles along with empires menacing from every side. Others respond with equally inappropriate revulsion against physicality in worship—that is, against what they deem to be the crudity of associating religious devotion with emotionally driven physical expression. Religion, they say, is supposed to be dis-embodied, a matter for the spirit and intellect but not the body. We ought not get up spontaneously to dance, nor shout, clap or wave our arms. We stand or sit, or we rise and bend our knees to bow, according to an established choreographic plotting that has no room for ad-libs. It is as scripted as the service leader's "Please read responsively" or "We continue on page 37," and in some traditions it is still more detailed.

Yet even adherents to such practice might not notice how the established shape of the space and liturgy may limit spiritual expression. In synagogues, like other "houses of worship," we might sit in uncomfortable, un-houselike rows, facing forward. We are cramped, we cannot easily see one another, and too often we are often effectively cut off from contact with nature or artistic beauty.

Yet, if asked to describe an intensely spiritual experience that they have had, most people will readily cite their spontaneous reaction to something richly physical, such as standing before the Grand Canyon, hearing an especially moving performance of a great musical work, savoring an exceptional dinner superbly prepared and elegantly served, being in a group that relates significantly as a community of shared experience, seeing Michelangelo's "David," recalling the first meaningful kiss, giving birth. Or they may acknowledge being moved toward the spiritual by a physical illness, a close escape from a terrible accident, someone's death, or a gripping fear that is as visceral and painful as any visible wound. As Emily Dickinson wrote, "I like a look of agony / Because I know it's true." That moment of truth pushes us to the full awareness of living and of the aura of life that surrounds and transcends our individual moment of being.

In other words, our bodies do not get out of the way so that we can have a spiritual event. They are part of that experience and the medium through which we take in the stimuli to which our spirits respond.

✳ ✳ ✳

Wrapping in fringed light

The tallit is frequently called a prayer shawl, though that is not its original meaning. A tallit was simply a cloak-like garment; Orthodox Jewish males today may wear a simple tallit with fringes at the corners as as undergarment beneath their shirts. As a prayer shawl it used to be predictably white with black horizontal stripes; blue stripes were stylish modern innovations. The modern revival of interest in fabric arts and designs, which has also affected the design of the *kippah* or *yarmulke*, has resulted in a marvelous variety of colorful *tallitot*, hand woven of fine wool or linen, or hand-painted silk, some shawl-like and others large enough for wrapping oneself, visually vibrant with biblical scenes or other motifs meaningful to the wearer; they might contain texts in fine calligraphy other than the customary blessing for wearing it lettered on the *atarah* (neckpiece). The rules for a tallit are few. It may be made of linen, silk or wool, so long as linen and wool are not combined in the fabric, which is prohibited in *Leviticus 19:19.* And it needs four distinct corners, near each of them a hole through which are threaded the strands that will be wrapped and tied to form the *tzitzit,* "fringes." It is the four sets of *tzitzit* that make the tallit a Jewish garment rather than just an ornate caftan or scarf.

While most *tallitot* come with them already attached and tied, there is merit in tying one's own, since by that process we can better learn the meaning of the ties. This craft has been called Jewish macramé. Regardless of the style of tying, they all have in common four threads for each corner, doubled into eight strands in order to tie them in the requisite knots. Numerologically, the letters in the word *tzitzit* have the value of 600; add 8 to that for the eight strands, and 5 for the five knots, and each set of fringes should recall that there are 613 biblical commandments. Each of the various methods of winding adds to the numerological symbolism by reminding a knowledgeable wearer of one of the sacred names of God through the pattern of coils between the knots.

There is deep wisdom in the code of the fringes. Theologically, we do not see the whole fabric of God. What we see instead are the strands of creation, much as God tells Moses, "You will see my back, not my face" (*Exodus 33:23*). Ethically, we need on one hand to be conscious of those who are marginalized and on the fringes of the community, who are literally or figuratively exiled or estranged, and on the other hand to be aware of our own borders and boundaries as members of a society and as Jews.

None of this is specified in the written Torah, which only gives the commandment that we wear fringes on the corners of our clothing. That was taken as applicable to men. Now, some women also wear the tallit as a prayer shawl during morning prayers, and a *kippah* while at prayer or otherwise; a smaller number wear *tefillin*, described below. The oral Torah takes on the practical task of clarifying according to tradition what is acceptable as fringes and how they are made, but just as importantly it fulfills the homiletic function of providing an ethical lesson for a ritual whose written mandate has a form but no meaningful content. Of course, we may suppose that there was a social function of *tzitzit* for men wearing them all the time. To themselves and to all whom they meet in public, these are visible reminders of their Jewish identity, their membership in the community or nation of Israel, their service to Y-H-V-H. Such identification would be particularly significant for men as they traveled, conducted business and interacted among other peoples. Wearing the *tzitzit* as a sign means that what the wearer does, and how, reflects not only on the individual but also on the Jewish people. Moreover, by specifying particular methods for tying, the oral traditions refine and deepen the lesson for their wearer, since each knot conveys an element of a coded reminder that we bear ourselves as witnesses to a sacred covenant.

Preparing to put on a tallit, we stand to hold it in both hands, reciting the two opening verses of Psalm 104, *bar'khi nafshi et-adonai*, "Bless Y-H-V-H, my soul, clothed in majesty and beauty, wrapped in light as with a garment; You spread the heavens like a curtain." Then, while reciting the blessing for wearing *tzitzit*, we cloak ourselves in the tallit. Some who use a large tallit rather than a scarf-like one cover their head, shoulders and back with it, or swathe themselves such that they are enwrapped by it, before perhaps letting it drape across the shoulders. The consonance of word and gesture, of verbal and visual imagery is perfect. We are virtually robed in light, enfolded in the teachings of Torah.

Tefillin

A pair of phylacteries: Are they two items or one? In Hebrew, they are called *Tefillin*. How odd that in English biblical translations, an unfamiliar Hebrew word, *tefillin*, which might or might not be related to the word meaning *prayer*, is "translated" by the Greek word *phylactery* that is just as unfamiliar, doesn't mean anything to anybody, and furthermore doesn't even equate well in Greek with the objects it is supposed to name. *Tefillin* consist of two small black leather boxes, each one attached to a specially wound black leather strap whose knots and windings have the shapes of certain Hebrew letters, although we need to use our imaginations to perceive most of those. During weekday morning prayers, one is worn on the worshipper's arm and hand, the other going around the worshipper's head so that the box is centered on the forehead above eye level. Until recently the wearing of tefillin was generally reserved for men, although the daughters of the great medieval commentator known as Rashi were known to have worn them at prayer.

Inside the boxes are little compartments in which are placed a scribe's hand-written parchment scrolls consisting of the four sets of biblical verses from *Exodus* and *Deuteronomy* in which *Tefillin* are commanded (Exodus 13:1-10, 11-16; Deuteronomy 6:4-9, 11:13-21). The tefillin *bayit*, "house" or box, for the arm is divided into four small compartments while that for the head has only one, though they contain the same four passages. This was characteristic of the earliest known tefillin as well. While there is no stated rationale for the difference, we might make an inference on the analogy of the question as to whether or not a separate blessing needed to be said when putting on the tefillin for the head after wrapping the tefillin for the arm, in other words, whether this constituted one obligation or two separate ones. This was solved in good Jewish fashion with two distinct blessings. Similarly, since there are four passages but they relate to one mitzvah—the wearing of tefillin—there might have been some early uncertainty over whether that implied one scroll containing all four passages or four scrolls with one passage each, consequently, we settled on both. There was also an ancient disagreement over the order of the passages, prompting a small number of worshippers to change from one set of tefillin to another during their prayers.

One never opens the boxes; those little scrolls inside are not taken out and read; but the texts are quoted in the liturgy, the most familiar of the passages being the Deuteronomic commandment, "Take to heart these instructions I give you today. Instill them in your children. Consider them when you stay at home and when you are away, when you lie down and when you arise. Bind them as a sign on your hand and let them serve as a frontispiece between your eyes. Inscribe them on the doorpost of your house and on your gates." (Of course, the usual translation, "frontlet" rather than frontispiece, is another English word that really means nothing to anyone, but at least it gives an inkling of an idea.)

Wearing *tefillin* at prayer is generally regarded as implying that one accepts the biblical commandments and considers them binding, in this case literally, on one's actions—the hand and arm—one's impulses—because the box on the arm is angled toward the heart—one's thoughts, and one's way of looking at the world—the other *bayit* on the forehead between one's eyes.

For some who wear *tefillin*, however, the most important part of the ritual is not wearing but putting them on. This begins after one has already wrapped oneself in a *tallit*, and it is conducted effectively in silence, because it is supposed to take one's entire attention. First, one has to remove any watch, rings or bracelets on the hand and arm on which the *tefillin* will be wound—left for right-handed people. We take the *tefillin* from their cloth case. They and their straps are always shiny black leather; some sets, crafted from an especially fine piece of hide, are handsome examples of a leather-maker's skill, although I admit to fondness for more ordinary but well-used *tefillin* that are beautiful for having been worn frequently for prayer. The process of putting on the *tefillin* entails placing the box on the arm, tightening the strap, wrapping the strap in a certain way on the upper arm, then seven times around the forearm as one recites a blessing, temporarily winding the strap around the hand while one places the other *tefillin* on the head and recites yet another text and blessing, then returns to finish the process of binding the hand with the leather strap, wrapping around the middle finger while reciting a verse from the prophet Hosea that speaks of the betrothal between God and Israel, ending by looking at the back of one's hand and seeing that one has formed with the shiny black strap the Hebrew letter *shin*, the first letter of one of the special Hebrew names of God. And where else can that letter be found so prominently? On the outside of the *mezuzah*, the box containing a tiny hand-written parchment scroll with two of the same texts as the *tefillin,* placed as we heard before, "on the doorpost of" a Jewish person's house.

Through the wrapping of the *tefillin,* one virtually makes oneself the living embodiment of sacred teaching. For kabbalists, the seven windings around the arm and the three that form the *shin* represent the seven lower and three upper spheres of the mystical *sephirot* or dimensions that comprise all of existence emanating from the limitless source that we call God, sealed by the ring-like winding around our finger and crowned by the *tefillin* encircling our head. The letter formed by the strap on our hand and standing for a divine name temporarily makes our physical being an inscription. It is as if we, like the specially trained scribe who writes the parchments—on animal skins—had temporarily turned ourselves—in our human animal skin—into sacred text; as if for this period of prayer we could inhabit the divine presence through the *tefillin* that help us in *tefilah,* prayer. Or as if one's own person houses the commandments, like the *mezuzah.* They are on the doorposts and gates of our very being. That much of the understanding is homiletic: one can preach about it.

What cannot be so easily understood or expressed in normal discourse is the effect of the physical process of the wrapping. The ritualistic element of putting on the *tefillin* takes us into meditation, into something akin to a yoga exercise and, almost paradoxically, to dance. It is like a dance done with the feet and legs perfectly still, the core of the body motionless, but hands and arms and mind and lips constantly responding to one's focused attention and intention.

In truth, most people who wear *tefillin* regularly may put them on with as little purposeful concentration as most of us put into driving a well-traveled daily route. But the opportunity is available for an inner turn, the unexpected rediscovery of awareness, immersing into a deeper consciousness so that the automatic twistings and windings become rather like the focused whirls of the dervish, simultaneously requiring and intensifying our concentration, helping us to reach the still core of being at the center of our own turnings—the stable point of gravity that holds together our winding ways.

Mezuzah

A "mezuzah" is a doorpost, but the term has come to refer to the small case containing a very small parchment scroll (*klaf*) on which a scribe has handwritten the biblical passages related to the appropriate commandments for placing the Torah's teaching "on the doorpost of your homes and gates" (*Deut. 6: 4-9* and *11: 13-21*). On the outside it bears the Hebrew letter *shin*, standing for the sacred name *"shaddai."* Nowadays the mezuzah is nailed or screwed to the surface, but in some old sites of our past such as Girona and Tarazona in Spain visitors can still see hollowed enclosures in the wooden or stone doorposts that once would have held a scroll beneath a cover. Along with other Jewish ritual objects, the mezuzah has recently become a genre for artistic invention. *Mezuzot* of colorful ceramics, metals of all sorts, wood, silver, enamel, plain and colored glass fill pages of Judaica catalogues. It has sometimes been called an amulet, though that is incorrect. We place the mezuzah and its texts on the doorposts of our house "and on its gates" to remind us of our obligations as we come in and as we go out. Many touch the *mezuzah* each time they pass it, bringing their fingers to their lips, completing the circuit of text, hand, mouth, Written Torah, deeds (*mitzvot*), Oral Torah.

At the core of the Jewish worship service we also place a kind of mezuzah, reminders to ourselves. But there, they are not to remind us of Jewish biblical and rabbinic commandments;

instead, they speak of our obligations and frailties as human beings, as we enter into prayer and as we move from it. Before the sequence of prayers at the heart of the liturgy, we enter into them asking, "Breath of Life, part my lips, that my mouth may open in praise." Once they are concluded, we need to be accountable for what those words said, and how we felt about them; we leave that time of prayer with the hope, "May the words from my mouth and the thoughts within my heart be acceptable before You, my Rock and my Deliverance." Just before we reach that prayer, we have a time to pray in silence. But silence might also need words, and tradition has provided them: "My God, preserve my tongue from trouble-making and my lips from speaking falsely." We need words to remind us of the danger of words.

We are continually undermined and betrayed by what we say, and when we say it, to whom and how, by the false ways in which we have knowingly or unconsciously distorted the truth because of our own needs, desires, vulnerability. No wonder that, as rabbis always point out on Yom Kippur, the prayerbook's list of sins that we confess and for which we ask forgiveness include only one that has to do with what we put into our mouths and over a dozen varieties of what comes out of our mouths. Naturally, "mouths" today must include not just cellphones but talky e-mails that can so quickly speed rumors and gossip. We are wired and wireless, and sometimes oblivious and clueless. Many of us are exasperated by the people who inflict their part of a cellphone conversation on everyone in the airport lounge, grocery store, bookstore, or restaurant. Imagine having to overhear every conversation, every prayer, every threat, every plea, every cry. Imagine being God.

Sometimes words are too much. Sometimes they are not enough. Not enough because they may drape themselves casually over the surface of life, leading the trusting and unsuspecting to assume that beneath them there is a solid place to stand, a safe place to sit and rest. Not enough because linguistic resources continually fail us. (Just think of how paltry the word "love" is for all its varied duties—everything from how we feel about chocolate to how we feel about our children or the chosen companion of our lives.) Not enough because our readiness with words can keep us from listening for the sanctified moment in the heart's silence, can keep us from hearing the "still, small voice" we need to hear clearly and honestly, can keep us from discerning amid the chatter the voice of another who needs to be heard, the silence of another that needs to be noticed. Not enough because too many words may keep us from being <u>still</u>, and in that stillness to know who and what we are, and where, and how it is with us.

Jewish tradition holds that the most sacred name of God is unpronounceable, unutterable; and that the highest level of divine existence is a Something that is indistinguishable from Nothingness, beyond the capacity of human beings to comprehend and far beyond the capabilities of any language—even Hebrew—to describe or define. We similarly struggle to speak of ourselves, fail again and again to say who and what we are, we individual and collective mortal creatures, who are indeed more than talking heads. Through music and ritual, through dance and the visual arts we try to bring ourselves into expressive being, doing the little that we can to speak ourselves to one another with whatever resources we can command, because words are not enough.

Sefer Torah

Whenever you have a chance to see a *sefer torah*, take the opportunity; and whenever you have a chance to hear a *sofer*, a Torah scribe, talk about the year-long process of preparing the many leather pieces of parchment and handwriting a letter-perfect *sefer*, go. Unlike medieval and renaissance illuminated manuscripts, the scroll is not illustrated; there are no ornate initial letters or marginal decorations, no gold leaf or colored inks. In a way, there is not much to see except to the informed or practiced eye. Lettering is the art form and basic black is the color. Yet being a handmade product, every one is different, even though the text in each one should be identical to all others, and many particular features appear as well in every scroll. While the Torah has no markings of vowels or punctuation, about 100 of its exactly 304,805 letters in its 79,976 words have specific, unusual calligraphic details, many of which have been the subject of homiletic *midrashim*. A *sefer torah* found to have even one erroneous or illegible letter when read in the synagogue must be set aside until it can be checked and corrected. The Torah's two poems, the exuberant Song at the Sea in *Exodus* and Moses' swansong in *Deuteronomy*, each have their own particular layout, as do the two occurrences of the Ten Commandments and various other passages. Although there are no indications of what we would call chapters or even verses, the traditional divisions in the text such as "open" or "closed" paragraphs must be scrupulously followed. References in talmudic era works, notably a minor talmudic book called *Soferim*, specify many of the characteristics of a valid scroll, including the "square" letter forms of which are different from that used for the mezuzah and tefillin scrolls; if these were printed texts, we would say that they are printed in different fonts.

Despite the numerous prescriptive details, the scribe's hand shows in the rhythm, slope and weight of the letters. This sofer's letters stand alertly erect, that one's scurry, another's trudge stolidly, yet another's dance. The scrolls themselves take on personalities from the interplay of the parchment, the lettering, and the visible wear and tear on both. They age, some more gracefully than others; and some young scrolls make a grand first impression, though without having interesting personalities. Some are distinctly blue collar scrolls, produced correctly albeit not artfully by diverse craftsmen in a busy workshop; others are elegant and precise, as perfectly turned out as a diplomat sitting for an official portrait. Some scrolls are composites patched together from different *sifrei* to replace irreparably worn or damaged sections, like war veterans with prosthetic limbs. Here we notice erasures of mistakes, there the darkening of the parchment that makes reading more difficult; one line is hard to read correctly because the letters are cramped; on another line the final letter juts a bit too far into the margin to look neat; elsewhere, a letter horizontally elongated to fill out a line affords an unanticipated moment of imaginative daring. Sometimes a scroll will need careful attention because its bindings are weakening, letters fading, ink flaking, sheepskin discoloring with age; occasionally, one is too badly worn and damaged to repair, like a body with multiple organ failures, and will have to be buried ceremonially in a Jewish cemetery. Another scroll after more than a century and a half of use remains vibrant and strong. And in those places where a *sofer* has completed a line by artfully stretching a letter to fill the space gracefully, the beautiful aesthetic effect is nonetheless subject to the same pragmatic legibility test as everywhere in a scroll, whether the letter can be recognized by a child who knows the Hebrew *aleph-bet*.

The scroll's importance in the synagogue is marked by its place in a special enclosure in the center of the wall toward which the service is literally <u>oriented</u> (from the word for "east"). The scroll's prestige is also indicated by it being the most elaborately decorated object in the synagogue. Enclosed in its own special case in a Sefardic synagogue, in an Ashkenazic one it is ornately garbed. Or perhaps we should say that "she" is ornately garbed, as the word "torah" is grammatically feminine. She wears a cloth mantle (white for major festivals) and often has a silver breast-plate and ornaments for the tops of the rollers, generally in the symbolic shape of a crown or pomegranate, a hard-shelled fruit filled with small yet tasty and juicy seeds, thus fittingly symbolic of the Torah. A special pointer called a *yad* ("hand") is used during reading so that the reader can follow the text without touching the surface of the scroll. The yad, which should not be made of base metal, is often fabricated of sterling silver or wood and ends in the shape of a hand with a pointing finger; visitors to Jewish museums might see some with tips of ivory or coral. Donors wishing to contribute to the beauty of synagogue ritual life sometimes donate or craft themselves new mantles or Torah ornaments, and in the past century many artisans have gone past the reproduction of styles from 18th and 19th century Europe to deck the *sefer torah* written with an ancient art in stylish contemporary adornments.

Before and often after the reading, the scroll is removed from the ark with special music and paraded around the congregation. (In a Christian church, a remnant of this ritual is the ceremonial raising of the pulpit bible to show the congregation when the priest, minister or deacon takes it into the center aisle for the recitation.) From the time that the ark is opened until the scroll is placed on the reading desk, and then again whenever the *sefer torah* is raised, we stand, for we are in the presence of (so to speak) a royal messenger. The words deserve respect even when we need to struggle with the message. The anticipatory *hakafah* before and subsequently the celebratory one after the reading are the most jubilant moments in the synagogue, a parade each week to rejoice with our most ancient treasure, other than the living world itself.

The scroll is bound between two wooden staves (*atzei chayyim*, "trees of life"), each having a circular wooden disk above and below the parchment. When we look from the congregation at the ends of the two wooden rollers on the reading desk, we might imagine them looking like the infinity symbol ∞ before the scroll is opened. The full scroll itself, in being read continuously through each liturgical year, ending and beginning again on the same festival day of Simchat Torah, models infinity. When we open it, wherever we look we glimpse a moment in time, which reflects back to us and we in turn reflect back to it, continuing a dialogue between an ancient text and our new understanding of it as the scroll of our life also turns.

Chapter 4
Sabbath pantomime

The mime speaks through the body. The mime's hands tell a story, whether in ballet or solo performance. The mime teaches us to perceive the essence of an act expressed through simple physical gestures, so that we "see" the wall, the invisible presence of which is marked by the mime's flattened palms, or the ladder that the mime "climbs" standing on the floor while performing the climbing motions. Formalized by choreographers, mime has a vocabulary of gestures to articulate emotions eloquently. A hand circling one's face means, You are beautiful. Pressed to the chest, it expresses a vow: I mean this from the bottom of my heart. An index finger pointing to the ring finger signifies marriage.

We use such pantomime in daily life. Palms held together with the hands angled next to one's tilted head means sleep. We may adjust the signs dynamically to changing circumstances. Not very long ago, one signaled the intention to speak by telephone through a circular dialing motion, which became obsolete and then incomprehensible to a new generation that knew only push-button phones, not rotary dialers. For a very few years, an index finger pushing imaginary buttons replaced the dialing motion, before being almost universally supplanted by the cellphone sign, thumb toward the ear, middle fingers closed, and pinkie toward the mouth. We'll talk.

And now sunset time approaches on Friday evening. A woman traditionally has the honor of welcoming the sabbath through lighting candles or (less usually these days) oil lamps and reciting the blessing; however, a man may do this if no woman is present or able. We take two white candles, place them in holders and stand still before them for a moment. We remove a match from a box, strike it, then carefully hold it toward the candle on the right, letting the wick catch fire, then do the same with the other candle. Waving our hands two or three times toward ourselves over the lights, then we cover our closed eyes with our hands while reciting the blessing, *Barukh atah adonai eloheinu melekh ha-olam asher kideshanu be-mitzvotav ve-tzivanu ner shel shabbat*, "Praised . . . whose commandments show us the way toward sanctity through the kindling of shabbat light," opening our hands and eyes as we finish.

The meaning of the text is clear, though it is not without its own enigmas. For example, Where does God command the kindling of sabbath light, a *mitzvah* not to be found anywhere in the Torah? And why is it the singular *ner,* "light," when the universal practice is to use two lights? Why the mime accompanying this? What are its purpose and meaning?

The purpose actually answers a dilemma in *halakhah*, the legal aspect of Jewish practice, posed by the conjunction of lighting and blessing. Usually the practice is to say a blessing *before* performing an act, though *after* passively receiving or experiencing something. For example, we say a blessing for bread *before* we taste it; however, we say an appropriate blessing *after* hearing good news or seeing lightning. We either anticipate an experience or we recognize one that has occurred. Shabbat, however, is singular because of restrictions about its observance once it has begun. Consequently, we need to determine at what point Shabbat begins, not in a chronologic sense but in spiritual and communal terms: When do the restraints commence that turn Friday-night-and-Saturday into Shabbat, including the traditional prohibition against kindling fire? Conventionally we speak of "making" or "bringing" Shabbat, the verbs denoting the fact that although the sun will set on Friday evening, it is something that we do that will turn the passage of time into the sabbath.

If saying the blessing that acknowledges Shabbat marks the onset of the holiday, then once we conclude the blessing with the word *shabbat*, it is (according to *halakhah*) too late to strike a match because technically the sabbath has already begun. If it is the kindling of the light itself, along with the intention that this be *ner shel shabbat,* the light for the sabbath, saying the blessing after the lighting seems like an afterthought.

The mimed ritual described above serves the purpose of halakhic compromise. The lights are pragmatically kindled first, the blessing is recited while the lighter's eyes are occluded so as not to see the light, and the uncovering of the eyes at the conclusion brings together text and act. This is the purpose; and even someone who does not accept the premise of the halakhic stricture may appreciate the elegance of the solution.

What, though, of the meaning of the ritual waving of the hands? Jewish tradition holds that on the sabbath we each receive a *neshamah yetirah*, an extra measure of soul. By the waving of our hands, we draw to us that additional soul with a generous, open, two-handed welcoming "Come hither" motion.

How about covering the eyes? After all, if the main point is not to see the flames, one could accomplish that simply by closing one's eyes. True, but when our hands shield our eyes, we do two things. In community, we <u>demonstrate</u> that we do not see the lights. That is, we communicate to everyone around that we are following the letter of the teaching. Simultaneously, in our own inner life, we <u>focus</u> ourselves inward to the spiritual message of the sabbath, a day when the "labor" from which we are supposed to abstain is the work of changing the physical world to suit ourselves. In *Exodus 31: 16-17* we are told,

> Therefore the people Israel shall keep the sabbath, to observe the sabbath throughout their generations, for an everlasting covenant. It is a sign between me and the people Israel forever; for in six days Y-H-V-H made heaven and earth and on the seventh day rested and was refreshed.

The Hebrew original contains a lovely play on words in the poetic last phrase. It says, *u-va-yom hashvi'i* [Y-H-V-H] *shavat v'yinafash.* The word *shavat* is the verb form of the noun *shabbat.* The second verb, *yinafash,* translated sometimes as "refreshed," comes similarly from the word *nefesh,* "soul." One of the great songs welcoming Shabbat greets her (Shabbat, we have said, is often imagined in feminine terms) as *Yedid nefesh, Beloved soul.* In the trifold conceptualizing of the soul in Hebrew—*ruach, neshamah, nefesh*—the last is regarded as the most basic to the physical being, in a sense the least elevated level but the one at which body and spirit touch. Therefore we can understand this passage as saying that on the seventh day (*yom hashvi'i*) Y-H-V-H stopped working on the physical universe, on matter, to become the essence of Being. Or, as Aryeh Kaplan translated the verse, "ceased working and withdrew to the spiritual."

That withdrawal of the divine essence from physical action into contemplation, into inward reflection on one's own nature and the inner nature of all that is, finds its physical expression in the act of covering the eyes with one's hands, as if drawing the shutters on the outside world. The woman shielding her eyes in lighting shabbat candles in this way truly expresses *imitatio dei.* She becomes the expression and the reminder—*shamor v'zakhor,* preserve and remember the Sabbath, we are told in the two versions of the Ten Commandments—of divine creativity returning to re-gather its spiritual energies. The commitment to preserve and remember is that impulse of piety that we noticed at the beginning of this book

Lighting two lamps or candles has a homiletic point, in other words. Kindling "a" light—even one lamp—is sufficient for the rabbinic interpretation that one observes shabbat with lighting, rather than with making sure that no fire is burning on shabbat (which was apparently the Sadducee halakhah on *Exodus 35: 3, lo t'va'aru eysh,* "you shall not kindle fire"). In the Talmud, *Shabbat 25b,* R.Abbahu refers specifically to kindling *ner b'shabbat,* "a flame for shabbat." In *Berakhot 31b* we also find a reference in the singular to *hadlikat ner,* "the kindling of a flame," where the shabbat light is obviously intended. Talmud references often simply refer to *or l'shabbat,* light (singular) for shabbat.

In the fourth "Commandment," the precept for shabbat observance, the Exodus version asserts, *zakhor,* "remember," but Deuteronomy mandates *shamor,* "preserve" or "guard." Tradition deals with the discrepancy by claiming either that some of the people heard one word, the rest heard the other, or that the divine voice miraculously spoke both simultaneously. Notably, the sequence of the words is reversed in the first verse of the 16th century kabbalistic mystic Shlomo Alkabetz's Shabbat hymn *L'cha dodi,* still sung on Friday nights in most synagogues and many Jewish homes to any number of melodies: not *zakhor v'shamor* but the other way around. In that way it parallels the great affirmation of faithful obedience by the Israelite people attested in Exodus 24:7, "All that Y-H-V-H has said, *na'aseh v'nishmah,* we will do and we will understand [literally *hear*]." This odd sequence—we would expect to <u>hear</u> first and then understand—is usually interpreted to imply that one understands a commandment through doing it. In other words, we do not let our intellects, our rational mind, determine what we do; rather, we respond to the imperative to act, and through the action we comprehend the meaning. That perhaps seems uncomfortably irrational to many of us. We might better say that the Torah recognizes that we learn through experience. As George Balanchine liked to say, "Don't think, dance." The Torah knows that not all meaning is encompassed by logical analysis, nor is reason always the surest way to understanding. Were it so, what hope for romantic love?

How else might we understand this? Think for instance of swimming. A book can show the ideal motions for various swimming strokes, providing instruction and practical tips about the synchronized movements of the arms, head, torso and legs, and when to breathe so as to move most efficiently. But we learn to swim by getting in the water. More importantly, it is by getting in the water and moving through it that we find why we want to swim for any reason other than the strictly utilitarian purpose of keeping from drowning. If we go to a crowded pool or beach on a mild, sunny day and ask everyone splashing in the water why they are doing this, how many would reply, "I'm practicing saving myself from drowning"? The one who swims cleanly, elegantly (in the mathematic sense of elegance, with no wasted motion) is the one who seems best to show the pleasure of knowing the medium of water intimately.

Another way is through the kinesthetic experience that we have been considering—apart from the words that define its meaning, the physical ritual associated with kindling the shabbat lights. Imagine that you stand before those lit candles. You extend your arms in an embracing gesture, then draw them toward you once, twice, three times, sensing the warmth of the flames below your hands. What does it feel like? Does it feel as if you have embraced that warmth to bring it to you? Now place your hands over your downcast eyes, blocking your vision. Can you sense your mind turning its focus from the room "out there" and even from the candles that you know are lit to the world inside your head? You have gone through *mimesis* or imitation into learning by experiencing. The act is the message.

The act may seem strange to those who don't get it. A hassidic parable uses this analogy to explain ecstatic prayer movements, in other words, prayer moving the practitioner to physical expression. Suppose a totally deaf person walked by a house and saw through the window people leaping and turning around, waving their hands and making strange facial expressions. They are mad, the viewer might conclude, because the deaf person was not hearing the music that was moving these enthusiastic celebrants to dance. From the outside, even if we see ourselves from the outside, we might not have the inner experience that gives the ritual a meaning beyond the mimicry of a learned pattern of formal actions.

This takes us to the next step of recognition. If the ritual movements accompanying the Shabbat ceremonies feel awkward or embarrassing, perhaps that is because you are not yet comfortable with this particular dance. It may become one that you enjoy practicing. Or it might not be your dance.

But there is more than one dance for shabbat. The 16th century mystics of Tzfat (Safed) developed a ceremony of welcoming the sabbath, *Kabbalat Shabbat*, by going to the fields and hills as the sun departed on Friday evening. There, they invited the regal sabbath bride to join her husband, the people Israel, welcoming her with psalms and hymns. Today we too welcome our heart and soul's desire in the open air or our homes, or in the synagogue, where it might be preliminary to the evening service, even if the male mystics' bridal metaphor calls for re-imagining. We have countless lovely melodies, old and contemporary, for greeting shabbat in a range of moods and musical modes expressing the styles of Jewish communities around the world, and there is always room for more, or for your own spontaneous invention. Appreciating the most ingenious moment, however, depends on us having a little bit of information.

In the time of the Temple, the Levites (who formed the Temple choir) sang a certain designated hymn on each day. When the kabbalists arranged *Kabbalat Shabbat*, they designed it with both a mystical and a dramatic sensibility. Often the ceremony according to a traditional "transmission" (literally, *kabbalah*) begins with the hymn *Yedid nefesh,* "Dear soul," by R. Eliezar b. Moshe Askari, 1584, a kabbalistic poem expressing in four stanzas the soul's yearning for God. Jewish traditions, both exoteric and esoteric, often use the number four, which also has many other cultural associations, such as the four seasons, "the four corners of the world" and so on; the mystics teach that there are four dimensions ("worlds") of being, from the material to the divine. In this poem the initial letters of the four stanzas form an anagram of the sacred name Y-H-V-H. The well-known *Shalom aleichem,* now so often used in this part of this ceremony, was first printed in Prague in 1641; based on the Talmudic notion of two angels accompanying us on shabbat, it moves us from the holy love of *Yedid nefesh* to the spiritual connection between the divine and the human that is expressed by the imagery of angelic messengers or companions. These two poems, often sung, braid together the transcendent and immanent, the divine and the human.

Following are six psalms. Therefore we have one for each day of creation, each day of work, each shofar blast signaling onset of shabbat, and each of the *sefirot* that equate with the six days or stages of creation. The practice of reciting these was begun by another teacher of mysticism and ethics, R. Moses Cordovero, in 16th century Tzfat. Purposefully, we may presume, the numerical value (gematria) of the initial letters of these psalms add up to 430, the same value as the word *nefesh*, "soul." Some prayerbooks emphasize that by printing the initial letters in bold face or a larger font. Typically, the antepenultimate item is another hymn to the beloved, *L'cha dodi*, the stanzas of which form an acrostic of the author's name, R. *Shlomoh Ha-levi* [Alkabetz], yet another of the leading mystics of 16th century Tzfat. Acrostics are a clever and lovely way of permanently "signing" the text, forever weaving the author's presence or some covert meaning into the art. It is customary to rise at the last verse to face the west and greet the arriving royal bride called Shabbat with a bow. Although that is not required, and seems artificial or excessively literal to many, the expressive physical gesture adds a moment of choreographic beauty and drama to the ceremony. At this point any mourners in the community would join the synagogue service, thus our gestures also acknowledge them through a congregational bow and a wish for peace.

It is at the end of the ceremony that the kabbalists' imaginative power comes through in the drama of the liturgy. *Kabbalat shabbat* concludes with two psalms. In order, they are *Psalm 93*, which was the Temple's Shabbat hymn, and *Psalm 92*, the Temple's hymn for the sixth day, Friday. If we think about that sequence, it should seem odd to us. Friday is just ending, Saturday is arriving. Why not recite the hymns in the proper chronological and numerical order, first Psalm 92 and then Psalm 93?

This is the mystics' brilliant *grand jeté*, the daring dance leap across the stage of time. The sixth day of this hymn does not honor the Friday that is just ending but the one on the other side of the arriving shabbat, as if it were possible to leap from one shabbat (celebrated in Psalm 93) to the next Friday (celebrated in Psalm 92) without having to trudge through a week of labor. We find ourselves at the end of the ceremony welcoming this shabbat as if we were already on the other side of the week, again anticipating shabbat. It is as close as one can get liturgically to a foretaste of the time beyond time, an endless cycle in which one shabbat leads to the anticipation of another shabbat, as if we could live continually in the realm of physical ease and pleasure along with spiritual anticipation and joy. Ideally, Shabbat is not a period dominated by "You may not . . ." but "No need to." No need: that is completeness and rest.

✳ ✳ ✳

Havdalah

We have welcomed Shabbat as an honored guest, indeed, as a royal bride. Therefore, it is fitting that we honor her departure as well, escorting her out of our life as night begins on Saturday until the next Friday evening. *Havdalah* ("the separation") is the bride's recessional ceremony, the royal withdrawal accompanied with wine, sweet spices to make her memory linger in our senses, and a torch to light her way.

Beautiful havdalah sets in metals or ceramics can be purchased, or you can make up your own from treasured items, so long as you have a goblet for the kiddush wine, a container for the spice, and a preferably a holder for the multi-wick havdalah candle. Candles specially braided for havdalah are commercially made; some have six strands intertwined for the six days from one shabbat's ending to the beginning of the next. These havdalah candles, each of which can be used several times, are delightfully artful examples of *hiddur mitzvah*, a beautiful way of satisfying the halakhic requirement that this light, *eysh*, "fire," be strong enough to make an illumination that is not just ceremonial but practical. Even with this we can improvise if necessary by bringing together the wicks of at least two candles. We can make our own spice blend from cinnamon, cloves, or whatever mixture pleases you. Some make pomanders of last year's Sukkot etrog studded with cloves; many Sephardim use flasks of rose water.

Havdalah begins when we can see three stars in the sky, shortly after sunset, a perfect reason to take the ceremony outside if the weather cooperates. We can make the separation later, in fact as late as Tuesday, though we have to make do without the spice and light if we postpone too long. Lingering for a while to recall the sweetest and best parts of shabbat, thanking any family and friends present for helping to make the holiday good, carries the shabbat mood with us.

Wine and its blessing always come first in our ritual life, and traditionally this cup is filled to overflowing. Next we offer a blessing for the *b'samim*, the spices, passing to everyone the spice container so that each person can take the sweet shabbat scent into the workweek. Last, the fire. As this light is for use, we want to find a way to use it sacredly. Cup your hands behind the light; appreciate the divine work shown in the human hands. Hold up your hand in front of the candle with the fingers spread so that the light shows the blood of life through the fingernails; around the edges of your fingers you can see the red and black boundary between light and darkness, the separation, *havdalah*. And even that we must bless, for separation allows for meaningfulness. The Hebrew term for what is usually translated as "the ordinary" or (worse) "the profane" in contrast to the sanctity of Shabbbat or the festival is *ha-kol*, literally, the all, the universal, the generality of life. Without demarcation, nothing is special.

Yet with separation comes the desire for integration. Consequently, we sing longingly for the prophet Elijah, *eliyahu ha-navee*.
Some today add Miriam the female prophet, *miryam ha-navee'ah*.
The prophet is harbinger of the longed-for messianic time, when
the sacred may be well integrated with *ha-kol*, the generality of
life. If we imagine Miriam as also inspiring our transformed future, we can hope that the masculine and feminine will also be
reintegrated, that we fully realize once again what it means to be
human, *ha-adam*. No matter how lilting the melodies may be,
havdalah music is a song of yearning, simultaneously holding on
to the day gone by, longing for the perfect time yet to be. When
Goethe's Faust makes his pact with Mephistopheles, he does not
trade his soul for wealth, power, knowledge or lust. What he
wants more than anything, this man who has conquered so many
fields of knowledge, is to feel completely satisfied. The devil can
have him, he bargains, when at last a moment arrives at which
Faust can say, *"Bleibe doch, du bist so schön,"* "Stay like this, you
are so beautiful!" Our Shabbat hints at that perfect moment, so
beautiful that we wish it would never end and our soul feels that
there is nothing more to desire.

Chapter 5
Annual Rings

Jewish holidays celebrate our encounters with deep meaning in three realms: nature, especially in the agricultural cycle; history, particularly the development of the people Israel; and learning, notably through the teachings of Torah. Each year and maybe for each of us, the blend of these three strands will be slightly different, for life's experiences will change what each observance means. That is exactly what happens as we engage with works of art. Depending on our perspective at any time, Kafka's *Trial* (to take this one example) might be about the relentlessness of totalitarian tyranny, or maybe the bewildering workings of an impersonal bureaucracy; sometimes Joseph K. seems a haunted victim of psychological guilt, at others we think he is the individual isolated in modern society; sometimes the novel clearly looks like an autobiographical parable, at other times it seems like a tantalizingly oblique traversal of the genres of literary fiction; and maybe it suggests our frustrated efforts to grasp life's truth before we die. The words of the book remain the same but the text shifts colors in different lights.

Similarly, in any year or from another perspective in life, a different layer of meaning will stand out most strongly for each of us in Jewish rituals and readings.

We get small moments of insight or large movements of comprehension. What Abraham hears is not the same as what Sarah does, or Hagar, much less Ishmael or Isaac. Jacob's visions are unlike those of Moses, whose concept of what God wants of us also takes shape quite differently from Abraham's. Hearing the prophets' critical accounts of the gulf between the ideals set for us and the reality of how we act, we might think, *plus ça change, plus ça meme chose*, recognizing with some sorrow that our "civilization" seems to make small progress over the centuries.

The Torah itself is also a paradigmatic life story in five "ages," to borrow Shakespeare's term. We love stories, and *Genesis* is certainly a collection of colorful ones in which we encounter interesting and even fantastic characters, great journeys, dramatic confrontations, successes and dangers, kings and mysterious strangers, lovers and husbands and wives, fathers and mothers and children. Some of the stories are definitely meant for adults and adolescents but not younger children, and if we look at what they all reveal about the human family, we see how difficult family relationships can be. What translations called *Genesis*, we know as *Bereishit*, a compound word stemming from the Hebrew *rosh*, "head." *Bereishit* takes the world's story, as a musician might say, "from the top." It also starts where we begin understanding our life, from the first moments of consciousness when we formed notions of selfhood, time, place, other people as separate identities. If we think of it as beginning with the childhood and adolescence of the human race, it also brings to mind the childhood and adolescence of the individual. From stories, we learn who we are, where we came from, the chronicle of our ancestors, our family, what our grandparents and parents experienced along the way.

Exodus chronicles the young adult's task of breaking away from the patriarchal family (the household Pharaoh), the people who make the rules that oppress us, though they do not have a clue as to who we are nor do they really understand us or our needs. Because we follow our own god who speaks to us clearly and decisively, we need to make that break. Doing so, we go into the wilderness, a place not yet defined and determined by their attitudes and belief systems nor yet by our own. In that place, guided by some sort of revelation through which we perceive some imperatives for our life, we begin to construct our own beliefs and values as well as the hopes and dreams that might also be called our Promised Land. These become formalized into our own set of absolutes and rituals in behavior and values; we acquire as well the practical obligations of adulthood (*Leviticus, Numbers*). In old age (*Deuteronomy*, the "second statement of the Law"), like Moses we earnestly retell the narrative of our life, imparting the lessons we have absorbed in order to transmit them to the next generation, here nagging and insisting, there alternately encouraging and admonishing, occasionally revising the tale a bit, either because we misremember or because we know that it needs to be altered to make it pertinent for changed circumstances of a new era. Eventually, our individual time runs out, like the great prophet's on Mt. Pisgah. If, like him, we are most keenly aware of what remains undone, of what more we hoped that we would live to see, we might ask, "Why me?" or "What did I do deserve such disappointment?" But there is no use bargaining for a few more years, months, days; we can discern that there is a future, but those we leave behind will live it, and we have entrusted it to their care, knowing that each journey will be unique, as yours and mine have been.

So your narrative of the Torah might be very different. This is good, for without such differences and the conversations to which they give rise, we only move in a circle. But a living torah, *torat chayyim*, should lead us into a spiraling dance.

✳ ✳ ✳

Andrew Vogel Ettin

Rosh Hashanah

Rosh Hashanah is the one festival on which the *shofar*, re-calling the binding of Isaac, is still sounded ceremonially in all Jewish congregations as a reminder of human fidelity and divine providence. Around the sounding of the *shofar* an elaborate litur-gy and an even more extensive context of biblical interpretation has developed to draw spiritual meanings from the use of this archaic instrument. The liturgy also brings together numerous biblical references reinforcing three large themes suggested by the *shofar* calls.

First is divine sovereignty. Like the monarch heralded by trumpets, the ruler of the universe is announced by the shofar, whose upward-turning notes link the earthly with the realm of spirit, and whose call celebrates order and good governance in the cosmos. Pluto might or might not be a planet according to mortal definitions, but it goes about its path unfazed by any-thing we say or do, following an impulse over which we human beings have no control. We might seldom think that we under-stand why the universe is as it is, but we may nonetheless want to believe that it follows at least normal logic. Fish got to swim and birds got to fly.

Second is the theme of remembrance. The separate note patterns of the shofar have been described variously as like an alarm, a trembling, a wailing. They are said to remind and move both us and God of the possibilities for change, improvement, an-nually turning and returning, alerting us to keep those promises that need to be kept for the sake of the moral order of the world. The shofar's sound jolts us into awareness that our accustomed patterns are not inevitable. It also reminds us of times when, individually or collectively, we were able to arise hopefully and sustained from life's ashes—the destruction of the Temple, the loss of a homeland—and another—and another, the Holocaust, the excruciating agony of personal losses, the grieving spirit and aching heart that is the sacrifice endured by all in this world that risk hoping, and all who dare to love.

Third is faith in messianic deliverance, like Shelley's "trumpet of a prophecy" ("Ode to the West Wind"). We live with the desire nourished through biblical voices with their prophetic visions that at some point in the future there will be an earthly state of living as harmonious as the apparent stability that we see in the stars and planets. A state of living in which indeed we shall no longer study landmines and rockets but instead study how to live in peace and harmony with one another under vines and fig trees, addressing the needs of the widows, the orphans, and the resident aliens living and working in our midst, documented or not.

What none of this commentary really accounts for is the extraordinarily compelling presence of the shofar itself and its voice. It is usually called a ram's horn in English, though it might be from a sheep, goat, or many varieties of antelope. We cannot use a cow's horn, a *keren*, because that recalls the apostasy with the Golden Calf. Each species has its own size, colors, shadings and twists; and each one looks exactly like what it is. There is raw integrity to a shofar.

The shofar remained the instrument of choice for religious ceremonies of the Jewish people long after silver trumpets (which are mentioned even in *Numbers*) came into routine use in palaces and the Temple. Without valves, without an artificial mouthpiece, the shofar is unpredictability itself. Each differs in sound and responsiveness. One raises it, attempts to place it properly against the mouth, blows, and has no idea what sound will emerge. The *baal tekiah* tries to adapt, but on some days and with some shofars, there seems no way to succeed in producing anything beyond a splat or fizzle. The word *baal* sometimes means "master" but that rarely describes the actual relationship of the blower to the instrument. Sounding the shofar is, in short, a lot like living, an unpredictable act over which we do not have total control, try as we will to master it. When the call does emerge, it is absolutely visceral and animal, and each sustained note is like a bridge across the void.

All the commentaries of the prayer book and the rabbis seem merely a series of postulates without the shofar. Human beings are not just talking heads. After the ceremony, what people remember, far more than any of the associated biblical texts and their themes, is the *kol shofar*, the voice of the shofar. A voice demanding attention. A voice that gets attention without words. A voice speaking of our own yearning, hopefulness, uncertainty. A voice pulling us from the mundane and expected into the realm of the unpredictable; into the realm where changing and turning oneself is the practice of the moment, and the results uncertain even if the intention is clear; into a realm where the presence and the working and the abiding sustenance of what some of us call God is as certain as the laws of physics and just as impenetrable by even the keenest sensibility.

On Rosh Hashanah we also engage seriously with the story of creation. "And God said, Let us make an earth-being in our semblance." *Vayomer elohim na'aseh adam b'tzalmeinu.* Looking at the plural ending for "<u>our</u> semblance," *b'tzalmeinu*, kabbalists interpret that God was addressing everything already created to become collaborators in the making of *adam*. This is not a man named "Adam" since the verse will also refer to *adam* in the plural. Rather, it is a human creature formed from *adamah*, earth.

If human beings were created by God from all the elements of creation, we ourselves are "lions and tigers and bears—oh my!"

And so we are more like the poetic metaphors than we might have thought, compounded not just from the various chemical elements of creation but from the nature of all that is. We are at times soaring eagles, whales plumbing profound and mysterious depths, the solitary, daring mountain goat. We are also the sparrow pecking for whatever we can find, the ant hurrying about our own business and the worker bee hurrying about somebody else's. At times the lion within us roars or defends its lair; at other times, we are the wary, unpredictable snake, and maybe sometimes even the worm.

Our flows of moods and feelings, transformations in our thought or "humors" move like the clouds in the sky, fog across the damp field, fluids coursing through our body. Each of us has had moments of feeling the weighty mass of oppression, anxiety or depression like a rock inside of us, and we have known stoniness in the heart and soul. We all have clay feet. Sometimes we feel like dirt, especially when we are treated like dirt. We must know this but also remember that we can soar, plunge deeply, climb bravely. And we must know too, and live as fully as we can to the end with this knowledge, that one day we may vanish, insubstantial as air, or reverberate like a note of Bach, or the voice of the shofar.

❉ ❉ ❉

Yom Kippur: Why do we need t'shuvah?

According to the Talmud, "Seven things were created before the world was created, and they are: The Torah, repentance, the Garden of Eden, Gehenna, the Throne of Glory, the Temple, and the name of the Messiah. . . . Repentance, for it is written, 'Before the mountains were brought forth . . . You turn people to contrition, and say, Turn back, you children of flesh and blood {*shuvu, b'nei adam*}'" [*Pes. 54a,* citing *Ps. 90, 2-3*]. No sooner is the Torah created than is repentance possible.

I recall overhearing a conversation that said a lot about the importance of nourishing one another and the difficulty of doing it wisely. But before we can absorb its lesson, we need to be clear about the repair of our failings, the process of *t'shuvah*, "repentance." The noun *t'shuvah* comes from a root that means both "to return" and "to answer." *T'shuvah* is a word closely associated with action and reaction, and that is quite different from the English "repentance," which means "to feel remorse, regret, or self-reproach." *T'shuvah* may begin with such feelings, but most important are the resulting actions: our return, and the answer—the reply—that we get. In the *Tanakh* the focus of *t'shuvah* is national, not individual. God is concerned about the waywardness of the people Israel collectively. Hosea expressed the need for *t'shuvah* in words that we read on Shabbat Shuvah, a plea that inspired the sages after the destruction of the Second Temple when we needed to shape a Judaism replacing sacrificial offerings with prayer. Hosea urges:

> Shuvah, Yisrael—O Israel, return to the Lord your God; for you have stumbled in your iniquity.
> Take with you words, turn to the Lord and say: Forgive all iniquity, and receive us graciously; so will we offer the words of our lips instead of calves for sacrifice. [*Hosea 14: 2-3*]

The prophets claim that it is because of "iniquity" or bad behavior, especially by not trusting enough in God, that Israel as a people was punished with exile and misery. So we hear Jeremiah, the great prophet from the time of the Babylonian exile, promising,

If you will return, O Israel, says the Lord, return to me;
so long as you will put away your abominations out of my
sight, and do not waver,
And if you swear, The Lord lives, in truth, in judgment,
and in righteousness; and the nations shall bless themselves in the Lord, and in the Lord shall they glory." [*Jer.*
4: 1-2.]

Only much later, in Talmudic times, did rabbinic texts
focus on each individual's personal need for *t'shuvah* even in personal relationships. The fight for a nation that was independent
of Rome had gone badly; the last hold-outs, the fighters at Masada, had died. We could still pray for a restored homeland, and
some form of collective *t'shuvah* was an important part of that;
but we were scattered, settling all over the Mediterranean basin,
and wherever we were, we had "issues." Along with the national
galut, the exile, we experienced individual and personal discords
with God; and contentions among us as individuals contributed
both to our own griefs and to the national distress.

That second idea was so powerful that the tractate of the
Talmud devoted to Yom Kippur [*Yoma* 9b] says that the Second
Temple was destroyed because of hatred between Jews. A midrash [*Lamentations Rabbah 4:3*] tells of a quarrel between two
men in the last days of the Temple. One gave a party and told his
servant to invite his friend Kamza; but the servant mistakenly
invited Bar Kamza, the host's enemy. Bar Kamza, taking the
invitation as a peace offering, went gladly, joining the gathering
of Jerusalem notables. The host, however, furiously ordered him
out of the house. Being rebuffed in his attempts to avoid being
thus humiliated, Bar Kamza left the house, vowing vengeance
by turning the Romans against the community. So he did, mar-
ring the emperor's Temple offering to make it unacceptable for

sacrifice. The insulted Romans rose up and destroyed the Temple. This anecdote, also told with some variations in the Talmud (*Gittin 56a.*), is often quoted as the example of animosity carried to destructive extremes.

However, what is seldom if ever noticed is a tiny detail, the mention of a character off in the corner of the story who does not speak. The midrash says that a rabbi named Zechariah ben Avculas was present at the banquet and could have prevented the host from mistreating Bar Kamza in this manner, but he remained silent and did not intervene. The midrash's judgment on him is breathtaking and unsparing: "The timidity of R. Zechariah ben Avculas," it says, "burned the Temple."

The House of God, in other words, is destroyed because human beings tear one another down, while those who should be peacemakers lack the courage or willingness to speak up when they should. Minding your own business is different from turning your back, or covering your backside. The place of sacredness is not set apart from the lives we live. Or, we might say that we cannot be righteous in our relationship with God unless we mend our relations with one another. The sacred and the human are not compartmentalized but connected to one another.

So far so good, but all of that is, in a sense, theology and ethics. If *t'shuvah* is a reconnection, a repairing of relationships, then the benefits and the costs can be sensed within the flow of our lives, in the health or sickness, the joy or pain that we experience directly in our relations with one another.

So, here's the true story that I promised.

I stopped in for a quick lunch at a restaurant. As I sat down, one of the two men at the next table was asking the other, "Is your son in school?"

"My son" –he shook his head—"my son is not in school," he answered. Without intending to eavesdrop, I could not help but hear. His son had received a full scholarship to a branch of the state university, where he got straight "A's" during his first term. Then he discovered girls and pot. In his second semester he didn't finish any of his courses. He lost his scholarship. But his father, wanting him to continue, paid all the expenses for him to return. The son promised that he'd learned his lesson and would do better. In his first semester back, he got three D's and two F's.

"I was incredibly disappointed in him," the father said. "I thought I'd raised my son to have a stronger character than that."

So he's now out of school, with no particular plans. And where was the son now, the other man asked? "He's living with his mother." the father answered; then he explained,

"After he left school he stayed with me but it was only for a couple of weeks. I couldn't stand looking at him." He paused with his head down, staring at his full plate of uneaten food. "Every time I saw him, I saw failure. His failure as a student and mine as a parent."

Like his luncheon partner, I could do nothing but leave this stranger facing the wreckage of this precious relationship, laden as he was with both resentment and guilt, contemplating which failure was the greater and more painful, the son's as a student or the father's as a parent. For him, the plate heaped with food might as well have been as empty as a pauper's. And the mother—in Jewish terms, the feminine manifestation of the divine, immanent, with us, *Shekhinah*—has taken in the son, the exile in *galut*, with his flaws and failings, much as we ask God to accept us with all of our flaws and failings.

Here, it seems, is the key to *t'shuvah* on the human scale. For without that process—and it is a process, not simply saying a magical phrase that changes everything—that <u>process</u> of recognizing and returning and reconnecting, we are left staring sadly and bitterly into the downcast face of our failures and disappointments at a meal of life that has lost its savor. This too is theology <u>and</u> ethics, but it is theology and ethics that are traced through the fault-lines in the human heart and soul.

We like to imagine "repairing" the world but that is a monumentally imposing task. We have to begin somewhere. And who knows if, without our *t'shuvah* to close the gap between us, we might even leave God like that father in the restaurant, unable to look at us, seeing only failure—our failures as students of the Torah's teachings, and God's failure as a parent. Who knows but that it is God speaking through Hosea who says, as the father in my story was not yet able to do, "Turn—turn and return—*Shuva, Yisrael*," calling us back because God needs us, wayward but loved children, to heal that pain of holy disappointment, longing for us to say the words and do the deeds so that God and we can face each other again. Just as we need the divine call, the invitation, the *sheilah* that asks *Eyecha?*—*Where are you?*, inviting us to turn, to return, letting us know that the point is not to have a relationship with the sacred, but rather, to learn that what is sacred *is* the connection of relationship itself. That our act of healing the strained or broken relationship is a sacred act, even as God, *Rachmana*, the Merciful One, is the Healer of Broken Hearts. With what, with whom, does each of us need to re-connect? <u>Make</u> *t'shuvah?* That is the question we probe during *Yomim Nora'im* each year. Every Yom Kippur we pray for many happy returns of the day.

✳ ✳ ✳

Yizkor: Memorial Services as Living Water

One summer while I was at a retreat in rural New York just before my rabbinic ordination I had an afternoon off from studying and made a long excursion into my distant past, to see if I could find the isolated late 19th century farmhouse in which I once lived amid farmland north of Ithaca, where I had my first academic job many years before. It was a spot filled with memories, some of them happy, some of them poignant; regrets and nostalgia were so complexly mixed that although I had been tempted to make this journey in previous years, I had always resisted. At a significant time of moving forward in my life, this seemed to be the right moment for time travel into an age gone by. I thirsted to know whether the house still stood. I wanted to re-member it, not just recall images from the past but, whatever had become of it, to integrate that image into my present life.

I had a rented car, a not good enough map, years of memories and my instincts, so I was both under-prepared and over-prepared. I headed off on a route that took me through the farms and deep forests of the Catskills, up and down and around wooded mountains and rapidly flowing rock-strewn streams, in and out of thunderstorms. It was a long trip—actually longer than it should have been, because of that not-good-enough map and the fact that I was trying to drive and navigate by myself. More than once I got lost, but it was usually "good lost," taking me into villages with Algonquin and Mohican names, anchored by flamboyantly painted nineteenth century inns with gracious wrap-around porches and elaborate wooden gingerbread trim, and the squarish gray stone homes, solid as forts, that had been built when America was not yet a country. I drove past disused railroad stations that were now the offices of the local tourist agency, and dairy farms with meandering Holsteins that could have fooled anyone into thinking that years, or in fact centuries, had never passed.

In one stretch of the road through the mountains I noticed a kind of highway marker I had never seen before and wasn't sure I was reading it correctly. I slowed the next time I saw one coming so that I could read it better. Yes, it did say "Former site of . . .". "Former site of West Hurley," but what could that mean? What was West Hurley, and what had happened to it? Why was it commemorated? Several miles further on was another: "Former site of Ashton," and then a few miles later, "Former site of Glenford / Brown's Station / Olive Bridge." I began to wonder if I'd slipped into the set of some bizarre B-grade made-for-TV sci-fi horror movie. Finally I had a chance to slow down to read the rest of the next sign. "Former site of Broadhead," it said, and under that, "Ashokan Reservoir."

Now I understood. These signs recorded the names of towns that had stood where the 13 square miles of water contained by the Ashokan dam system now stretched. These places, along with Shokan, West Shokan and Boiceville, had been villages where people much like us had lived and worked, cooked and gardened and played, raised families and ran businesses, taught school and farmed. Early in the twentieth century the residents had been bought out and moved, as the great project of building a ring of dams and locks progressed. The system was ready on June 19, 1914. For a full hour on that day all the area's sirens and steam whistles blasted a warning; then the floodgates were opened so that torrents of water rushed into the basin and began covering farms, orchards, stores and houses.

So the submerged villages had long vanished except for their names memorialized on these signs, and with them had gone the particular relationships that had held the people in them together as a community. What stories, what memories of people and events had been drowned here, along with the homes and gardens and farmlands, the places where corn and beans and wildflowers had grown, pastures where cattle had grazed? Gone along with the houses and barns were the lanes and groves, the fences and fields that for who knows how many years had been the familiar neighborhood landmarks that would have brought to mind shared pasts and certainties about the lives they expected to continue living. I wondered whether any of the displaced people, perhaps curious, awed youngsters with the fantastic religious school story of Noah in their heads, had stood along some safe, high ridge to watch the rising waters swallow up the familiar places where they had lived and explored, their yards and farms, their pasts, what they had thought would be their futures—or whether any place could be truly safe enough for watching such a sight.

Perhaps it was the coincidence of my own journey that made this accidental discovery so poignant. There I was on the road, hoping to be able to locate a house I'd lived in more than twenty-five years before, having no idea whether it still existed, a house that was nearly new when these towns were deliberately drowned, a house that had outlived them—but for how long? Was it also gone, and with it, the visible link to a vital part of my own past?

But drowning history is not the purpose of a reservoir. The purpose of this one, which it has been fulfilling for over ninety years, is to provide part of New York City's water supply. Water flows from this reservoir eventually reaching Staten Island 120 miles away. Those villages are no more, but the place where they had been has become the *mayyim chayyim,* the living water, for generations of people numbering in the millions. Few know or care about where their water comes from, or what sacrifices made it possible. Rare indeed would be the New Yorker with an archival interest who could name even one of those villages whose remains lie somewhere beneath the great metropolis's water source. Open the tap and the water comes. Few ever think, From where? Only the wise realize that it pours from the deep reservoir of the past.

Yizkor is not only our opportunity to erect a sign saying, "Former site of . . . ." It is also a chance to remember how those who are no longer visible in this world have provided our *mayyim chayyim*. How can they be gone when I can see them as if they'd never left this world? Not all the names on the Yizkor list are familiar. But years or generations after they have passed on, their reservoir of practical gifts—we ourselves, a synagogue building, for example, and the scrolls that it houses, and its prayerbooks, and its many years of prayers—and the teachings about life and Judaism that have quenched even thirsts in us that we might not have known that we had, continue to be our *mayyim chayyim*. From them the cells of our lives take substance. From the watershed of their years on earth, and the years of countless generations in other places and times, we still gratefully drink.

The record of names remains. It is said that during periods of low water in the Ashokan Reservoir the foundations of old houses and sites of orchards and gardens are still visible after all these years. And from there nearly a century ago 2800 graves, some going back to the Revolutionary War, were moved to new locations. Those who went on before, we bear with us still, not always like Joseph, whose sarcophagus was borne from Egypt to be buried in Canaan, but in the caskets of our hearts and memories.

The house that I sought, I found, yet standing and in good repair. The black walnut and pine trees around it are much larger now and will shield its current family from the winter blasts that shook us. I could be gratefully happy for a new name on the new mailbox, though the inhabitants might never have heard of mine, and I could drive on from there, my thirst quenched, remembering the past into my new life. And those new residents never suspected the appreciative glance and silent benediction given by a transitory specter from the past.

Those who were once partners with us in this world and, passing on, have helped fill the reservoir of living water of our community and our own lives, we re-member at the time of *Yizkor*.

✳ ✳ ✳

Entering holiness, closing the gates

The liturgies of Yom Kippur would never be described as economical. They are vast, complexly built, and repetitive, though in liturgy as in music (where *repeats* may be essential to a composition's structure and effect) repetitive is not the same as redundant. They draw our imagination back to the Temple, which for believers was the gateway to the divine realm, with the inner sanctum—the Holy of Holies—being the womb-like space in which human met divine, at least on that one day a year, The Day of Atonement, when the linen-clad *Kohen ha-Gadol* (High Priest) entered that space and articulated the sacred, most private name of God, Y-H-V-H, that was never otherwise to be pronounced. The uniting of human and divine is accomplished through an act of speech, a naming, that declares intimate knowledge and in so doing also lays claim to a singular relationship. The rite recalls the *hieros gamos* (sacred marriage) of other religious traditions, which was sometimes enacted through the sexual union of priest or king with a priestess or goddess representative (for instance, Inanna in Sumeria). In Christianity, the union of spiritual and physical takes place in Mary and is announced by the archangel Gabriel (from *gibbor el*, the mightiness of God). The significant power of knowing the someone's personal name and knowing thereby their essence is attested to by the many popular stories in which such knowledge is hidden or forbidden, such as Rumpelstiltskin, Lohengrin, or the Flying Dutchman. In the Torah, at critical moments Abraham, Sarah, Jacob and Joshua all receive new names; Moses is eager to know what name to call the God who speaks to him at the burning bush.

According to our sages, the correct pronunciation of those four letters (the Tetragrammaton, or *shem hameforesh*, the distinctive name) was lost from oral transmission during the talmudic period; and even if it were not so, the cessation of Temple rituals and the absence of the Holy of Holies deprive us of the one occasion for pronouncing the name. Not knowing how or not being able to pronounce the *shem hameforesh* expresses our ruptured connection with God. How hard it is to talk to God, to relate directly to God, when we cannot even articulate The Name, inscribed on our consciousness but denied to our lips.

As the long day concludes, the ceremony is pared to an exceptionally succinct ritual, the eloquence of which becomes clear only when we recognize the elegance of the construction. The trope or motif on which the Yom Kippur rites are constructed is that the heavenly gates of repentant prayer are open for our heartfelt commitment to change ourselves for the better—to "make *t'shuvah*," the turn that places us back on the right course. As the sun sets on the day of fasting and prayer, the concluding *Ne'ilah* service imagines that those gates are closing, prompting us to focus ourselves on the needed dedication. As it ends, the congregation standing before the open synagogue ark proclaims once, "*Sh'ma yisrael adonai eloheynu adonai ekhad*" [*Understand, Israel—the Source and Sustenance of all life: One!*] then three times "*Barukh shem kavod malkhuto l'olam va'ed*" [*Blessed be the Name and glorious honor everywhere and always*] and seven times *"Adonai hu ha-elohim"* [*Adonai is all divinity*].

Look at the numerical sequence: three texts recited in the pattern 1 + 3 + 7 = 11. We start with one statement of God's uniqueness. (Tradition advocates stating the *sh'ma* only once whenever it is recited, lest we seem to be acknowledging more than one god.) That is followed by two prime odd numbers adding up to 10, the total resulting in the next prime odd number. (The apparently interesting result of 11 appearing as "1" and "1" works , by the way, only in Arabic numerals.) While 10 may bring to mind the 10 Commandments, the division into a set of three followed by a set of seven suggests even more significantly the kabbalistic division of *s'firot* into an upper group of three (representing the spiritual emanations of the divine) and a lower group of seven. The *Zohar* teaches that reciting the *Sh'ma* facilitates the union of the upper and lower level of perfection, the transcendent and immanent manifestations of the sacred. We can imagine the divine unique unity flowing downward into our world through the conduits of these *s'firot*, being unified through our affirmations of the oneness of the source, and in a sense vaulted upward again through the one upward-curling long final note of the shofar sounding its *tekiah g'dolah,* ending the service with its call that is simultaneously visceral yet not embodied.

The ritual still has much more to say to us. Earlier in the day's services, the section known as the Avodah recounted the Yom Kippur rites in the days of the second Temple, during which the High Priest perilously entered the otherwise prohibited Holy of Holies to pronounce the *shem hameforash.* He did that three times while confessing and atoning for the sins of himself and his family, the community of *kohenim*, and the people Israel. Each time he began to speak the name, the Levites led the crowd in declaring, *"Barukh shem kavod malkhuto l'olam va'ed."* Consequently, when we proclaim the *barukh shem kavod* phrase three times at the end of *Ne'ilah*, we have the opportunity to recall the drama of our ancestors affirming the same within the walls of the ancient Temple while the *kohen ha-gadol* precariously placed himself at the intersection of the human and divine realms, a moment that should live within us, particularly in this moment of solemn commitment.

Even this drama is surpassed by the third phrase, *"Adonai hu ha-elohim."* Literally, it means *Adonai {he} is the God {or, gods}* and is often translated as, "The Lord is God"; it might also be understood as translated above, *Adonai is all divinity*. It derives from *I Kings 18:39*, the culmination of the extraordinary account in which *eliyahu ha-navi,* the prophet Elijah, defeats the 450 priests of the deity Ba'al in the presence of King Ahab and Queen Jezebel. The assembled Israelites, who had followed their monarch in Baalist worship, are first silent when challenged by Eliyahu to declare their faith, until the sacrifice on the altar that he has built miraculously flames in response to his invocation:

> Lord God of Abraham, Isaac, Israel, let it be known this day that you are God in Israel, and that I am your servant, and that I have done all these things at your word. Hear me, O Lord, hear me, that this people may know that you are the Lord God [*ki-atah adonai ha-elohim*], and that you have turned their heart back again. (*1 Kings 18:.36-37*)

According to Maimonides, this declaration of faith before Eliyahu on Mt. Carmel was the third and last time in the entire Tanakh when the Israelite people spoke in faithful unity. The first was their pledge receiving the Torah, *na'aseh v'nishmah, We will do and we will understand,* in *Exodus* 24; the second is recorded at the end of *Joshua* 1, as the people united and about to cross the Jordan River vow to follow their appointed leader Joshua and the Torah. By our unified declaration each Yom Kippur, we renew the pledges of our forebears at Mt. Sinai and the banks of the Jordan, committing themselves not only as individuals but also as a community. Proclaiming *adonai hu ha-elohim* at the end of the atoning day, we align ourselves also with those ancestors who miraculously found new faith and new commitment and well as acceptance by the God from whose worship they had been led away, their faith restored only by a miraculous manifestation of the divine power to transform nature, including human nature. And we then proceed to the culminating ritual of this day of *shabbat shabbaton* ("sabbath of sabbaths"), which is the Havdalah ceremony marking the division between the sacred day and normal time, a ritual in which we voice our hope for the reappearance of Elijah, that same Eliyahu ha-navi, now the herald of messianic deliverance. This, after all, is the end of our day.

✳ ✳ ✳

A wave of blessings

Waving hands over shabbat candles is an expressive way to bring the day's blessings to us. Waving of another sort is essential on Sukkot. As told in *Leviticus:*

> Also in the fifteenth day of the seventh month, when you have gathered in the fruit of the land, you shall keep a feast to the Lord seven days; on the first day shall be a sabbath, and on the eighth day shall be a sabbath.
>
> And you shall take on the first day the fruit of grandly beautiful trees (*p'ri eytz hadar*), branches of palm trees (*lulav* in the singular), the boughs of thick trees and wil-

lows of the brook; and you shall rejoice before the Lord
your God seven days. (*Lev. 23, 39-40*)

The Mishnah speaks of the lulav as being "waved" at particular moments in the *Hallel* [praise] psalms recited on Sukkot,
a statement for which the talmudic commentary raises the question, "Where is the precedent for talking about 'waving' it?," to
which the Talmud provides its own reply, "That's what he says."
In other words, there is no clear textual mandate in the Torah for
this practice but it was by then regarded as so absolutely authentic that it stands without external support.

Let us step back into the development of the lulav-waving.
Here we are with a fruit (maybe it was always an etrog) and
branches of three trees, two of them of specified species. Torah
tells us, Rejoice! When we look for the link between these, we
sense that since the festival celebrates the in-gathering of the
land's fertility, it must have seemed apt to rejoice with products
from the fertile earth. But what do we do with them? Our impulse might be a good guide. We want to pick them up and wave
them about, acknowledging the energetic flow of creation.

Perhaps some unrecorded Martha Graham understood viscerally that this was all around us, knew that we needed its bounty
pouring into us as much as into the soil, stretched her arms in all
directions as she held the lulav and etrog together, and yanked
them toward her from each direction, the lulav shimmering and
snapping—first point it to the left, then swing to the right, out
in front and over the shoulder to pull in the energy from behind,
pointed down from skyward and then pulled up from the earth.
Maybe these movements were not detached and mathematical as
they have become today through halakhic attempts to prescribe
what is required but dynamic, liquid swirls. Maybe she did not

stand with her feet together as she tried to remember at what verse we are supposed to shake the lulav and when to hold it still, as we are likely to do, but moved herself, responding to sacred music sensed but unheard, "felt in the blood, and felt along the heart" (Wordsworth, "Tintern Abbey," 28). She perhaps knew not only that the life-force encircled her around the horizon but that it flowed down from above through the sun, rain and dew, and that it came up from below ground where seeds, roots and bulbs were nourished through the soil, kept in dormant safety or warmed into life until they became the sustenance of people and animals. She knew that this same energy source had flowed into the present moment from the past that lay behind her and would continue ahead into the future, which she also acknowledged in her motions.

Our waving of the lulav may be viscerally deadened if we perform it only as an arcane, confusingly elaborate sequence of dictated movements that we carry out with anxious glances at a book to be sure we are doing them correctly—*Oh, wait, that was supposed to be east and then west. Uh-oh, I wasn't supposed to shake on God's name!* But it does not have to be: the prescribed motions by which we acknowledge and seem to salute and also draw divine creative power toward us expresses exactly the purpose of the ritual. Even if we follow them with such punctilious attention to halakhic requirements that we miss the inner life of the experience and feel anything but spirituality in the moment, the in-drawing of the lulav and etrog in our hands gives us a simulacrum of the experience as we express to the life of the world our intention to draw it into us.

Waving and shaking seem perfect analogous gestures for the central symbol of Sukkot, the fragile *sukkah*. Like all the holidays and every one of the annual Torah readings in the ever-

107

turning scroll, Sukkot takes on a new meaning each time we think we have already discovered its essence. On September 11, 2001 I was serving a rotation as a chaplain resident at Baptist Hospital in Winston-Salem, North Carolina. Unaware yet of what was happening in New York City, Washington, DC and Pennsylvania, I walked into the room of a young patient recovering from surgery to find her and her husband transfixed by the television set; we watched incredulously when before our eyes the second airplane exploded against a World Trade Center tower. A few minutes later, in a temporarily vacant room, I stood with a nurse as one of those towers disappeared in smoke and dust, while she tried in vain to phone her daughter, a civilian employee at the Pentagon. A few weeks later, in the handsome Tudor-style chapel of that hospital, I led a Sukkot service that has become an annual event, with a fresh comprehension of the fragility of all human structures, including our constructs of certainty in our life.

A hospital is of course nothing like a halakhically built sukkah and yet everything like a sukkah. Massive and well constructed though it be, it is but a temporary shelter and surprisingly fragile because we who dwell in it as patients or caregivers are fragile. The bodies that we come to depend on are like homes vulnerable to wind and water, to fires and earthquakes and mudslides, to damage and collapse; and those who care for them are like the thin walls and flimsy roof of a sukkah, unable to keep out the wind and rain. We end up trembling like the shaken lulav.

Even the assumptions on which we build our lives are fragile. The people we most love, the ones on whom we most depend, are finite; and sometimes, so are their commitments. The faculties of our senses are vulnerable. Our "vital organs," the ones that enable life itself, are finite. To approach Sukkot knowing this, knowing the multitudinous threats to the ecological system that fragilely shelters all life on this planet, knowing that people go to sleep in fear and wake in danger in their own homes because they cannot fully shield themselves from the violence swirling in their neighborhood or in the heart and mind of the person with whom they live or in their own anxiety or desperation, is to understand profoundly why we need the lessons of Sukkot and why the tradition tells us that we need to invite friends into the sukkah, both spiritual kinsfolk with the varied wisdom of the ages and the friends to whom we can turn today for sharing comfort, reassurance, and the blessings of hospitality.

Sukkot ends with a flurry of holidays often compressed into a blur. The succession of celebrations—*Hoshanah Rabbah, Sh'mini Atzeret* and the post-biblical *Simchat Torah*—acknowledges that we are reluctant to let go of the festival's joyful and comforting communal spirit: These concluding ceremonies of the season colorfully blend biblical, rabbinic and folk customs into a living tradition. If the weather cooperates, and (even more important) if the congregation cooperates, the holy days filling the month of Tishrei benefit from being taken outside the synagogue, and not just for *tashlikh*. A second-day Rosh Hashanah ceremony in which we read and discuss the biblical account of the binding of Isaac while we ourselves are on a mountain or hilltop, or even at the base of a great rock, takes the text off the surface of the page and into the imagination. From that place on a holiday when we commemorate the "birthday" or new year of the world, we can also explore dimensions of nature through Jewish texts, moving on to social action. The Sukkot ceremony during the time of the Second Temple featured drawing water to be poured on the Temple altar, in addition to its regular anointing with wine. Our ancestors acknowledged the connection between water and sacredness in life. We today are renewing our grasp of that connection. Revisioned, the ancient festivals retain the capacity to teach and motivate us.

* * *

Hanukkah and Purim

What an odd pair of stories these make, each a tale of improbable Jewish successes against seemingly overwhelming odds. Purim claims to be historical; it is defended as such by Orthodox Jews but by virtually no other streams of Judaism, though we nevertheless celebrate it as historically meaningful. Hanukkah definitely is historical but the books in which its story is told has never been part of Jewish scripture, and the defining miracle commemorated by the nightly illuminating of the *hanukkiyah* is almost certainly not historical, though virtually all Jews retell it as if it were.

Though separated by some calendar months, they are as closely related thematically as a pair of bookends facing in opposite directions. Hanukkah is a story of Jews living in the land of Israel but fighting literally to stave off assimilation as well as break the foreign dominance that threatens their culture. Purim is a story of assimilated diaspora Jews, living abroad but fighting literally to stave off destruction and in the course of doing so claiming their dual identity as Jews and as citizens of another culture. Separating them in the liturgical calendar is only Tu b'shevat, a celebration of the creative energy working in nature through invigorating vegetative life, as if this were the necessary a-historical stabilizing element poised between conflicting representations of the Jewish condition in history. Nature follows universal and cyclical patterns; politics, history and religious identity depend on <u>where</u> and <u>when</u>.

We do not know the exact reasons why the sages who negotiated the final canon of Jewish scriptures left out the four books about the Maccabees, which have been included in the Apocrypha of the Christian church. Maybe they saw the Maccabean victory as leading before long to a self-serving dynasty of puppet regimes under foreign imperial domination. Furthermore, the Bar Kokhba revolt of 137-38 C.E. against the Romans, which could be seen as analogous to the Maccabee revolt against the hellenistic Seleucid regime, had led to a disastrous military defeat culminating at Masada, worse oppression, more far-reaching exile and enslavement. The rabbis and sages had saved Jewish practice, transforming it into what became rabbinic Judaism. The now-famous Hanukkah story of the cruse of sanctified olive oil used to light the menorah in the rededicated Temple lasting for a miraculous eight days instead of one appears for the first time rather casually in the Babylonian Talmud (*Shabbat 21b*), where it is given as the reason for the holiday, with no mention of the Maccabees. It is this rabbinic intervention that turns the menorah into the quintessential symbol of the festival, leading eventually to the development of a special *hanukkiah* rather than the Temple's seven-branched menorah and recasting Hanukkah into "the feast of light."

The battles of the Maccabees were only partly directed against the occupying hellenized Syrians, the inheritors of the eastern part of the late Alexander the Great's empire. In recent Jewish history our experiences of living under oppression has led to greater emphasis on that aspect of the story. Mattityahu along with Judah and his brothers, and Hannah who nobly sacrificed her seven sons in defense of Israel's cause, have become our superheroes. For the impoverished, powerless and victimized Jews of eastern Europe in the days of the tsars, the example of these ancestors taking up arms at the initiative of their religious leader and rising up successfully against a mighty empire was inspiring, albeit fantastical. As the Yiddish "sweat shop poet" Morris Rosenfeld wrote yearningly in a song for the holiday early in the previous century,

> *Host a moyl a land gehot* / Once we had a land,
> *Host a moyl a hant gehot* / Once we had a hand.
>   *("Oy ir kleyne likhtelekh")*

Once, that is, in days of old but not in his lamentable time, we had our own home and could fight for it. In addition, in countries where we have not been persecuted but must be continually vigilant against infringements of our religious freedom, the Maccabees' revolt has been reinterpreted as a great victory on behalf of religious freedom, with the central act being cleansing the Temple that had been polluted by foreign practices. In the United States, for instance, a fairly common way to justify putting a hannukiah on public property is by claiming that the festival celebrates a great constitutional liberty, freedom of religion.

However, the Maccabees' first victims and (some believe) the main targets were hellenized Jews whose adoption of their foreign occupiers' culture threatened the hegemony of the traditionalists, who were championed and thrust into military action by the *kohen* Mattityahu, ironically often known as Mattathias (the Greek version of his name) and his warrior sons. Seen this way, for not all the Jews joined the Maccabees' cause, the conflict was internecine. It was less about freedom of religion and more about the freedom to coerce co-religionists. It was fought over orthopraxy, what being a Jew meant, over how much of a dominant culture Jews could absorb and still remain integral members of a community that followed Jewish practices. For more Jews today, inside as well as outside of Israel, these have become again the more immediate question. Not long ago at a convention representing a fairly unconventional mix of Jewish outlooks, a writer chatting with a group of rabbis was asked whether he ever did yoga. "Why would I do yoga," he replied rhetorically, adding with a defensive tone, "I'm a Jew"—as if the yoga-practicing rabbis to whom he was speaking were not. In small ways or large, we continue to ask how and what we do as Jews, what or who we shun.

Similarly, we struggle over how to understand what might equate with Hellenism today. The Maccabeans saw the influence of an alien culture as corrosive when Jewish men attended the gymnasium to bathe and compete in athletics naked like all the others; foreign cultic practices became tolerated in the Jewish Temple and sacrificial rites; secular and pagan arts and learning, food, dress and manners attracted Jews away from Torah study and practice. Some Jewish traditionalists today might compile a similar list of *bêtes noir* of the sort formerly evoked by *The Jazz Singer* and *My Name Is Asher Lev*. Others of us might understand the modern damaging values to be a sybaritic addiction to accumulating profits in place devotion to the teachings of our prophets; to love of fortune, fame, prestige and self rather than one's neighbor or God. The danger, we might argue, is not in foreign cultures but adopting materialistic imperialism as the religion of practice.

As within a burning flame, there is visible darkness within the light of Hanukkah. Violence is there, an inner violence that flares up against the external enemy; however, the foe outside may also be that which we fear within ourselves. Amid the glare of the holiday lights that we are instructed to show to the world outside, the joyful and proud songs, rich food and gifts, that darkness is what we want to believe we have blotted out. In the words of a popular Hanukkah song, *Ba-nu cho-shech l'ga-reish,* sung in English as "We have come to banish night," although in the original it is not "night" but <u>darkness</u> that is chased away. It is easier to see and deal with the darkness outside than that which is inside. It is easier also to know how we feel toward a foreign enemy (the Seleucid occupiers, for instance) than to acknowledge our hostility toward our own people with whom we drastically disagree.

Perhaps sensing this tension, as well as recognizing that the Maccabees' military victory of two millennia ago was too short-lived to warrant a modern celebration on its own abiding merit, in recent years some Jews have taken up a custom of lighting their candles in honor or memory of someone whom they want to acknowledge as a bringer of light in the spirit of the holiday. It parallels the Sukkot practice of inviting spiritual "guests" to join us in the sukkah along with family and friends. The custom is still just that, rather than "Jewish tradition," so it is all the more open to personal interpretation. We can think of light-bearers who set inspirational examples, or we celebrate a particular quality or virtue each night; we might connect these with the levels of kabbalistic *s'firot,* the seven "lower" levels and one unifying transcendent dimension on the last night, when all the lights blaze, suggesting that Hanukkah is a model for realizing the usually unseen coherence of the physical and metaphysical. Our intention, in other words, is to make the light expand more broadly, having it burn more intensely, not to overshadow but to "overlight," or as the song says, to "accentuate the positive, / eliminate the negative."

Purim also has a dark element in its finale of wild retributive justice. The mood, however, is very different from that of the Maccabees' story. In *Esther* the Jews are unified (surely proof that this is a fantasy), all the way from the vulnerable but faithful queen in the palace to the unnamed Jews throughout the one hundred and twenty seven provinces. There are no subversive enemies in our midst against whom we must also war. Even the highly placed, safely hidden, covert Jew "outs" herself at the moment of greatest danger in order to save her people, and a Jewish minority that has been submerged amid an alien culture emerges as a powerful force capable of defending itself.

Around the margins of Esther and Mordechai's story, realism is provided by the references to numerous busy and sometimes named eunuchs as well as unnamed maids. For instance, Hatakh, a court eunuch appointed as Esther's attendant, serves as a crucial messenger between her and Mordechai. This story suggests the importance also of sexually marginalized yet politically and economically important segments of the culture.

While the story of the Maccabbean revolt is as factual as any historical account can be, *Esther* is a carefully crafted fictive narration featuring farcical characters and cartoonish violence, encouraging the festive abandon of a Mardi Gras. The *halakhah* (more often rabbinically discouraged nowadays) is to get too drunk to differentiate between "Blessed is Mordechai" and "Cursed is Haman" (*Megillah 7b*), phrases that in Hebrew numerology (*gematria*) have the same numerical value. Therein we find the key to understanding the holiday. We become intoxicated by a state of mind in which distinctions between good and evil, blessing and curse disappear. This is not immoral or even "amoral" as that is usually understood but rather the most profound understanding of the divine transcendence. It parallels the

115

prophet Isaiah's reports of God's words: "I form light and create darkness; I make peace and create conflict [*ra*, usually translated "evil"]; I, Y-H-V-H, do all these"(*Isaiah 45:7*). Internalizing such a state of mind, we can laugh at evil, confident that if we could only see it properly we would understand it as only part of a coherent wholeness in which God is at once the source and the transcendence of all that exists. That we do not yet ordinarily have such a mind is reflected in the fact that when the sweepingly grand verse of Isaiah was incorporated into the *Yotzer*, the benediction for daylight recited after the call to morning worship, the rabbis changed it to say, "I make peace and create <u>everything</u> [*ha-kol*]." Apparently it was simply too disquieting to affirm each morning, "I make *shalom* and create *ra*."

Purim is a riotous feast of pretense, intoxicated and intoxicating even when one drinks nothing alcoholic. It depends on a secret identity, a train of sometimes-absurd improbabilities as well as more than one clever ruse, and it is characterized by make-believe that is also part of the story and perhaps the nature of the story also, a fable or short story (like something from Scheherazade's *1001 Nights*) pretending to be true history. The traditionalists' insistence on the story's historicity seems belied in the zany comedy that is the traditional reading of the Purim *Megillah*, punctuated by the racket made by *graggers* and congregational booing at each mention of Haman's name; in the story, the silly but well-timed verbal wit of the Marx Brothers coexists with Jerry Lewis's goofiness and the slapstick rudeness of The Three Stooges.

From the mid-twentieth century a shift has taken place in our perceptions of the female characters. Esther or Vashti are now seen not as historical figures so much as disparate role models. They are role models for women; yet they also represent differing

116

ways of dealing with authority. Rabbinic tradition, while often describing Vashti as immoral and evil, the antithesis of Esther, nonetheless also holds that she rebelled when the king commanded during his ongoing drunken revelries that she display herself to him and his subjects. Vashti's approach of direct disobedience is problematic despite being taken in a just cause, as it leads to her banishment, at the very least; of course, since we cannot really believe that an imperious monarch would merely exile a publicly defiant consort, the Talmud and the midrash *Esther Rabbah* claim that she was executed. Such midrashim were composed by Jews who knew what it was like to deal with the Roman, Parthian and Sassanian empires. As much as we may now admire Vashti's sense of herself, we want to ask the cost of it.

By contrast, Esther's tactic may appear skillfully diplomatic rather than merely compliant if we look at the entire story and see a woman who uses her wits despite arriving at prominence by winning a beauty contest to be queen. We can also perceive it as the necessary technique of the subaltern, someone with no inherent power other than the ability to manipulate the powerful adroitly; this is the servant who knows how to play the master; yet we might also say that it is the chess player facing long odds but armed with courage, insight and the potential for making a surprise move. It is crucial for us to understand that as Mordechai warns Esther (and as more than one "court Jew" learned in history), should disaster fall upon the Jewish people, she will suffer the same fate as all the rest, despite being the queen.

Maybe it is helpful to think about the two women named Vashti and Esther also as two parts of one person, or even two stages in everyone's socialization. Something happens, something is said that offends us, hurts us, even threatens us. Our "vashti" side immediately responds to the threat in a confrontational way, as Vashti does when she refuses the king's order. Maybe we are right in principle. Jewish tradition, after all, never says that she is wrong to refuse the king. In fact, it actually makes his command seem more outrageous than we would suppose from the biblical story itself. There, he only commands her to "appear wearing the royal crown" at his party; midrash infers that he ordered her to show up wearing nothing but the crown.

Yet it is possible to be right in principle and wrong in tactics. A temper tantrum might have a totally legitimate cause, but it is likely to get the child disciplined and the adult fired. Our sages and leaders were always convinced that in a conflict between "the way of Torah" and alien ways, the right is on our side; however, they also knew that some ways of showing it can get us and the whole community exiled or killed.

The side called "esther" (perhaps related to the Hebrew *hester*, "hidden") emerges next in response to the former experience. This aspect is more guarded, cautious, circumspect, analytic, diplomatic. It is also more effective. Esther, like Mordechai, operates the way Jews have done in many places for centuries, using a diplomatic strategy for working effectively on the real source of power. She takes advantage of the opportunity to get a good job and become a "court Jew" by the simple expediency of not mentioning that she is Jewish. Then she also takes a big chance, risking everything by declaring her identity and arguing for her people, but the risk is calculated and she takes it only when the issue is essential to the community's survival. It is a more disciplined form of heroism than Vashti's outright defiance, which might also come from Vashti's pride. It is also more successful and motivated by a public cause, not just her private one. Suppose the Megillah is meant to tell us (at least in part) about surviving in the world as an individual who is a member of a vulnerable minority. If we imagine the "vashti" response to be more instinctive and personal, the "esther" response is more calculated, wise, and political. She knows who has the power and she devises a strategy to win him to her side.

God's role itself is hidden or shadowed in both *Esther* and the Maccabbee accounts. These tales emphasize human courage and dedication, the former also showing a triumph of wits, the latter of military skill. God is not even mentioned explicitly in the Book of Esther. To someone devoutly religious, the text demonstrates what the Tanakh refers to several times as the *hester panim*, the "hidden face" of God. We see the divinely worked effect but are not aware of the active presence of the divine. Mordechai's one allusive reference to help coming from "another place" if Esther does not act is the only hint that there might be a higher authority than King Ahashuerus. In the same verse he advances the rhetorical possibility that this opportunity might be the reason why she has been brought to this place, a subtle gesture toward divine providence. We might perceive such a powerful spiritual force also at work in the fortunate timing of events and the Jews' eventual success against their foes, but the text itself never makes the point explicitly. By the power of the transmitted word, rabbinic tradition has defined Hanukkah also in religious terms. We quote, and perhaps sing to Debbie Friedman's popular melody, *Zechariah 4:6*, "Not by might and not by power but by my spirit, says the Lord of Hosts." This is as forthright a rejection of reliance on force as one could imagine. After Roman legions smashed Bar Kokhba's revolution in the early 2nd century, Jewish leaders were not avid to celebrate military rebellions against great empires. Hanukkah had to be about God's faithfulness to us even in adversity, not brave men with swords fighting a world power for short-term gains.

We today want both stories, "the feast of lights" and "brave Maccabeus," and more, for we also say that Hanukkah marks a victory for religious freedom and minority rights, a message that most people can honor, though it would have seemed a peculiar claim not only to Mattityahu but also to the talmudic sages. Religious liberty as we understand it was no more their intention than it was the purpose of the pilgrims who left a religiously tolerant 17th century Amsterdam to journey to the New World so as to establish a colony where their own religious beliefs were not threatened by those of heterodox Christians.

We return to the rabbis' original question, *mai hanukkah*. Why do we observe Hanukkah? There is no way to know whether the Jewish religion would have survived without the Maccabees' rebellion. But, the rabbis through the story of the miracle of oil seem to imply, if the only lesson or even the most important lesson to remember is the rebellion against the Seleucid dynasty and its Hellenic cultural trappings, then there is little substance to keep it going throughout the generations. We might reply, however, that we should not forget the war waged by the Maccabees, if for no other reason than this: it nudges us to fill in the blank, "I care more about being Jewish than . . . ." As we face other cultures with our curiosity and suspicions, hostilities or embraces, we continually confront that challenge, hedged with our uneasy, restless uncertainties: "But even so..." and "Yet what about . . . ."

Writing of our festivals in this way, however, intellectualizes them too greatly, at the cost of the multilayered experience of living with them. Remember Balanchine's, "Don't think, dance." Jews intellectualize, but we also eat and sing and dance. The value of the Hanukkah and Purim celebrations should not be calculated only in terms of the ideological constructs we perceive in our own moment. There is life lived fully in the moment. There is also the gift of a tradition, transmitting and remembering experience across place and time, a "civilization" as Mordechai Kaplan termed Judaism. Memories, the sensory experiences of the scent and sizzle of oil from latkes frying and served hot with applesauce and sour cream, or the synagogue tumultuous with jeers and foot-stomping and gragger-twirling against Haman's very name, the joy of klezmer music and dancing at Hanukkah parties, tastes of a half dozen different hamantashen recipes, colored candles ablaze in menorahs, the costumes and games of a Purim play and fair, tearing open Hanukkah gift wrappings are cultural legacies. As much as a name and genealogy, they help us know who our family is, who we are and who we want to be, if we are but given the chance to know them, and if we take them to us not only as customs but as living faith.

✳ ✳ ✳

Tu b'shevat and Shavuot – immanence and transcendence

Here is another seemingly improbable pair, the first a relatively minor post-biblical festival marking the New Year for Trees and therefore often called "Jewish Arbor Day" and the other, known in English as the Feast of Weeks or Pentecost, a biblical harvest festival on the magnitude of Pesach and Shavuot that also became through rabbinic interpretation a celebration of divine revelation as it was experienced through the giving of the Torah. Jewish mysticism points to a deeper connection between them.

Tu b'shevat has been observed since before talmudic times as an agricultural beginning, the New Year for Trees. The date for marking the start of the trees' new annual growth was a matter of utmost practicality, for the obligation to tithe the annual produce of nut and fruit trees growing on the land of Israel was a religious legal responsibility requiring a common understanding

121

of when one arboreal year should end and the other begin. The pragmatic aspect of the holiday continues in our day as the Jewish National Fund focuses on Tu b'shevat for its campaign of reforesting Israel, and religious schools teach about the importance of the land of Israel and its agriculture in Jewish tradition. The recent concern for ecology and environmentalism has deepened as well as broadened the reach of this material. If Hanukkah is the post-biblical holiday that expresses the political yearnings of modern Jews, Tu b'shevat with its modern heritage of tree-planting seems likely to take on a similar role for Jewish environmentalists.

The Tu b'shevat seder has especially captured the fancy of Jewish schools and communities. Initiated by the kabbalists in 16th century Tz'fat (Safed), for whom it had metaphysical dimensions, the seder offers opportunities for many levels of physical, intellectual and spiritual engagement, from the most basic to the most esoteric. Many of the central features come from the teachings of the brilliant, short-lived rabbi Isaac Luria, as transmitted by his illustrious student Rabbi Hayyim Vital. In their view, this is the time to "get the juices flowing," renewing the spiritual flow between the upper realms and lower realms of being, from the dimension of the physical to that of the metaphysical, and back again.

In contrast to the seder for Pesach, that for Tu b'shevat does not have one commonly accepted text, a haggadah, that has been transmitted and adopted across generations and throughout the Jewish world. Nor did rabbinic tradition assign either a particular liturgy or biblical readings specific to Tu b'shevat for synagogue use.

The kabbalistic origins of the ritual provide a structural outline that many practitioners find meaningful or at least useful; and there are particular traditions among Sefardic and hassidic

Jews regarding the structure of the seder and choices of tree-related readings from the *Tanakh*, the talmudic tractate *Zera'im* ("Seeds") and the *Zohar*. Nonetheless, the absence of halakhah on the order or content of the ceremony allows for a lot of independence in practice. Many have compiled their own haggadahs for this holiday, perhaps emphasizing connections with Eretz Israel or rich with esoteric kabbalistic constructions, with psychological insights about human nature, with teachings based on environmental concerns or informed by feminist political and psychological theory, each interspersed with thematically chosen readings and songs in addition to the blessings for the wine and foods

The seder will usually include in some form the seven foods specifically identified with the land of Israel in *Deuteronomy 8: 8*: wheat and barley, grapes, figs, pomegranates, olives, and dates. (The "honey" of the "land of milk and honey" was actually date jam.) The early flowering almond tree is also often represented by its produce, as is the hearty carob that grows in Israel. Some strive to have a total of fifteen varieties of fruits and nuts in three groupings. As at the Pesach seder, that of Tu b'shevat features four glasses of wine or grape juice, carefully sequenced, however, beginning with all white, then mostly white with a bit of red added, next mostly red but with some white, and finally all red. While this might remind us of a classic meal, the point is not to go (for instance) from sauvignon blanc through rosé, pinot noir and end with port but to pattern the flow of divine energy through the four "worlds" or dimensions of existence; the most transparent, the white, correlates with the lowest spiritual dimension, that of practical action (*assiyah*); the deepest red is the fullest and richest, the highest realm we can understand, that of emanation (*atzilut*), the flowing forth of energy. So, too, in a full-scale seder, we enjoy a similar arrangement of foods, in each group trying to taste first one of the species associated with Israel, and moving from the lowest order, fruits and nuts with inedible exteriors, the ones in which we are most aware of the harder material shell surrounding a rich, softer and nourishing interior, a metaphor for the physical matter enclosing the spirit, ending with wholly edible fruit with small seeds, like figs, evoking the realm of *b'riyah*, creation.

Why was the Tu b'shevat seder this important for the kabbalists? They had many reasons, and in understanding them we better appreciate how their grasp of the interrelatedness of plant life and human life resonates with our more scientifically expressed perceptions of nature. Although it is unfair to represent them as if they all taught and said the same things, represented their ideas in the same ways, and developed just one system of representing their concepts, we can still set forth some general ideas and frequently recurring images from their teachings.

Remembering that they expressed themselves with a poetic sensibility through often-bold visual images, metaphors and fables from unexpected angles of vision, we realize that this was also how they interpreted biblical language. Their techniques coalesced with the midrashic tradition. After all, if the Torah tells us that human beings were "made in the image of the divine," how could we possibly understand such an idea except as a metaphor for parallels and analogies that have not been spelled out? Their approach to biblical language led the mystics to bold interpretations derived by raising the Torah's text from the level of its plain sense in order to arrive at what they believe to be its esoteric teaching.

For instance, *Deuteronomy 20: 19* asserts an important practical and ethical commandment that while besieging a city, we are not to destroy the food-bearing trees. Having made that point, the Torah challenges us with a statement generally taken to mean something like the rhetorical question, "For is the tree of the field a human being that will oppose you in a siege?" The exact phrasing, however, is difficult; the syntax of the Hebrew puts *ha-adam*, meaning "person," in the position where we would expect to find the subject of the phrase rather than the object. Customary interpretations, looking at the sense of the passage, have treated that syntactic inversion as indicating a question. By contrast, the *Zohar* leaps upon the analogy compacted into these few crucial words, lifting the phrase from the field of the text like buried treasure: *ki ha-adam eytz sadeh*, "because the human being [or, Adam] [is] a tree of the field." Its analyses go in both possible directions, exploring the ramifications of "the person is a tree" and "Adam is a tree," writing of the primordial human being in quasi-mythic terms.

The tree, beginning from a kernel and developing underground as well as above ground, spreading roots and branches, bringing forth leaves, flowers and fruit, is the image of organic growth, emerging from that which is unseen to that which we harvest to sustain our lives. Differently from the kabbalists, we appreciate aspects of the analogy in other terms. We are likely to describe our "roots" as somehow connecting us to earlier generations and their homelands not only in genetic but also in cultural ways. We also understand trees as (so to speak) inhaling carbon dioxide and exhaling oxygen, and their roots anchoring vulnerable soil, making them crucial in the survival of the ecosystem. We know that the destruction of rainforests and ancient woodlands, clear-cutting and the deforesting of hillsides have consequences affecting human beings and all the creatures of the planet, not just the ones in that particular habitat.

Of course, the *Zohar* is especially attentive to the implications of the biblical "tree of life," referring to it over 150 times. Despite its significance in cultural history, the Edenic tree of life is specifically mentioned only three times in *Genesis*; a critical element in the story of Adam and Eve (Havah), God places it in the garden, implicitly sustaining the generative powers of life on earth. *Proverbs 3: 18* furnishes the metaphor about wisdom that the *siddur* applies to the Torah in the passage read and often sung as the scroll is replaced in the ark, *Eytz hayyim hee,* "She is a tree of life to those who grasp her, and all who cling to her are happy." It is for this reason that the two wooden staves holding the Torah scroll are known as *trees of life.* That "tree of life" became proverbial for something that furnishes an essential quality for satisfactory human living in the emotional and the ethical dimensions is proven by that same book of the Tanakh. *Proverbs 11: 30* adds, "The fruit of the righteous is a tree of life," while in *13: 12* "desire fulfilled is a tree of life" and in *15: 4,* "a healing tongue is a tree of life."

When we imagine that wisdom and Torah are like trees connected with the effluence of divine creative energy, and then we imagine that the human being, albeit created in the semblance of the divine, is like a tree ideally bearing good fruit, indeed that the original person was like a primordial tree, we can understand the next imaginative step. Not only are earthly trees rooted in *adamah,* "earth," stretching upward with branches, leaves and fruit being fed by the sap rising into them; but also the creative force that radiates to us, which we can also call the influence of divine creativity, can be thought of metaphorically as a tree (kabbalistically, this is the sefirotic tree) rooted in the realm of the divine and reaching down into the physical universe. Flowing through that downward-facing tree like sap are the qualities (the *sefirot*) that comprise the totality of balanced qualities that make our world what it is and allow it to leaf, bloom and bear fruit. These emanate from the realm of the divine and include wisdom, understanding, beauty, strength, endurance and so on, the ten various qualities usually designated within kabbalistic systems.

In their visual representations the kabbalists often superimpose those terms on a human figure but also frequently represent them in the form of a stylized tree, with the understanding that this "tree" comes from above, where its roots are located, and from which it derives its life-force. Kabbalists, in striving to evoke how the flowing emanations derive from a powerful source above us (in all senses) and how they connect with one another in dynamic relationship, most often resort to metaphors pertinent to lives of human beings and trees and prominent in the biblical description of the creation of the universe, light and water. These primal elements (unlike earth) flow. The *sefirot* can simultaneously be fed by water or light and they can be composed of water or light, with which they nourish animal and plant life as well. Inside the hard shells of fruits and nuts, or around their pits, the edible portion is suffused with the primal creative energy that goes back to the beginning of the universe. In expressing gratitude for our food, eating and being nourished by what we eat, we then have the opportunity to liberate the sparks of energy in the service of God by doing *mitzvot*, living according to the Torah.

The kabbalists take the notion that we are created in God's image to mean that we too are active participants in the work of repairing whatever is wrong or damaged in creation. If we think of those *sefirot* as representing what the world has or lacks in greater or lesser degrees, we can imagine that we can help by pruning, watering or feeding attentively, wisely, the tree of life, indeed the two trees of life, the one rooted in the earth and reaching upward yet also the one rooted in the divine realm but stretching into ours. In other words, we are not just recipients but givers. Sacrifices were acceptable in the Temple as ways of expressing gratitude to God; they also prepared the way for our approaching and influencing God, as would be the case with human monarchs. The Temple was formerly the meeting place between the human and divine realms, the place (so to speak) where the branches of the earthly tree and those of the celestial tree could intertwine. Now the need remains but we must meet it in other ways. In the exchange between us and the divine as some kabbalists imagined it, we are supposed to perceive how our actions and feelings (which are actions of the emotions) strengthen or diminish the flow, replenish or weaken the source that supplies the world with the light and water of life.

As with any profound ritual, one hopes to choose an ideal place and an ideal time. Tu b'shevat, the day when flowing sap signaled the end of winter dormancy for the trees of the land of Israel, was obviously a propitious time for a ceremony to free the divine energy of creation from its entrapment in the material form of what we call food from trees. With liberation as the theme, the obvious model would be the Passover seder, as *Pesach* is called *zeman heiruteinu*, the season of our liberation. Furthermore, mystics interpreted our enslavement in *mitzrayim* as the literal expression of the human spirits' entrapment in the service of the physical, before being liberated to receive the enlightenment embodied through the teachings known as Torah at the high and wild point of Mt. Sinai.

As for the ideal place, that would surely be in the land of Israel because of all of its associations. When Canaan is described in the Torah, it is not characterized as a place of revelations and spiritual living, it is described in agricultural terms, a land flowing with milk and honey, bountiful with wheat and barley, grapes figs, dates, pomegranates, olives. But there was a particular poignant tension here for the 16th century kabbalists of Tz'fat who developed the ritual for this holiday. Many were exiles or descendents of the exiles from the former center of Jewish mysticism and the arts, Spain, after the 1492 expulsion, or Portugal after 1496. This forcible uprooting along with the exiles' subsequent uncertain and hazardous peregrinations was still a strong part of the communal memory. Moreover, while they found refuge in *eretz yisrael*, the land of Israel, that was not *medinat yisrael*, the nation of Israel, but a rather provincial territory of the Ottoman Empire.

Here was a double paradox. They were home, but it was not really home since it did not belong to them as a Jewish people. Also, while they had returned from exile, in this case the long exile of Jews from the land of Israel following the expulsions of the second century C.E., yet now again they were in exile, the more recent exile from their home at the other end of the Mediterranean in Sefarad, the Iberian peninsula, where they and centuries of predecessors had lived in a flourishing Jewish culture that had been shattered. So near, so far! Consequently, they understood and expressed through their ritual the yearning and urgency of their generations' experiences, along with their spiritual grasp that complex forces are working on and through the material life in us and on the earth as well as in the cosmos. Eating and drinking as described at Tu b'shevat with the intention, the *kavvanah,* of spirituality nourishes our bodies and souls but through that process we return the precious sustaining life-energy to the source of life.

This process is sometimes termed *tikkun olam*, the repair of the world. The phrase is widely used today in non-mystical circles

Andrew Vogel Ettin

as a synonym for "social action," a way of sacralizing our pragmatic societal commitments, but that has not been its traditional
meaning. Rather, Lurianic kabbalah envisioned disruption and
breakage during the forming of the universe, for physical matter
was not perfectly capable of containing the powerful spirituality
emanating from the sacred source of life. The shattering (according to some kabbalists) was the source of the loose, harmful energy that we perceive as evil, really the undirected or misdirected
potential that we can transform into power for goodness through
mitzvot, thereby helping to reconnect that *yetzer*, or impulse, with
the holiness from which it has become separated.

Tu b'shevat lets us map our understanding of the world.
A Tu b'shevat seder therefore is not just an occasion for enjoying
a plate of fruits and nuts accompanied by wine or grape juice,
all arranged as an arcane vegan tasting menu, though perhaps
it frequently seems that way. The essence of the seder is *kavvanah*, the intentional focus with which we go through the process.
The date of the holiday remains constant but the seasons of our
lives do not. In one year, connecting with modern Israel might
be uppermost, and we are not only sampling the fruit of that
"good and ample land" (*eretz tovah v-rachavah*) as it is called in
Exodus 3:8 but also considering what we learn from the seder
about the land and its people. In another, we are most aware of
worldwide ecological interdependence, appreciating biodiversity,
talking about what we eat and how it is produced, and by whom.
Again, the most compelling perceptions could be the spiritual
and emotional truths that (for instance) below a tough shell, rich
sweetness exists, or that inside of a soft and welcoming exterior
there needs to be a solid core; or perhaps we unexpectedly find a
hardness within that breaks the teeth. At another time we grasp
at least from a distance the metaphysical relationships comprised

130

by *tikkun olam*, purposefully willing that our actions help to energize for the wellbeing of everything the power of spirituality incarnate in all that we eat, drink and do, for the sake of both the world's good and God's goodness.

The flowing of divine creative energy into the earthly dimension of nature connects Tu b'shevat with the biblical festival of Shavuot. Like Pesach and Sukkot, the other pilgrimage festivals, Shavuot fuses the vegetative cycle with the historical moment that interjects a singular revelatory experience into nature's repetitive pattern, the day linking the grain harvest with the giving of the Torah, the bread of our life. Between Pesach and Shavuot those seven weeks of seven days each stretch like a power line. Kabbalists perceive during this period a process of spiritual movement in which each week contains the principle expressed through one of the seven lower *sefirot*, beginning with the most elemental and working toward the uppermost, and similarly each of the seven days of that week expressing analogous gradations within that *sefirah*. At the culmination, Shavuot itself, we reach the fiftieth day; as this is the transcendent day of revelation, we thus move spiritually beyond the seventh level (what other ancient cultures called the "seventh heaven") into the upper *sefirot*, the region of the divine.

Like all the festivals, Shavuot occurs along both a horizontal plane, on which it has its place in the linear time sequence of the yearly cycle, and a vertical plane, on which it connects with sanctity that we can think of as emanating from below and above. On the plane of time, it is linked with Pesach, marking another interruption of the predictable continuum of normal life. The exodus was a singular experience; the Sinaitic revelation was another. Each in its own way burst the hitherto-presumed limits of possibility and understanding. As we say during the Passover seder, if God had only brought us out of Egypt, *dayyenu*, that would have been enough for us. But there was to be more. Without the exodus, no Torah; then the Torah becomes the point of the exodus. The temporal path from one to the other is a kind of spiritual odyssey, a journey of inner transformation compressed into forty-nine days that will be "repeated" every year, but not merely repeated because the traveler is not the same each year. Even the experience at Sinai sent us forward. That mountain was not to be the destination of pilgrimages.

The all-night study session is another Shavuot tradition dating from the 16th century kabbalists, who understood that this might induce a state of mind susceptible to a mystical experience. It is called *Tikkun leil shavuot*, meaning the "repair of Shavuot night," referring to a midrash in which Moses had to awaken the Hebrews, who had fallen asleep during the night while awaiting the revelation. (There is also a tradition of the bridegroom staying awake all night before his wedding, which we might connect with the marital analogy of Israel's covenant with God.) The list of readings remains open for our own additions to the chain of transmission. A customary curriculum for Sefardic and Hasidic communities consists of reading the first and last few verses of every one of the weekly biblical Torah portions as well as other selected passages, each section of the Mishnah, and mystical texts including passages from the *Zohar*. For people who regularly attend a synagogue where the entire Torah and its *haftarot* are read through each year, and who spend some time in formal Jewish study, a few verses will be enough to recall the entire passage, so the experience approaches something akin to a Sinaitic revelation, having at least the entire Torah rapidly downloaded into one's consciousness as something like a zip file. And there is more. If we look at this description of the night's syllabus, we see that it encompasses the written Torah, the oral Torah, and the mystical explication of the Torah. That is, it represents our receiving and accepting of the Torah on this day in all of its significant dimensions.

On the plane of sanctity, as Tu b'shevat is grounded by the earth and the flow of sap stimulated by the trees' roots, Shavuot holds to the barren mountain from which, amid lightning and thunder and in the absence of any other living creature, we pluck from the downward-growing tree the Torah, which is also called *p'ri eytz hadar*, the fruit of a splendid tree. It is not only given but received. The intimate intensity of that unfolding of divine complexity that Shavuot expresses perhaps explains why it is a one-day festival, unlike the other two *regalim*, Sukkot and Pesach. Truly, we are taught that Shavuot is called the festival *matan torateynu*, "of the giving of our torah" because the giving can be linked to a particular event but the receiving takes place all the time. "O taste and see that the Lord is good," the psalmist urges us (*Ps. 34: 9*) and the female beloved in *Song of Songs*, the poetical book that the rabbis accepted as a mystical testament of the relationship between God and the people of Israel, proclaims "His fruit was sweet to my taste" (*Song, 2:3*). "How sweet your words to my taste, sweeter than honey in my mouth" (*Ps. 119: 103*). This is how Ezekiel experiences the scroll God compels him to consume: "Then I ate it, and in my mouth it was as sweet as honey" (*Ezek. 3: 3*). The Torah's source may be transcendent but the experience of it is intimately physical, on our lips and in our mouth, as if the giving and receiving is a sublimation of sexual experience.

Why the Torah should be perceived in these terms is not obvious when we think of it as a compendium of "shall" obligations and "shall not" prohibitions, a tabulation of obligatory animal sacrifices and agricultural contributions, a building plan for an elaborate tabernacle, and the organizational chart for a national theocracy. Looking over its shoulder, so to speak, in order to look past the particular details, we may see that what the Torah sets forth is a plan for something new: leading a fully integrated life in which we are as consonant with one another as with our physical and natural environment and with ourselves, a life not compartmentalized as if we were built of separate components.

In other words, if God is One and we are made to be God's semblance, then the Torah is a pattern for our oneness. Think of the end of Yeats's poem "Among School Children," where he asks rhetorically,

> O chestnut-tree, great-rooted blossomer,
> Are you the leaf, the blossom or the bole?
> O body swayed to music, O brightening glance,
> How can we know the dancer from the dance?

What is imparted to us at Sinai is a certain taxonomy for the tree of life, a particular choreography for the dance of living. The sweet savor, the full taste in the mouth, comes from the transformative conviction that it is possible and good to live in such wholeness.

This implies neither obligatory acceptance today of every word of the written Torah nor rejection of the very idea of religion as being expressed through law. The concept and actuality of the oral Torah implies that it must be a living document whose vitality depends on our daily actualizing of it. Nor would even the most radical antinomian want to live in a world without law.

At some places, during the Shavuot Torah reading the entire congregation stands for the recitation of the Ten Commandments. An effective way of doing this, where possible, is to gather the congregation at the foot of the bimah while members carefully hold up an open Torah scroll on the bimah facing the congregation; the reader chants the text that the congregation can actually see, dramatizing the idea that they witness the document that they are accepting. Others make this a time for a congregational retreat, journey to Israel, or a trip to a nearby mountain. That will not be Sinai but it can still move those who make the journey into another approach to the day's spiritual potential.

If the absence of outstanding adaptations into other art forms is a measure of a work's stature, the Book of Ruth, which is the designated special reading for Shavuot, is great. Economic as a work of art, this novella is continually open to discoveries of layers of meaning within it. The relationship between the maternal yet also sisterly Naomi and her widowed daughter-in-law Ruth, two women partnered in life by fate and choice, emerges with particular complexity through feminist analyses. A family fleeing from their country to a neighboring one to escape a famine, the personal disasters that ensue, Ruth's treatment by Boaz and his harvesters as an resident alien farm-laborer—such themes compel us to comparisons with the stories in our newspapers and neighborhoods, and they touch our hearts and consciences as much as our minds. *Ruth* seems made for interpretation as drama, music, dance, bibliodrama or visual representation, but it rarely is. This work would call for a much more sophisticated treatment than the Purimspiel of *Esther*, subtler nuances than Handel needed for his oratorio on that narrative of a fictive Persia, with its big confrontations and emotions as well as clearly defined villains. There are no real villains in *Ruth*. It is a story in which the *yetzer ha-ra*, the impulse that causes distress, seems dormant. The 17th century French painter Nicolas Poussin caught the atmosphere effectively in his lovely pastoral harvest scene, "Summer: Ruth and Boaz," where the main characters, dividing the midpoint in the painting's foreground, seem dwarfed by the fertile landscape in which they are central yet barely significant.

Ruth was probably selected as the Shavuot reading because the barley and wheat harvests are critical in the story. Further, there are significant additional resonances that make it appropriate to this festival. One is that Ruth voluntarily accepts the Torah with all of its obligations, which is how the sages interpreted her famous pledge to Naomi, "Where you go, I will go, and where your dwell, I will dwell; your people shall be my people, your God shall be my God" (*Ruth 1: 16 ; Ruth Rabbah 2: 22*). Moreover, she was an ancestor of David, therefore also of Solomon, builder of the Temple, which became the new locus for the connection with God after Sinai, and therefore also an ancestor of the messianic line.

We may also feel a less explicit connection, that the quality of relationships developed in the story expresses the spirit of Shavuot. As they are usually perceived, the principal figures in the narrative relate to one another caringly and respectfully. There are deaths, but they occur "off stage" to characters whom we never really know. Situations that we might expect to be dangerous or tragic achieve peaceful resolutions because people surprisingly do not take advantage of one another's vulnerability. The Torah's commandments such as guarding the rights of "the widow, the orphan and the resident alien among you" and the responsibility of a kinsman toward a relative's wife and property are lived out in this text; they establish set obligations that work toward the benefit of the characters' lives or, in literary terms, the story's happy ending. For like a modern romantic comedy, *Ruth* ends with everyone apparently satisfied, Ruth and Boaz living happily as a married couple with a baby, and Naomi delighting in the grandchild who gives her new life. This grandchild leads us to the messianic line of David.

The balance between messianic hopefulness and individual responsibility was carefully but succinctly articulated in the Middle Ages by Maimonides to persecuted communities in the near East:

> There is no set time for the coming of the Messiah, so that one can say, 'He is near' or 'He is far.' ….The obligation to perform the commandments is not contingent on the coming of the Messiah, for we are required to be occupied with the Torah and the mitzvot and to attempt to complete their performance. After we have done that which is required of us, if God will grant us or our grandchildren to see the Messiah, then good; if not, we have lost nothing, for we have done that which is required of us.

We might ponder how the actions of the major figures in *Ruth* enact or facilitate the *tikkun*, "repair" that will make a future—a messianic time—possible. Thinking of the story in this way, we better understand how artfully the author has significantly paired minor characters with one another, one toward the beginning and the other toward the end. Orpah, the daughter-in-law who chooses not to accompany Naomi and Ruth to the land of Israel, and *ploni almoni*, "What's-his-name," the kinsman who chooses not to marry Ruth and take on the responsibility of continuing her husband's familial line are not able, willing or ready to make the connections that will effect such a repair of the social connections based on respect, selflessness and love.

A beautiful Sefardic custom is to read on Shavuot a ketubah between God and the bride Israel, as Shavuot was interpreted midrashically as a marriage. For instance, the Talmud (*Shemot Rabbah 41: 6*) proposes an analogy between the two tablets of the Ten Commandments and the two witnesses for a wedding. Some *ketubot* depict the Torah as the groom, brought by its parent, God; in others, God is the groom. Many texts have been used, going back to writings of 16th century mystics. Here too is an opportunity for artistic and creative re-engagement with the tradition. How might a modern ketubah text for this ceremony read? What would members of the community want to specify or promise as signatories? What are they bringing to this marriage? What do we bring to our relationship with Torah? What do we expect? And what do we bring to our committed relationships? These are questions for a day of receiving, thus of "owning" for ourselves, the Torah that we have been given.

✳ ✳ ✳

At the Seder Table

Setting the Pesach seder table is no simple matter. There will be candles, not just for decoration but for ceremonially welcoming the festival with appropriate blessings. A seder plate, maybe more than one, is customary. It could be an heirloom with a significant history, a finely crafted modern work, maybe a child's hand-decorated paper plate fashioned in a religious school classroom. Whatever it is, it will have places for the ritual foods mentioned or sampled during the service, all of which are set out before the ceremony starts: lamb shankbone or a vegetable surrogate for it, a roasted unpeeled egg, a fresh green herb, a bitter leafy green or horseradish, the fruit and nut mixture called *charoset*. Three matzahs are stacked on a plate or in a special holder used during the ceremony; other matzahs are available for general eating, their rippled surfaces mottled with brown flecks from the oven's high heat. The kiddush cup is provided for the leader of the seder; perhaps everyone has one instead of a conventional wine glass, and bottles of wine or grape juice are available for the four times that we drink ritually during the seder. Bowls of salted water sit ready for the dipping of green spring herbs. A beaker of water, basin and towel are convenient for ceremonial hand-washing. The table might be set with an especially beautiful cloth; the dishes are traditionally those used only during the week or eight days of this holiday. At each place is a Haggadah. A place is also set for the prophet Elijah, with an especially generous-sized kiddush cup. Some now also have a special goblet of water honoring the prophetess Miriam, Moses' sister, who was biblically associated with life-giving water.

All this, and we haven't even gotten to the meal!

In imagining the seder table, we have been looking at a stage set for a liturgical drama performed as home dinner theater with audience participation. The design of the items will reflect the taste and budget of the producers (i.e., the hosts); however, everything mentioned has a purpose. The production involves some action, pantomime, a bit of choreography, music according to the abilities of the participants, much story-telling, and preferably a lot of improvisation. It is, in other words, a hybrid form, in some ways more like a revue in its mix of musical styles, narratives from various sources, and spontaneous repartee, but fine-tuned over the ages into what Wagner called a *Gesamtkunstwerk*, a comprehensive art work.

The evolved structure of the seder is complex yet clearly marked out into fourteen acts or scenes, the fourteen sections of the seder that are our annual production.. Why that number? Perhaps because in Hebrew the number *14* is spelled *yud-dalet*, the same spelling as the word *yad*, meaning "hand." Passover celebrates God's "mighty hand and outstretched arm" that brought the Israelites from servitude to liberation; in the story of the Exodus we perceive God's "hand" working in human history. (Some follow a differentiation into fifteen sections by considering the blessing for matzah and the eating of matzah as two elements rather than one. The result is also significant as the number *15* represents the first two letters of the Tetragrammaton, *yud-hey*. [7]) Typically the seder begins with a melodic review of the names, the rubrics, of each part, reminding us of the order, which is what *seder* means. Noting that an order exists is probably just as important as recalling what the order is, for this is a liturgy worked out intentionally, not a brief ceremony or only an elaborate holiday meal. The rollicking incremental tongue-twisting songs at the end may be designed to wake everyone up, yet even these are meaningful allegories of Jewish historical experience. The revue-like character is reflected through the variety of the music and the narrating techniques, with some seders being done in traditional nusach, others relying on recorded music for lively support; still others take a heterogeneous mix of styles from whatever voices are around the table. At a typical seder we might use a venerable yeshiva chant tune, a modern Israeli melody, middle-European and Yemenite musical settings, and an American folk song. The event turns into a pageant of Jewish culture. The breadth of the experience has become greater in recent years as Jews from Ashkenazic backgrounds explore Sephardic and Israeli cuisine, incorporating recipes from parts of the world far from where their own families formed their culinary habits a century or more ago. The European-style dishes containing walnuts, apples, cinnamon and the ubiquitous parsley are often joined by those featuring figs and dates, spiced with cumin, coriander and cilantro leaves.

Gestures made during the seder as well as the ones not made are deeply significant. Perhaps the most dramatic of the gestures occurs during the portion of the narrative when we recall the plagues that afflicted the Egyptians until the Exodus occurred. As each of the plagues is named (and in traditional seders, as each of the other catastrophes and the acronyms for groups of plagues is recited), each of us dips a finger into the wine glass, removing a drop of wine onto the plate or into the salted water, showing that the recollection of others' suffering lessens our joy (for Psalm 104:15 says that "wine gladdens the heart"). The litany accompanied by the dripping of wine, each like a drop of blood or a fallen tear, is eloquent and profound, all the more for memorializing afflictions of our persecutors. It is an extraordinary acknowledgement that surely developed long after the event. Could we imagine today dropping wine for the air raids that killed so many Germans and others during the Allies' struggle to defeat the Nazis and their allies in World War II?

Contrast this with an action in the part of the seder following the meal. The much-cherished ritual of sending a child to open the door for Elijah, perhaps accompanied by one of the familiar melodies for the song *eliyahu ha-navi*. That tuneful, comfortable welcome of the awaited prophet is quite different from the traditional reading probably dating to the Middle Ages denouncing those who perpetrate violence against us. Everyone rises to exclaim, *sh'fokh khamat'kha*: "Pour out Your wrath," we cry out to God, hurling phrases from Psalms and Lamentations into the night air, "on the other peoples [*ha-goyim*] who do not acknowledge You, for they have devoured Jacob and destroyed his dwelling-places. Pursue them, annihilate them from under God's heavens." It is an uncomfortable, even a frightening passage for many people, therefore it has been omitted from some modern haggadot. A few others balance it with a plea supposedly found in a 16th century haggadah from Worms, Germany and worded as its exact but contrary counterpart, urging God to "pour out" love on those peoples and nations who in love and piety toward God have shielded Jews and protected our communities.

We can certainly understand why some want to suppress the original text. Most of us live in comfort among and often with non-Jews, some of whom may be seated at our table but who might nevertheless imagine themselves included among the cursed *goyim*. Even more, we are likely embarrassed by uncharitably cursing our enemies to the extent of praying that they be annihilated. But there is a difference between not feeling anger and repressing the justified anger that one does feel. We cannot know Jewish history without knowing and being profoundly affected by the bigotry or persecution our people have experienced. To give voice to that righteous awareness of injustice is legitimate; indeed, we may say it is more legitimate than ignoring or evading it. We might need to be able to recognize how this historical experience has affected us inside. To be able to do so with the door open—think of the backlit solitary child facing the dark night—is a measure of our security or courage.

Depending on the way the imprecation is expressed and felt, it may be purgative as well. Calling on God to destroy our oppressors is a large step away from attacking them ourselves, and giving public voice to our hostile emotions can be a means to rid ourselves of them. We pour the wrath out of us as we call on God to pour it on our tormenters. It is our temper tantrum, our melt-down, but not arbitrary.

Nor does it occur at an arbitrary moment. Opening the door for Elijah during this passage is not paradoxical, although there is a vast difference in doing so accompanied by *sh'fokh khamat'kha* rather than *eliyahu ha-navi*. Might it be that recognizing and acknowledging the dynamics of violence, especially as it affects the outlook of its victims, is necessary to the bringing of the messianic time? That perhaps this great transformation has not taken place because we either repress or misunderstand the lesson buried in the Haggadah? That we remain silent or hide the resentments of the past, or take at its face the powerful condemnatory words that we hurl from the open door? A door that not only stands open to receive the hungry stranger and the awaiting prophet but also to give forth what has been closed up inside, hidden from the external world?

During the seder there are times when the haggadah instructs us to raise our glass without blessing or drinking. Again these gestures, approaching pantomime, are not explained by the text. If they are not commented on or pondered, they are merely odd rituals devoid of significance, tics in the smooth flow of text and action. They occur, however, at strategic moments. For instance, during the *maggid* (narration) of Israelite history, the text recalls God's promise to Abraham that his descendents will dwell under oppression in Egypt, after which they will be liberated and their exploiters judged for what they did. At that point we cover the matzahs (the bread of liberation, but now hidden by a cloth, kept from our sight) and raise the cup, which will be set down untasted, as we recite, *v'hi she'amdah avoteinu*, "And this promise has upheld our ancestors and us, for not merely one enemy has arisen against us to destroy us, but so in every generation, except that the Holy One, blessed be!, delivers us from their hand." At such a recollection, our emotions are too full to allow us to express thanks or to enjoy what we drink or eat. Recalling that we are still here, how can we not raise a glass of thanksgiving? And yet, in the moment of recognizing our ancestors' sufferings, the destruction of Jewish families and communities, our people's many near-escapes from total annihilation, how could we enjoy wine? It is as if we pick up the cup to drink and, realizing what we are talking about, put it down, too distracted by the memories that the narrative arouses.

Think of how different this is from simply not touching the wine glass at all. The gesture of raising the glass and then setting it down untasted communicates eloquently, even though inexperienced or inattentive attendees often sip before getting to the stage direction telling them not to, much as concert-goers sometimes applaud inappropriately at cadences that sound like finales but aren't. We will give thanks for the wine with the appropriate blessing, and we will be able to taste it with enjoyment, just not at this moment.

From what have we been liberated? *Mitzrayim*—the biblical name for Egypt. In Hebrew *tzar* (spelled *tzadi resh*) means "narrow." Not the historical entity known today as "Egypt" but *Mitzrayim* is a place of constraint, where we cannot grow or develop. That is another way of understanding the seder's remembrance, *avadim hayinu,* We were slaves in the land of *Mitzrayim.* Slavery here does not denote only forced laborers; it also means that we lived with culture-bound restrictions on our development. The Exodus is heralded by the repeated refrain, *sh'lakh et-ami,* Send my people out. We can understand this as a succinct way of saying, Free my people from living under constraints that prevent them from expanding their knowledge of themselves in the context of eternal truths (in the Torah's language, "serving God"). *Mitzrayim* can also be thought of as like the womb, the constricting incubator from which we pass forth through the birth canal represented by the parting of the *Yam Suf,* the Sea of Reeds. Only by going forth from that narrowness can we enter into the open, unmarked region of the *midbar*, the <u>wilderness</u> of Sinai where we mature through our own unpredictable, unscripted engagement with the life-source of the universe. The sages transmit the teaching (*Numbers Rabbah 1:7*) that the Torah was given in the wilderness to show that one must be totally receptive, open, in order to take it. Had we remained in *Mitzrayim*, we would have remained restricted from it, not open to receive it.

Questions and puzzlements are always good for this. For example, Rabban Gamliel ruled that we have to explain *Pesach, matzah,* and *maror.* So we speak familiarly about the sacrificial lamb offering, the unleavened bread prepared and eaten in haste by our ancestors, and the pains of slavery symbolized by the bitter herb. All of those need to be remembered and transmitted *l'dor v'dor*, from generation to generation. And they can be renewed symbols.

Suppose we think this year also about what "sacrifice" might mean to us today, and how we might be saved by it. Some might think in political or social or economic terms, and some in ecological terms. What might I give up or sacrifice in order to save not just my family or the Jewish people but a livable world? And some might think of it in terms of health. Might "sacrificing" by dumping out the rest of the pack of cigarettes or turning away from the super-sized French fries help keep away the angel of death? Could that be our *Pesach* this year?

Matzah is the opposite of *chametz*, the leavened or fermented food. Nothing but ground wheat and water that don't meet until 18 minutes before they come out of the oven, it is like a "reality check" on bread. Matzah was also part of the regular offering in the Tabernacle and later the Temple, so it is bread appropriate to be a sacred contribution. What is the *chametz* in <u>your</u> life? What is the extra, unneeded ingredient that keeps you from "getting

Andrew Vogel Ettin

real," from living the kind of life that would put you closer to the Creator? What's keeping us "puffed up" with some leavening agent that we don't really need in order to "be real"?

In the Jerusalem Talmud, Rabban Gamliel refers to the third item as *merorim*, the plural form of *maror*. "Maror" can mean any sort of "bitterness," not only "bitter herb." Maybe the plural version can help us rethink the idea and ask what "bitternesses" we want to register at this point in our lives, whether as individuals or as a group. Some may feel free enough to name those openly. Perhaps we need to make a breathing space in the narration for those bitternesses that need to be acknowledged silently in our deep core.

We remain open to whatever the seder brings to us each time. A charming story in the Talmud recounts an anecdote about a seder at the home of Rabbah, one of the greatest sages of the great academy in Pumbedita (Iraq) during the third century, CE. His pupil Abaye, who would succeed Rabbah as head of the academy, was present. After the first of the four cups of wine, and long before the meal was served, Rabbah's servants came and removed the serving tray. Abaye exclaimed, "What's this? We haven't eaten yet and they've taken away the tray?" Rabbah responded wittily, "Now we don't need to ask '*ma nishtana*' ['Why is this night different?']."

This story is worth recalling because it reminds us that reading every word of the Haggadah is less important than making the seder a living experience for the participants. It should be real. That might come about spontaneously (like Abaye being surprised) or it might have to be planned. What can we each do this year to make our seder seem new?

It is important here to be open and accepting: someone else's *merorim* might include items that please you, but we need

146

to grant other people the <u>freedom</u> to declare (as we might say) where their shoe pinches them, even though your shoe fits you better.

Let us remember that *"cherut"* or liberty includes even ideas with which we disagree

✳ ✳ ✳

Tisha b'av

How do we turn disaster into ritual? Judaism has funneled its chronicles of losses into the commemoration known as Tisha b'Av, literally the 9th (day) of the month of Av, which occurs in the Gregorian calendar between mid July and mid August. Both the first and second Temples in Jerusalem were destroyed on or about that date, the first by the Babylonians in 423 BCE, the second by the Romans in 69 CE. This was also, according to the sages, the date on which the Romans ploughed over the ruins of the city; and in 133 CE the town of Betar, the last Israelite stronghold of the Bar Kokhba rebellion, was captured by the Romans on Tisha b'av at the end of a three-year siege, concluding an episode that cost many thousands of lives. The mishnaic sages calculated (*Taanit 4:6*) that it was on Tisha b'av that God decreed that the generation of the exodus from Egypt would die during the wilderness wanderings, never to enter the promised land that they had rejected because they were terrified by the scouts' reports (*Numbers 14: 22-23*). In later Jewish history, the expulsion of Jews from England in 1290 took place at Tisha b'av, as did the more momentous, consequential expulsion of Jews from Spain in 1492. (Ferdinand and Isabella's earlier expulsion decree had been postponed to give the exiles more time, moving the actual departure to this time.)

Lamentations of Tisha b'av start with history, and specifically with Jewish history. This is understandable: all commemoration begins with something specific that becomes the focal point for memories, much as the Japanese attack on Pearl Harbor and the raising of the flag on Iwo Jima focused American experiences of World War II. We cannot imagine memorializing "the war on terrorism" without centering it on "9/11." The single name "Auschwitz" has developed as metonymy for the devastation of European Jews and their communities by the Nazis and their allies. Tisha b'av commemorates what we have lost in the course of history.

Tisha b'av has been so clearly the focal point for Jewish commemorations of historical tragedies over the centuries that many religious Jews have objected to a separate Holocaust commemorative day, preferring to incorporate that memorial in the more ancient observance, even though we cannot identify a particular Shoah event singularly linked to the 9th of Av. They feel that it is improper to represent the modern destruction as unique rather than one more in a long line of afflictions.

Perhaps they are also responding to the general non-Orthodox disregard of Tisha b'av and all that it represents. Amid summer sun and heat, how many congregants can we induce to the synagogue on the 9th of Av, whatever day of the week that might be, to engage in rituals of community lamentations, a "black" fast of grieving? Shakespeare's Richard II facing the loss of his throne and inevitably the loss of his own life exclaims, "For God's sake let's sit upon the ground / And tell sad stories of the deaths of kings!" On this day for God's sake we sit upon the ground and tell sad stories of the deaths of king and commoners, priests and paupers, people like us, and a kingdom we called our own.

The importance of Israel as a kingdom of our own is even hinted at in one of the most famous biblical tales not usually associated with nationhood. In a famous anecdote in *I Kings 3:*

16 ff. two prostitutes come with an infant before King Solomon, proverbial exemplar of wisdom, each claiming to be the mother, and each tells the same story: I gave birth at the same time as the other woman, with nobody else in the house; her child died but the one that lives is mine. Solomon calls for a sword, proposing to settle the matter by dividing the child in half for each woman; the real mother at once resigns her right so as to spare the baby, whereupon the king, who discerns the truth, returns the child to her. This is so often told as an example of Solomon's cleverness and psychological acumen that we might not notice how bizarre it is, or we simply take its peculiarity at face value, as if the thought processes of ancient peoples were much less sophisticated than ours. Two prostitutes appear before the king of Israel asking that he adjudicate their child custody dispute? Everyone ought to recognize the improbability here. Even someone holding a low opinion of prostitutes' intellectual capabilities will know that no-one would suppose that half of a bisected infant would be of value to her.

The situation is analogous to one that begins the talmudic tractate called *Bava Metzia.* Two people have clasped a *tallit*, a cloak, and each of them claims that it is entirely his. The Talmud will take a different tack from Solomon's in addressing this dilemma, testing a great many permutations over a great many pages to do so. The key to the passage in *Kings*, however, is provided in the text, starting just three verses after Solomon orders, "Divide the living child" (v. 25). Concluding the anecdote, the narrator tells us that "all Israel heard of the judgment the king had rendered; and they were in awe of the king; for they saw that the wisdom of God was in him to deliver a judgment. And King Solomon was king over all Israel. And these were his princes"

149

(vv.3:25, 4:1-2—the verses are sequential; chapter divisions in the Tanakh are not of Jewish origin).

What do we learn from these lines? This tale about Solomon is a political allegory. He has united the tribes of Israel into one kingdom. It will be destroyed if it is subsequently divided into parts because one man or another selfishly wants possession so badly that he will split it in order to get a share for himself rather than let another have it all. The person who really loves all Israel, the story's "living child," would be the one willing to relinquish the entire claim rather than divide and thereby destroy the state, and it is that person who is the true "mother"—the rightful next king.

Fascinatingly, the text calls both women *zonim*, prostitutes. It would have been easy to make the unselfish one come from a higher class, or for that matter both of them, in which case it would be more plausible for them to have a royal audience. Instead, the story shows that even someone whose motives are usually thought to be venal can be moved by a higher value. Perhaps we are supposed to recall the most important *zonah* in Israelite history, the prostitute Rahav in *Joshua*, whose aid proved crucial to capture Jericho, the essential first stage in the conquest of Canaan. It is Rahav who bargains for safe passage by describing it as "*hesed* for *hesed*," bartering one loving-kindness for another loving-kindness. That concept might associate her and the compassionate prostitute of the Solomon story with Tamar, Judah's widowed daughter-in-law in *Genesis* who pretends to be a *zonah* in order to be impregnated by Judah, thus perpetuating her husband's lineage. One of the sons of that union was Perez, an ancestor of Boaz, who married Ruth; according to the fine genealogical economy of Tanakh history, three generations later the descendent of Ruth and Boaz was David, father of Solomon.

By the time *Kings* was written, the sequel was already known. What Solomon feared is exactly what happened after his death. His sons Rehoboam and Jeroboam fought against one another, splitting the kingdom in two with disastrous consequences for the line of succession and for the concept of the nation. It would be hard to say which was the worse king, and *1 Kings 14:30* summarizes succinctly: "There was war between Rehoboam and Jeroboam all their days."

Israel, we must remember, is not merely a political state, though it is also that. While even in biblical times there were varying accounts of its intended boundaries, it is continually cited in the Torah and several times elsewhere in the Tanakh as "the land [*ha-aretz*] that I [God] pledged to your ancestors." Biblical and rabbinic texts often refer to the land of Israel simply as *ha-aretz*, and so it is called by many Jews today. Dividing the land according to the biblically designated tribal inheritances and then by lots was intended to be fair to all, not to destroy the integrity of the people or the common inheritance, not to kill the state or damage as *ha-aretz ha-tovah*, the good land, as it is repeatedly termed in *Deuteronomy* and *Joshua*. In *Ezekiel 37: 22* God promises a redemptive future in which, "I will make them one nation in the land upon the mountains of Israel; and one king shall be king to them all; and they shall be no more two nations, nor shall they be divided into two kingdoms any more at all." The better we appreciate that love of the land transcends disputed real estate rights, the more sensitive can we be in balancing our criticism and support, as well as comprehending how emotionally charged Tisha b'Av can be, even apart from memorializing human suffering during wartime and exiles.

Yet the Ninth of Av is also a day of hope. Rabbinic tradition holds that the messiah (*moshiach*, "anointed one") was born on Tisha b'av. A legend? A quaint bit of folklore? We should prefer to think of this as a profound truth attested to by experience as well as psychology. In our deepest pain—the dark, seemingly hopeless moment, when we "bottom out"—restorative hope comes. We know how bad the worst is. When things can't get any worse, the hopeful sense of a possible better future slips into our awareness.

Imagine the synagogue on the evening of Tisha b'av, dark except perhaps for some flickering candlelight. The open ark is bare of its beautifully ornamented Torah scrolls that we are accustomed to see glistening with their silver ornaments; instead, it is empty, shrouded in the black cloth of bereavement. Worshippers sit or lie on the floor, or perch like mourners on low stools. Perhaps a figure rises from the shadows, stretches yearningly toward the barren ark, body swaying in silent grief before sinking again to lie prostrate on the floor.

For what do we mourn? Some, perhaps most in traditional congregations, recall the long history of Jewish suffering, vulnerability and powerlessness, or center on the still-raw recollections of the Shoah and perhaps on modern Israel's losses during its vulnerable youth. Others may perceive these Jewish experiences as paradigms of other communities' griefs, while still others move outside of collective historical experience to their personal experiences of persecution and loss.

However we shape our understanding of the day, Tisha b'av becomes the locus for the ruptures in the fabric of the universe. The Bible offers one familiar paradigm in what Milton termed "loss of Eden." His phrase aptly embraces more broadly, "all our woe" (*Paradise Lost*, 1: 3-4). In other words, the expulsion of Adam and Eve from the Garden of Eden stands for every form of misery. When we examine this idea in the context of Tisha b'av, we begin to take in the scope that it encompasses.

The expulsions of Jews from England and Spain meant the loss of community. Amid all of the other fears and horrors, tearing of the fabric of lives and relationships must be included in those caused by these expulsions and the countless others recorded through Jewish chronicles (not to mention those of other groups expelled from their places of residence or indeed their ancestral homes). Letters and other accounts of the victims record the poignant, bitter rupture of friendships and family groups. Being forced to leave behind not only homes and businesses and synagogues, familiar landscapes and neighborhoods, they also lost their communities and communal organizations (for a synagogue is not just a building with a Torah scroll). In place after place they recorded the excruciating pain of being uprooted from what they called "the Jerusalem of . . .," that center of Jewish civilization having become the paradigm of all others, expulsion from it being the paradigm of all others, its destruction the paradigm of all others.

Of course, this sort of disruption carries with it something yet more fundamentally universal, the loss of one's sense of safety. We know from victims of natural disasters how profoundly disturbing it is to the psyche to feel that not even one's own residence is protection, and in knowing that neither can they defend their family's home. How much more frightening it is to live with the knowledge that one can be expelled arbitrarily from one's dwelling-place, indeed, banished from what one had always taken to be one's own country. No wonder that the refugees took refuge in what was most easily transportable, such as recipes that could be imitated elsewhere and in songs to be sung and stories re-told in any time or place, in the constancy of the languages that they took with them into exile and preserved wherever they went in the world. For the Jews of Iberia, that meant Judeo-Spanish (also called Judezmo or Ladino) for conversation and music, and Hebrew for learning.

We do not have to cut Tisha b'av from its traditional moorings in Jewish history to appreciate and extend its applicability to life. Not only do entire communities live in continuing diaspora or *galut* from their home or ancestral land, whether that be Tibet, Nigeria, Libya, Armenia, Laos, Guatemala, Russia or any number of other places. We as individuals often feel that we are uprooted or even rootless in the modern world, with no clear sense of "home." We also feel insecure. Those who grew up during the Great Depression, WW II, the Cold War, the epoch of *film noir*, the Vietnam Era—indeed, most of the 20th century—recognize insecurity as endemic. Magda Sorel in Menotti's opera *The Consul* gives a particular human voice to the catastrophe: "To this we've come: that men withhold the world from men."[8]

Tisha b'av posits that this is not a normal or natural way of life, nor inevitable, by posing that we mourn for the absence of security and the confidence of knowing that we are "at home" and safe being there. Consider the reorienting, potentially restorative value of that recognition, that mourning, channeled through a public and, importantly, community observance. Imagine the power of a community lamenting the ruptures in the universal or common notion of community itself!

The Hebrew *galut* is too often translated as "diaspora." This ignores a crucial distinction. The Greek word *diaspora* simply means "dispersal." A diaspora may be made up of people who more or less voluntarily emigrated for any number of reasons, and their descendents as well, but are free to return to a native land that has retained a familiar identity with them. The Hebrew word, however, specifically denote exile. An exile has been cast out, along with subsequent generations of the exile's family, with no inherent right to go back. The separation is so radical that (as Gertrude Stein, an émigré but not an exile, remarked about revisiting the place of her birth after many years away) even if one could physically return, "There is no <u>there</u> there." Legally, spiritually and psychologically, the differences between being outside of one's homeland and being exiled from it are enormous.

The fall of Betar was a momentous and relatively recent loss in the memory of Jewish sages of antiquity, who mention it nine times in the Talmud. The last blow in smashing Bar Kokhba's revolt against Roman rule, this defeat meant the loss of the hope for political independence. Naturally, that cannot be separated from the previously mentioned losses of home and security. Not only in the political realm—essential as that is—but also in other aspects of human life, we yearn for self-determination. Rome (in rabbinic language, "Edom") is not only a place and an empire in chronological time. Quintessentially bearing all the worldly power that is invested in The State, it also represents coercion. In addition, because the biblical Edom is etymologically related to the name Adam and therefore also to the words for "red," "earth," and "blood," the sages associate it with physicality, violence and emotional impulsiveness.

On Tisha b'av we lament not being in control of our lives. That results partly from external forces, the political oppression explicitly connected with the day in history. We are subject to the power of others, whether governments or any others who have coercive influence over us. It also results in part from internal forces: we are not fully in control of ourselves but are driven by our passions, addictions, phobias and desires. Suppose we imagine Tisha b'av to be the occasion to lament our loss of self-control, to yielding (against our own will) to bad instincts, along with the loss of independence in the face of oppression.

The core experience represented through the destructions of the first and second holy temples, "with loss of Eden," is loss of connection with the divine, which is the root of it all. If Eden means the wholeness of sanctity within the natural world, the Temple stands for the structured access linking humanity with divinity. Animal sacrifices were historically real, yet we can imagine them metaphorically as the process by which we accept and go beyond our physical needs, becoming closer to the sacred. That is what the sacrificial offering, the *korban*, was for: its purpose was *karev*, "bringing close." In various ways we now acknowledge separation. Whether we say that God is absent or dead or hidden, or that we have become secularized, whether like the mystics we yearn to bridge the gap or like Wordsworth feel that we have become mortal "trailing clouds of glory" from a divine origin from which we have been thrust (birth as the Fall itself), the experience of being remote or even estranged from holiness is common.

The passions of *Eicha*, the Book of Lamentations, channeled through Tisha b'av allow lament, protest, grief, the frank recognition of horrors, brutality and brutalization to have biblical voices. The chronically suffering, those who have been victimized or cry justice for other people who have, may rarely feel empowered to express their feelings religiously. Too often they have been told that such attitudes are impious; anyone who utters them may be accused of weak faith not trusting sufficiently in divine providence and justice. The traditional chanting of *Eicha* distinguishes between the melody used for the third book and that for the first two and last books; in the third, the text speaks to us not in the communal voice of collective historical experience but in the first-person "I" of personal memory. Both kinds of testimonies have integrity, but because they are different sorts of expressions, we need to hear them differently, which is easier to do within the Jewish tradition of *nusach* than in simple reading.

Tisha b'av authenticates our plunge into grieving lament. We do so not just sympathetically and memorially, recalling what they suffered; but we lament empathetically, realizing that what they lost, we also lost, and therefore what they suffered is a type of our own suffering. Yes, we must see how sadly brutal the chronicle of history can be and remember the innocent victims of imperial conquests. Set aside this day to forget what can usually please and nourish the body. Forget about your physical image— never mind how you look to other people, or how you want to look to yourself. No matter how good we look at our best, we are vulnerable, every one of us. Accept how you feel when you are at your lowest, when you suffer and mourn for all that you have lost, or even all that you fear losing. Don't look in a mirror—but not because doing so is a symptom of vanity. No, avoid looking in the mirror for fear of what you might see there. For God's sake . . . for those like us, and for ourselves, creatures in the semblance of God, knowing that this day is also the birthday of the messiah, whose coming may be hastened by either the cry of human exultation or human pain, *geschrei,* Cry Out!

Chapter 6
Times of Change

A time for mourning

I remember Orthodox *shevas* in my childhood as fearsome events, morose, gloomy, the apartment rooms congested with tears and wails. Haggard mourners in torn black clothes sat on low stools as they clutched crumpled handkerchiefs to wipe their tear-swollen red eyes that might water at any moment, or they gripped their bodies as if to keep the sobs from shaking them apart convulsively. Off in a crowded room the minyan of men davvened flatly in Hebrew, murmuring at their small black siddurs.

I miss those *shevas*. I miss the raw, candid grief, horrifying though it was to me at the time. Relatives and friends may have gathered from great distances at the last minute but this was not merely a family reunion. There would be no photographs; nobody had to look their best. Someone who had been integral to these people's lives was newly ripped from them. The pain was intense, horrid, beyond any remedy, and there were no cultural inhibitions restraining the survivors from expressing that.

Too often these days, the reception following the funeral seems delicately managed to avoid excessive expressions of unguarded emotions. The event, and whatever minyans may follow in the next days, look and feel like catered affairs, though the catering may have been arranged by congregants and friends. The mourners do not behave in unseemly fashion, sometimes even ignoring the fact that they should remain seated, which is why this practice is referred to as "sitting *shiva*," sitting during the seven (*shiva*) days. Honestly, this is not a time for sociably comfortable behavior. Jewish traditions encourage us to contend with the emotional and physical experience of a loss, regardless of what you or I might believe about an afterlife.

From the preparation of the body and the practicalities of funeral arrangements through the actual burial and during the months and years beyond, halakhah offers teachings that function as religious law for some people and for others guidance through emotion and memory. Particularly in the earliest stages immediately following a death, when the survivor's second instinct is likely bewilderment ("I don't know what to do"), Judaism teaches, This is what you do. While we are feeling overwhelmed by emotions, unable to function normally or to work, Judaism teaches that grieving is our normal function and our work at this time in our life. When time passes and the daily presence of sorrow and pain recede, much as the physical presence of the close relative has slid away from our places and days, Judaism gives us the practice of reciting kaddish for a year with a minyan, and on every anniversary of the death, when we also light a 24-hour memorial candle, and on those major holidays when *Yizkor* prayers are recited in the synagogue. There is no "closure" in the sense of putting the relationship away and out of one's consciousness. From stage to stage, the place of the dead person in one's life will shift. Nevertheless, as my grandmother taught by example, the conversation continues.

Not knowing what to say is so common an experience following a death that tradition encourages us to say little. Going into a house of mourning, we are supposed to wait until a mourner, seeing us, invites us to approach and thereby signals the willingness to speak. "I'm so sorry" is sufficient consolation and "Thank you" sufficient acknowledgement at this point unless the mourner wants to say more, in which case our primary function is to listen. We console by literally being there, not by imposing on a grieving person our own notion of whether this was "for the better" or that "we know just how you feel." True, we might remember how we felt after the death of a close relative; but each mourner merits the uniqueness of that particular relationship and that loss, if "loss" is even the right word.

What must be said and what can be said? A bad eulogy is not one that admits an unflattering observation; a bad eulogy is one that is either so generic that it could be about anyone or so stereotypically encomiastic that guests wonder if they wandered into the wrong funeral. What we miss there is the particular multi-hued personality. It may fall to the eulogist as an ethical duty to frame some uncomfortable truth in the best way possible. The funeral oration should shape a portrait of the life for those who remain in this world. Many of them have their own experiences of the deceased, so ignoring what is most obvious to them about those experiences unintentionally insults the living by denying their experience. If there is an elephant in the room, it has probably stepped on someone's toes.

I think for example of the funeral for a man who had lived a productive life of professional responsibilities for many years but whose late decade or more had been clouded by his wife's long terminal illness, his own health problems and his independent temperament that had left him socially isolated. I knew him slightly; I appreciated his skills and sacrifices, along with his candor; yet meeting with his adult children, I was struck immediately by how much pain his emotional distance from them and his demands on them to meet his standards of achievement had caused during their youth and affected their lifelong relations with him. One after another had left home as soon as he

161

could, retaining a polite and respectful but usually long-distance connection with a father for whom verbal or physical expressions of love never came easily. Their lives with him needed to be acknowledged in terms that were honorable to the man's memory but truthful to their experience of him. This was a time for generosity, which was the art of framing a difficult life in the best terms possible, but not for dishonesty. It would not do simply to describe him as a loving father and devoted grandfather. If they had been cool toward him, the fault was not entirely their shortcomings as people. Following the burial, his sons asked for a copy of the eulogy. One of them, whose wife had refused to attend the funeral, said that he wanted her to read it because she had never understood either his father or their relationship. This was an opportunity for a *tikkun*, a repair.

The description of a funeral assumes that there is a body and it will be buried in accordance with traditional practices. We know of situations beyond our control when this is, as Milton wrote in "Lycidas" about a drowned schoolmate whose body was never recovered, "frail surmise." Sometimes the body cannot be retrieved; in other circumstances it must be embalmed or cremated. Further, some Jews now prefer cremation. Their reasons are varied. My resistance to considering voluntary cremation as a valid Jewish option was softened first when a couple I know, long-time environmental activists, spoke from their hearts about their distress over the amount of usable land taken up by sprawling cemeteries. Another person who had experienced considerable physical and emotional pain yearned to be released from the body and set free into the air. Some of us perceive this as another occasion for a conversation, preferably well in advance and with the principal person, not with the mourners as they address practical concerns in the throes of fresh loss. For me, no less than for many others, the significant connections are those we carry within us. The grave is there, along with a disintegrating body, but not the person. Relatives whom I have mourned are buried in six states on the east coast and the west, most of them in locations I never visit, yet they are seldom out of my thoughts for a week. Especially in our mobile society, the cemetery grave often seems like the virtual location, while our memory holds the real place of the dead.

And after all, what else but memory and imagination can hold the astonishing uniqueness of a human being, each of us carrying the primordial elements of the original creation, and each of us singular, unique in our memories and experiences?

※ ※ ※

A time for celebrating

Weddings are the subject of books. Even more so in the 21st century, trying for completeness would mean taking in various permutations for interfaith and same-sex couples, or couples who have children already from their own or other unions, as well as a range of traditional or creative ceremonies and the adaptations for special needs, for blended families or for ones that resist blending. Rather than attempting that, we will seek in a few pages to appreciate better the aesthetic and ethical value of some long-sanctioned elements of the wedding ceremony. Along with being "traditional," what do the customs offer us?

Polonius in Shakespeare's *Hamlet* properly squawks his protest when reading a letter to his daughter in which Hamlet describes her as "the most beautified Ophelia." It is, he objects, "an ill phrase, a vile phrase" (II.ii.111). Sometimes we think that the way to make a ceremony beautiful is by personal innovations and we end up instead with something that is "most beautified" rather than beautiful.

Andrew Vogel Ettin

Ask someone to explain what they mean when they describe a particular wedding ceremony as beautiful. Usually they will talk about the gowns, flowers and décor. Occasionally they will mention an inspired innovation in the liturgy, a poem or special music. More often than that, however, they will speak of the spirit (*ruach*) or *kavvanah* conveyed by the couple and the officiant. This comes from people who know and trust one another and who are at one with the ceremony that will connect the couple's lives in a unique relationship. Beauty does not have to come from doing an ancient ritual in a different way for the sake of creativity. It only needs to be done with conviction and attention, as if nothing mattered except this performance. The words in the liturgy are merely notes on the page. A great pianist on a good day will make them mean something that is beyond the expressive reach of a performer who is just competent; but two great pianists—say, Mitsuko Uchida and Murray Perahia—will each express something different without changing a single note of the score. Yet in truth, when we are in need of that particular piece of music, we can be honestly grateful for sheer competence.

Two of the most beautiful parts of the wedding are private moments before and after the public ceremony. Following the signing of the ketubah and just before the wedding procession, the groom draws down the bride's veil, which he will raise during the ceremony. Immediately following the breaking of the glass, the couple (who traditionally were fasting) go to a private room for some food and drink, and whatever else might inspire them in the short time of seclusion, known as *yichud*, togetherness.

We might think that these rituals of *bedecken* (veiling) and *yichud* are antiquated, maybe more pertinent in arranged or early marriages where the bride and groom have been living in their parents' homes, not with one another, as is often the situation

164

now. However, even if the bride and groom have cohabited for years, the Jewish rituals intensify the private meaning for the two people most directly involved, the bride and groom. Couples with no connection to Judaism have used these practices and found them meaningful and gratifying. If for no other reason, they are ways of extricating the couple from well-meaning people devoted to managing every ceremonial detail; reminding them that the performance is being stage managed by others, we let the bridal couple know all that is required of them is being fully aware of themselves and one another in the moment.

The customary explanation of the veiling ceremony traces it to the story in *Genesis* of Jacob, whose crafty father-in-law Laban substituted his older daughter Leah in place of her younger sister Rachel after making Jacob labor seven years for him in order to marry his beloved Rachel. The veiling custom presumably affirms the association with our eponymous patriarch. Further, on the off-chance that the bride's family might have another daughter in urgent need of marriage and be tempted like Laban to substitute her for the intended bride, the groom himself draws down the veil immediately before the procession begins and will raise it before the wedding. (After all, Jacob could marry both sisters, though it took him fourteen years to do so, but for the last thousand years Jews outside of Muslim countries have been monogamous.) An historical explanation reflects our resourceful attempt to link customs with biblical precedents, but it offers little else as a reason for following this practice except the inevitable fall-back, "Tradition, tradition."

There really is another good reason. This moment should be considered part of the ceremony because it is the knowing, private, face to face acknowledgement by the bride and groom of the momentous step they are about to take. Here, they look at one another with understandings, promises, hopes and acceptances that are theirs alone. At this moment they know one another deeply and they resolve to take one another as a life partner in as full awareness as they can possibly have before marriage itself. Properly framed by the officiant, it can be a holy moment of great beauty. The couple should focus at this point on one another. Often the bride is distracted by well-intentioned fussing going on around her, for usually immediately before the ceremony someone is doing the final repair of her makeup and adjusting the drape of her dress, while the groom paces elsewhere as if waiting to be escorted on stage. Even if the bride chooses not to wear a veil, in taking the time to look quietly at one another in anticipation, to say "I love you and I want to marry you" whether with words or looks, the couple emerges not into a moment of anticipatory, superficial surprise (as in, "I can't wait to see what she looks like") but thorough, intentional, focused commitment. The bride or groom's tears of joyful love during the ceremony really will be no less spontaneous.

Similarly, after the glass-breaking, if there is no prearranged *yichud*, the couple is swept up immediately into the swirl of phototaking and well-wishing, worst of all the receiving line, and then the reception crammed with socializing and dancing to music that makes conversation nearly impossible. It could be hours before the now-exhausted wife and husband have a private moment to look at one another in the full recognition of how their relationship is changed by this experience. They have missed the opportunity to take it in together in its fresh, bright novelty immediately after the public rite brings their futures together.

The ceremony itself may be enriched by personal elements, like a favorite poem of the bride and groom, a huppah adorned with a beautiful fabric from the bride's Japanese family or the couple's travels in Kenya, a kiddush cup that belonged to a grandparent. Because these will vary from couple to couple, they ought to be worked out with the officiant, who might explain the significance during the ceremony. While creative liturgies and texts seem good in principle, often the actualities are limited by the couple's own preferences and their particular family circumstances. For instance, a beautifully devised special ritual incorporating the families may sound fine in the imagination but it probably will not work when the real bride's or groom's divorced parents need a ten-foot demilitarized zone between them and negotiating the stepmother's presence threatens civil war, or children from a previous marriage would really prefer not to be drawn into a ceremonial role. If the immediate family accompanies the bride and groom or stands at the huppah, they supportively acknowledge the marriage.

The entire ceremony is built on two defining moments that require little or no innovation. One is the ring ritual. In Orthodox practice that means the groom giving the bride a ring, with one spoken sentence, the only words either of the principal parties says during the entire wedding; in non-Orthodox ceremonies, it is an exchange of rings. This act is so significant that the traditional ritual is to place the ring on the bride's index finger in order that it may clearly be seen by everyone at the ceremony. Tangible as the rings are, they are still merely tokens, but the close encircling clasp of the unmarked bands expresses far more than can easily be articulated. In a Christian wedding, the vows are central; however, they are not customarily used in Jewish weddings, during which traditionally the only words spoken by either party are the one line said by the groom when bestowing the ring; rather, the *ketubah* or *te'udat ahuvim* (lovers' declaration) that is read aloud during the ceremony may declare what else needs to be said. But we might also claim that in a sense the commitment to marry says it all. How could any vows uttered encompass all that is meant by marriage? How can those who are not yet married to one another express all that marriage embraces, and will need to embrace? Instead, vows usually say both too much and too little.

Most people would expect that the other significant moment is the officiant's announcement that the couple is now married, but that is merely a formal redundancy in the Jewish wedding, recognition of the general society's interest in their legal status. Rather, the other significant moment is the kiddush, the sharing of wine by the couple. This properly balances the ring ceremony. As the gift of a ring represents the outward, visible and halakhic commitment of mutual marital responsibility of two individuals living together responsibly, consuming the same drink from the same cup represents the private empathic delight that others may glimpse from the outside but is most fully experienced sensually and emotionally within the distinctive marital experiences of a wife and husband. The community's and tradition's voice of celebration enters the ceremony through the *Sheva Berakhot* (Seven Blessings), which may be recited by the officiating rabbi or cantor or by friends and family members.

Placing the ring and sharing wine might be understood best as romantic metaphors. The former act expresses the encircling public embrace that we permit others to witness. The latter is the intimate erotic and emotional experiences that take place between these two people, symbolized by their drinking from the same cup. If the person officiating also drinks, it is not as a private individual but as a representative of the religious tradition or community that the couple embraces.

※ ※ ※

A time for welcoming

Most cultures develop some ritual for welcoming a child into the immediate and the larger family. The ancient Jewish ritual, biblically dating to Abraham, is the circumcision of a boy on the eighth day. (Muslims also circumcise, following the tradition of Abraham's circumcision of Ishmael, but generally at an older age, albeit before puberty.) This is a sign of the covenant, *oht ha-b'rit*. There are many hypotheses about the origins and purpose of this particular procedure, which the Torah presents as a distinguishing mark of the Abrahamic family. There have also been many claims made for and against the health benefits and the safety of circumcision. These are not new, though some of the particular strategies for arguing the case on either side date from modern times; they include everything from family expectations or wanting the son's penis to resemble his father's anatomy to the highest claims of religion and ethics.

In the medieval period, some philosophically minded rabbis proposed what are known as *ta'amei ha-mitzvot*, explaining the purposes of the commandments. In doing so, they were reacting to the facts of Jewish cultural life at the time, when most of us lived under either Christian or Muslim rule. In both situations, albeit to varying degrees depending on time and circumstances, there were disabilities and even dangers in remaining Jewish; at times, the incentive to convert was extreme duress, including the threat of death. To some rabbis responding to their own and their followers' plight, it was vital to justify honoring and preserving Jewish practices despite the cost, and one way that they chose was to argue that the *mitzvot* were not merely cultural practices that could easily be set aside by an apostate and replaced with some ethical principles that the monotheistic religions shared. Instead, they wanted to show that the Torah's commandments for religious practice existed to instill essential moral and mental qualities.

Andrew Vogel Ettin

Christianity challenged Judaism on the value of what it called the "ritual law," practices including circumcision and the dietary rules that, according to the writings of Paul, were made irrelevant by belief in Jesus' divinity and in his crucifixion as redemption from sin. Islam, by contrast, placed as much importance on ritual practices as Judaism but had its own equivalent of *halakhah*, called *shari'ah*, which it claimed was better, along with its own versions of Abrahamic stories. As these theologies developed in the Middle Ages, Aristotelian logic was often their dominant mode of thought, exemplified by Maimonides (Moshe ben Maimon) in Judaism, Thomas Aquinas in Christianity and al-Farabi in Islam. Propounding rational reasons for the *mitzvot* was a way of defending for rational people the value in practicing Judaism. Maimonides, the pre-eminent Jewish philosopher of the era, taught that the literal level of commandments simply accommodated the literal-mindedness of ordinary people; more sophisticated readers would grasp the intended higher ethical meaning as well as the practical wisdom. Therefore, as a physician as well as a rabbi and a philosopher, he advanced the benefits of health and the lesson of governing sexual instincts as biological and ethical motives for circumcision.

Other rabbis opposed applying reason to the performance of *mitzvot*. First, it seemed presumptuous to them that any human being could claim to fathom God's unstated purposes. Second, they recognized that this was the first slip on a slope toward non-observance. If a *mitzvah* is not really a divine commandment but behavior that should be done for rationally understandable reasons, we can use our own reasoning in deciding whether to perform it or not; and if that is true of written Torah commandments, so much the more for the oral Torah, the rabbinic ordinances or interpretations of commandments. That is essentially

170

what took place much later, starting in the early 19th century, stimulated by Romantic individualism as well as the beginnings of the social and political emancipation of European Jews. The reforms and reactions that began in that era have continued; these include questions about circumcision's value, and whether or not it is essential to Jewish male identity.

Some questions will inevitably remain unresolved. We cannot really trace the supposed origin or purpose of circumcision, nor can there be a final scientific answer as to whether it is healthier for a man and his sexual partners. There are simply too many variables; there will always be some new findings involving a previously unexplored medical question or a different result from more recent research. Neither can anyone conclude scientifically whether or not circumcision or its lack will cause emotional trauma to the infant that has lifelong consequences, or whether circumcision increases or decreases the male's sexual pleasure. All we have regarding these are individual claims for or against, none of which is empirically verifiable or applicable to anybody else's experience.

In many families the questions never arise when they anticipate a son; if they have any qualms, those are minute compared to the anticipated joy represented in the *b'rit milah* celebrated with a big party in the company of relatives and friends. For them, no decision is involved. They would deem not doing this as equivalent to denying the boy his Jewish identity. For medical or personal reasons, some who want their sons circumcised nonetheless want that done in a hospital soon after birth, rather than having it performed by a *mohel* at home with a ceremony on the eighth day. Of course in many smaller communities a family wanting a *mohel* would have to import one from a considerable distance. With the circumcision already done, the ceremony on the eighth day turns into a baby-naming, perhaps with a retrospective reference to the covenanting intention of the circumcision that was already done.

Whether circumcised or not, a child whose birth mother is Jewish is a Jew; nonetheless, the uncircumcised Jewish male is atypical. For a male who converts to Judaism and has been surgically circumcised already, the drawing of a drop of blood is considered sufficient, but most rabbis require an uncircumcised male convert to have the surgery. A rabbi working with a family that is considering not circumcising their son needs to listen attentively to their reasons and to respond thoughtfully, honestly but fairly about the halakhic and social implications. At least some of us are ready to offer options for those who reject circumcision but are committed to raising their child as a Jew. For me as a rabbi, taking in the tradition, what I know of Jewish history, and ethical sensibilities, this is one of the topics about which I prefer to say that I do not have a policy; I have conversations.

What seems safest to say is that the only certain reason for a *b'rit milah* (*bris*) is not rational but religious. Though I am not a *mohel*, I have officiated at numerous *brises* done in homes by medical professionals. What I tell the assembled family and friends has nothing to do with health benefits and everything to do with religious belief. At a time in the child's life when we want him not to cry and will do absolutely anything to protect the child from harm, the *oht brit milah* ceremony reminds us that the child is a creature of God and a member of the Jewish community and will have a relationship with both that transcends even his relationship with his parents. It does not matter whether "God" means a figure much mentioned in Jewish scripture or the child's own eventually-developing inner sense of moral direction; the child, like Abraham, will learn from his parents but follow what he believes. We as parents and grandparents understandably want to protect our infant, yet there is a prior claim on him, marked by this sign.

But here are difficulties as well. There are legitimate concerns over the ethical principle involved in causing even brief pain and permanently marking the boy physically because of the parents' religion. Circumcision, like all other surgical procedures, is not immune from complications. A parent's worries may be more pronounced when she or he has experienced physical or sexual trauma, which is likely to increase the normal anxieties over this procedure. With no male children or grandchildren, I cannot write about it from the standpoint of a parent who has circumcised his child, only as a rabbi who has listened and read the words of those who have and have not.

The most glaring of the problems from a religious standpoint is the absence of a suitably analogous traditional ceremony for welcoming a girl, and here I do write as a father and grandfather. Some ingenious arguments have been advanced as to why that sort of ceremony is not needed, but none is really persuasive. The fact that no one of the numerous ceremonies devised recently for welcoming a girl has become standard suggests that none has quite met a broad range of needs. Some ceremonies have used anointing of one sort or another for girls, but here too the ritual and symbolism fail. The specifically Jewish "marking" in the circumcision of a boy at the age of eight days is not paralleled by the various proposed rituals such as dabbing a girl with milk or water or partuitional blood, none of which has a uniquely Jewish content to it. Further, these approaches are at one and the same time superficial and yet biologically essentialist in ways that seem limiting. Inventing some ritual that insists on the literalness of anointing turns us in the wrong direction. For similar reasons, some of us are not persuaded either by the claim that following the Jewish teachings about menstrual purity serves in place of circumcision, a procedure that marks a male permanently from his eighth day of life.

Ceremonially welcoming all children is worth a new ritual. By all means, have soft music if feasible; scented candles or other fragrances might be used, keeping in mind that some people are sensitive to these. In short, do what you are able to do in order to make the ceremony beautiful and ethically principled. It ought to be one that does not merely obligate the child but commits the parents to doing something actively beyond having this one ceremony, and that is a feature not explicitly part of even the *b'rit milah*. It should be suitable to our era but not seem like a period piece five years from now. It also should be built on a principle central to Judaism, the performance of *mitzvot*.

For we have essentially two forms of a covenantal lineage. We are (along with those whom the Talmud called "Ishmaelites") members of the monotheistic family of Abraham, though the Torah only provides for that membership to be marked ceremonially among our males. We are also familially *b'nei Yisrael*, the children of Ya'akov (Jacob) who was re-named "Israel" because he wrestled with God and was progenitor of (as Arthur Waskow writes) a family of God-wrestlers, people whose relationship with God is not merely passive acceptance but active struggling. And we are members of the covenant made with Moses and our ancestors at Sinai, confirmed by the communal affirmation *na'asei v'nishma*, "we will do and we will understand." (*Ex. 24: 7*), bound together by the common intergenerational acceptance of *mitzvot*. The traditional *bris* celebrates only the first of these at most for male Jews, not the *kulkhem*, "all of you," that Moshe *rabbenu* summoned to be a covenanted community *lif'nei adonai eloheichem*, "in the presence of Y-H-V-H your God."

A *b'rit mitzvah* such as I describe speaks instead of the parental obligation to raise the child as a Jew, meaning to teach Judaism and inculcate Jewish values in their child, female as well as male. Because the *b'rit mitzvah* is based on Torah precepts that the parents pledge to teach to their child, it pertains alike to boys and girls, to adopted children, and to children of same-sex couples. A traditional *b'rit milah* can be incorporated into it, though it can also stand on its own. Such a rite of *b'rit mitzvah* can also incorporate the designing of a wimpel (*mappah*), which would also work for girls as well as boys as a Torah wrapping for their bar or bat mitzvah ceremony and as a huppah ornament. This ceremony thereby links the covenanting with the child's growth into personal religious responsibility celebrated when she or he becomes a *bat* or *bar mitzvah*. That ought not be a passive act: we do not "bar mitzvah" but acknowledge the young person's growth into personal religious responsibilities.

Chapter 7

Conversations in Prayer

Do you know the song that Irving Berlin wrote toward the end of World War I about the soldier's response to the bugler's call, "Oh! How I hate to get up in the morning"? We all know the feeling because we all have days when we don't want to wake up, get out of bed and start the day. Judaism, never forgetting that it might be otherwise and that the capability of even waking is somewhat miraculous, teaches a different attitude. *Modeh anee {for a woman, Modah anee} l'fanekha,* we say when we awake. "Grateful am I before You, eternal sustainer of life, generously restoring my soul to me in your great faithfulness." Of all the blessings and prayers with Judaism adorns life's morning routine—using the toilet and giving thanks for our body's working, that orifices open and close as they should to enable us to live and be grateful, washing our hands while being aware that by doing so we follow a biblical commandment in dedicating them to good hygiene and good labor—the benediction at waking seems the most poignant. In its phrasing, in its structure itself, opening with the word for gratitude, it recognizes the fragile pretenses of certainty on which we construct our daily lives. The sudden death of a friend, a serious illness or surgery, a news report of a natural disaster or unnatural crime: if we give a solemn moment to ponder any of them, we grasp what it is to live in the presence of an ominous shadow and know that we must not take awakening for granted.

This is balanced at the end of the day by a kabbalistic evening prayer preceding the bedtime *sh'ma*. Each day has its pleasures, yet each adds slag. The accumulated weight can drag us down, not into the peaceful night's rest we crave. Setting ourselves at ease requires a miniature Yom Kippur in which we forgive those who have harmed us, ask that they not be punished for what they have done to us, and pray that we will not repeat our own sins or meet harm because of them. The sage Mar Zutra, according to the Talmud, would say when he went to bed, "I forgive all who have troubled me" (*Megillah 28a*). Perhaps more importantly, Rav Assi reminds us that Psalm 4: 5 teaches, "speak with your own heart on your bed, and be still. Selah." Giving priority to what is in our volitional control, the mystics' prayer emphasizes our forgiveness of others, including anyone who has angered, troubled or harmed us physically or financially, damaged our reputation, intentionally or not, in word or deed, and even in this incarnation or another. (Though belief in incarnation is not a mainstream Jewish belief, it has had and still has adherents.) A worthwhile discipline to reinforce this is to review the offenses that have occurred each day so as to concentrate oneself on the intention to forgive the perpetrator and seek divine forgiveness. In the same way, it can be helpful to include in prayers for health and wellbeing someone against whom we have hard feelings, not necessarily forgiving them but consciously trying to wish them well and not harm.

But this is a difficult teaching. It is not included in most Jewish prayerbooks nor does it appear to be widely followed beyond some Orthodox practitioners. In fact, it contradicts our usual understanding that forgiveness depends on the offender making *t'shuvah* by recognizing and asking pardon for the harm that she or he has caused and attempting where possible to rectify its effects. When the injury and its consequences still smart, why forgive someone who has pained and damaged me, perhaps even deliberately, but shows no understanding or remorse? Morally and viscerally, we resist. Why, then, do some follow the practice, and why might it be worth considering?

From the kabbalistic context in which it originated, this ritual of release and repentance is important in restoring harmony in our lives and the world. Instead of furthering bitterness and retribution, we take the evil that has been done to us and transform it from negative into positive by preemptively relinquishing any desire for retribution. More pragmatically, in doing this we also liberate ourselves from being chained by resentment to the person who has grieved us. We do not want to be bound continually to that person because of the unrequited, uncompensated offense. If we do not want to try to sleep burdened by the memory of our own misdeeds or errors, neither will we want to go to bed each night nagged by every unpleasantness or injury that we have encountered that day or are still holding from weeks or even years past, for there is no rest with these griefs. Although it is phrased as generosity toward others, the *mechilah*, the forgiveness, of this prayer works for our benefit. We say that we are releasing the offender when in truth we release ourselves from corrosive bitterness, anger or hatred. Perhaps there are times when we say it because that is our practice even when we do not think we mean it, and then we find that saying it makes it real for us.

Yet truthfully, this approach doesn't always help. The damage has been too grievous, the insult or injury too painful, the injustice too great for us to forgive, at least without the offender making an attempt at *t'shuvah*. Justice as well rightly claims satisfaction not only for us individually but for the moral good of the world. How big a debt are we prepared to write off for the sake of peace of mind? Like much else within the pathways of Jewish living, the ritual of the evening *sh'ma* is there to aid us on our life's travels if we want or need it. The message of its prayer of repentance and forgiveness is a good *torah* but it does not have to be your *torah*.

Here, therefore, is another way to bring *Sh'ma* into our life. It is a verse from the Torah, but we may hear the *pasuk* as a poem. Imagine it as a three-line stanza:

> Sh'ma yisrael
> Adonai eloheinu
> Adonai echad.

Notice the rhythm of these words:

Sh'—ma yis – ra—eyl
short-long short-short-long

a—don —nai e—loh – hei—nu
short-short-long short-short-long-short

a—don – ai e—chad.
short-short-long short-long.

In prosody, we use Greek terms for these rhythms:

iamb anapest
anapest anapest [with an extra short syllable; or, pyrrhic
+ spondee]
anapest iamb.

The general metrical pattern is a *chiasmus*, beginning and ending with the same familiarly emphatic iambic rhythm; in between, the "poem" is governed by the lilting anapest. No wonder this verse is almost hypnotically memorable.

We can use that characteristic, along with our understanding of the meaning, to develop a breathing exercise to supplement or invigorate our recitation of the *Sh'ma*. Let us look again at the text. The word *sh'ma* ("hear," "pay attention") calls us to personal awareness. The next, *yisrael*, is outwardly directed: originally it was applied to the patriarch Jacob after his struggle with the angel that made him, as Arthur Waskow says, a "god-wrestler," one who wrestles or strives with God. As descendents of Jacob and his children, we become the people *Yisrael*, not incidentally also struggling with God. The two words of the middle line of this poem are the two most frequently used biblical terms for God. The former, *"adonai,"* is the traditionally accepted periphrasis for *yud-hey-vav-hey*, the unpronounced Tetragrammaton or four-letter Hebrew name of God the Ineffable. That also is an inner perception of God, one that is too profound even to be spoken explicitly. The other, *eloheinu*, ends with the first-person plural suffix: <u>our</u> God. It is a notion of the deity that connects with outward rather than inner experience, the God experienced and recognized by our people. The final phrase repeats the alternation of inner and outer experience, as *adonai* is repeated and the concluding *echad*, meaning "alone" or "one" or "solely," affirms unity that binds God and all that exists. Hold the final syllable long, tradition teaches. Let the final "d" reverberate.

The rhythm of ideas, in other words, is the rhythm of normal breathing: in, out; in, out; in, out. We can therefore connect the words of the *Sh'ma* in our mind to conscious breathing, hearing them internally as we concentrate like yoga practitioners on taking in and letting out the breath of life. Since we are told to recite this passage in the evening and morning (if you attend an afternoon *Mincha* service, this is one familiar passage that will be missing), it becomes a perfect focusing exercise, connecting our own being with the text of Torah and with the profound belief expressed in it. Here is the way that works.

> *Sh'ma Listen!* (breathe in) *Yisrael My Community* (breathe out)
> *Adonai The Inexpressible* (breathe in) *Eloheinu Our God*
> (breathe out)
> *Adonai The Inexpressible* (breathe in) *echad All One* (breathe out).

We draw in attentiveness to the ineluctable: *sh'ma adonai adonai.* We breathe forth the unifying connectedness: *yisrael eleoheinu ekhad.* Do this often enough (indeed, twice a day for three days might be enough) and it becomes a habit. That doesn't necessarily mean that you will continue doing it every day. But it will become a groove for our memory. A deep breath or recalling the *Sh'ma*—either is likely to trigger the practice. *Sh'ma* (breathe in) . . . .

❊ ❊ ❊

According to the Mishnah the pious of antiquity "waited for an hour" before prayer so as to concentrate their attention on God (*Berakhot* 5). Though this practice is not explained in any detail, we may assume that it does not mean that they just hung about killing time before the service started. They surely prepared for prayer with thoughtfulness and intentionality, perhaps by means of deliberate meditative or focusing activity. That hour seems luxurious to most of us, certainly including experienced prayer leaders, who are likely to find that they are distracted from focusing on their intention to pray by all sorts of claims on their attention and time, many of them mundane ("Rabbi, did you see the article about . . .") but others pressing and needful ("Rabbi, could we say a prayer for . . ."). Many of us struggle to erect some mental boundary between us and the congregation to allow us to develop a focused approach to the service.

The tradition tries to assist us. Facing us on the east wall of many synagogues is a Hebrew sentence: *da lifnei mee atah omeyd,* "Know before whom you stand" (*Berakhot 28b*). It comes from the deathbed advice about the proper attitude at prayer from the revered talmudic-era sage R. Eliezar to his pupils who asked him for his final words of wisdom. In some Jewish homes a different focal point for prayer is placed on a wall, a text known as a *sh'viti* ("I have set") from *Psalm 16:8,* "I have set Y-H-V-H always before me; because God is at my right hand, I shall not be moved." Because Judaism has resisted using as a devotional focus any object that might be mistaken as sacred in itself, words are more likely to be chosen than a "graven image or pillar" (*Lev. 26:1*) or "the work of human hands, wood and stone" (*Deut. 4:28*). Visitors to the remains of the once-lovely small medieval synagogues of Spain in Granada and Toledo can still see the vestiges of elaborate calligraphic and geometric designs that made the interior of those houses of worship seem like the insides of magnificent sacred books. As much as one could, we have prayed <u>within</u> our texts and a harmoniously structured order of the universe that human beings could appreciate. The synagogues shared that with the nearby mosques and were often decorated by the same artisans using similar techniques. Thus they contrasted with the churches of the time, in which frescoes, sculpture, paintings and pictorial stained glass gave the effect of windows looking onto tableaux of persons and moments in religious history.

Visually and verbally we want to establish the proper *kavvanah,* intentional focus. When we arrive at the physical place of prayer, the custom is to recite the verse from the Book of Numbers that will help us become consciously attentive to where we are, *Ma tovu ohalekha ya'akov, mishkanotekha yisrael*, "How goodly your tents, Jacob—your gathering-places, Israel!" Though most appropriate for a synagogue, these words could also be said whenever we pray in our own space, even at home, as midrash understands that the "tents" are Jewish homes, "goodly" because they are arranged decently to allow for family privacy, and the "gathering-places" as our houses of worship. Another technique is simply to hum or quietly sing a *niggun*, a melody that sets the necessary mood for ourselves and, we hope, the congregation if we are guiding one. That mood could be joyful, reflective, yearning, mellow, indeed anything we want, and the tune could be familiar or extemporized so long as it suits the time and occasion. If we sing as though we are singing to and for ourselves rather than projecting like a soloist for a congregation, the song can shape an aural *tallit*, a prayer shawl of sound that we drape about us as shelter from distractions as we prepare for praying.

Jewish prayer is also replete with physical activity, both according to tradition and to its potential. We kiss the neckband of the *tallit* before putting it on and cover our heads with it like a sheltering tent to help us concentrate. Preparing to put *tefillin* on our arm and head, we kiss them before beginning the elaborate ritualized windings. Here we stand, perhaps bowing from the waist or with a bend of the knees, at this word we rise, and here we sit. At points in morning worship the *tzitzit* or fringes on the *tallit* corners may be gathered in the hand or twisted in our fingers. We may cover our eyes with our hand in reciting *Sh'ma*, or touch the *tefillin* if we are wearing them when the text refers to them. At this point we step back three paces, then move forward.

Bowing (also "genuflection," from Latin, meaning bending the knee) is still a significant gesture in Jewish worship, in some circles developed into a meticulously performed, obligatory rite.

Prostration, lying prone on the ground or floor, was once also regularly done; it is now rarely if ever encountered, the most notable exceptions being one time each on Rosh Hashanah and Yom Kippur in some synagogues. Removing the shoes before worship has lasted as a formal practice in Islam; R. Abraham the son of Maimonides tried unsuccessfully to revive it in his Egyptian community, and some today may make it their private practice, either out of reverence or to connect with the earth.

Regular *davveners* customarily sway or move back and forth (*shuckle*) rhythmically while praying, inducing a state of mind that the founder of Hassidism, the Baal Shem Tov, described in explicitly erotic terms as appropriate to *devekut*, "clinging," a devoted embrace. In his book *Tzava'at ha-rivash,* he says,

> Prayer is coupling [*zivug*] with the *Shekhinah*. Just as there is motion at the start of coupling, so one has to move at the beginning of prayer. After, one can stand motionless, clinging with *devekut* to the *Shekhinah*. In your movement, you get yourself excited and you think, "Why am I moving so energetically? Surely it's because the *Shekhinah* is in front of me," and so you get worked up into *hitlahavut* [enthusiasm, rapture].—*sec. 68 p. 55*

But notice that this movement is appropriate for the beginning stages, by which he means not just at the start of a period of prayer but when one is still an inexperienced *davvener* or perhaps one who is praying at a lower level of spirituality. The higher level is to experience the *devekut* wholly internally, where the intensity is contained within and doesn't have any physical release or sensory gratification, and to pray *sotto voce*. He acknowledges (sec. 105) that it might look from the outside as if there is no *kavvanah* at all. The Baal Shem Tov is building on ideas in the *Zohar*, except there the prayers of angels and Israel prepare the *Shekhinah* to unite with God—to repair the union of the separated lovers—while in hassidic thought it is the union of the *Shekhinah* and the worshiper [of course, presumably the male Jew]. He is also working with hints from the psalms, *Song of Songs*, and Maimonides on the love of God being like the desire of the human lover for the beloved.

Unfortunately, the ritual actions during prayer have become victims of two discordant approaches. One is the rationalistic and socializing tendencies that characterized progressive streams of Judaism during the last two centuries. These led to the suppression of such physical behavior as overly literal or overly dramatic, lacking in properly worshipful decorum. Good social behavior, which was expected in the house of worship as well as in any public space, meant not gesturing, raising one's voice, or behaving in ways that called undue attention to oneself. All that remained in many synagogues was the rabbi's instruction, "Please rise" and "Please be seated," or the even more discreet hand cues to stand or sit, reinforced by the requisite directions printed in Reform prayerbooks.

The contrasting hyper-traditionalist approach brought an obsessive punctiliousness to the physical activities. These usually are not announced, as the congregation prefers to pretend that everyone knows what to do and when to do it; but as the arcane directions need to be conveyed to newly observant Jews, *siddurim* such as the Artscroll series give precise choreographic instructions like "Take three steps back, bow left and say . . . ." Such control is as symptomatic of that variety of Orthodoxy as the disembodied approach is of its cultural context. In the rational modernist sort of congregation, someone who covers her head with a tallit might be the object of bemused looks from regular attendees. In the traditionalist, the person who gets the chore-ography wrong is likely to feel like the tourist who violated the local customs. Knowing that the tradition authorizes physical expression during prayer should give you the confidence to draw upon it ("I'm doing it the traditional way") or to find your own ways of incorporating it ("This is the practice I learned").

It is also a good idea to remember the importance of the person who only says, "Amen." In the Talmud *Shabbat 119b*, the sage Resh Lakish said, "The gates of Paradise are open for anyone who responds 'Amen' with full devotion. For it is writ-ten, 'Open the gates, that the righteous nation that keeps truth [*shomer emunim*] may enter in' [*Isaiah 26:2*]. Imagine that we read those two words as, *she'omrim amen*, 'those who say "amen."' What does 'amen' mean?—R. Hanina explained, *adonai melekh ne'eman*, God, faithful King."

✳ ✳ ✳

If you spend time with a prayerbook, you will find a section called something like "Morning Blessings," followed by another perhaps termed "Preliminary Service," replete with blessings and texts for study, mostly from the Tanakh and Talmud, as well as psalms. Some passages preview material that we will encounter again in the actual morning prayer service. Taken fully, these could provide the hour and more of preparation that the Talmud praises. Perhaps that was the original liturgists' intention. The selections, regardless of which *siddur* we have, will be historically and intellectually interesting. Like reading an anthology of po-etry and prose from another era, some passages will engross and others mystify us; some may seem irrelevant, some might be of-fensive, and here and there some will catch our imaginations and even emotionally move us. Each community and probably each person even within Jewish Orthodox circles finds a particular way of moving through these sections, focusing on some passages more than with others, reading silently here and chanting there. For some who *davven* regularly, these passages may be the most engaging, and they ponder different ones over time; others regard them as a *pro forma* warm-up that they skim or skip. One that should not be glossed over is the one-line blessing *l'asok b'divrey torah,* giving thanks for the opportunity to fulfill the commandment to "engage in Torah study," or as some say, punning on the pronunciation of the Hebrew verb, to "soak" in the words of Torah. It is truly a privilege to have the time to study. Just ask any rabbi or other teacher who is also a scholar, continually striving and often failing to find time for books.

Although it is likely that studying these prescribed passages is not what you think of as readying yourself for prayer, some sort of preparation is important. The dancer getting ready for her role in *Giselle* does some of her most important work at the barre, refining her technique while repeating warm-up and stretching exercises that she has practiced daily for years. Those warm-ups are, one might say, simple but not easy. They are necessary but they are not the reason for dancing, and although most dancers wish they could skip them, they do not. They are working on what athletic coaches like to call "the fundamentals," represented by the seemingly endless, painful drills of basic techniques that are part of each practice. The same is true of singers warming up. The exercises are neither interesting to do nor melodious; actually, some sound grotesque and ridiculous. But woe to the singer who goes on stage "cold," and woe to their audience, who will get a vocally undercooked performance.

We should remember also that "prayer" or (worse) "prayerfulness" does not mean a display of piety or ecstasy in the High Pontifical mode, when we take on an attitude that we have been told is sanctity, or contort our faces to show our ecstatic yearning. If we are directed toward God, our prayers are received even without the show. Music, whether it be quietly humming to yourself, singing a contemporary Jewish chant or listening to Bach, is one form of preparation. So are yoga-inspired breathing exercises. Or the analogous rocking back and forth that is a trait of Jewish *davvenen*. So too (if one is privileged in this way) is being in the presence of a spiritual guide or teacher who has already developed a prayer practice from which we can learn by experience. This is like being taught and coached by someone who has already done the role on stage. It is the difference between doing yoga exercises from a video and taking a class from a well trained instructor who is attentive to the pupil's progress. The prayer texts can show you what a tradition has accepted as a repository of resources. Each of us should be aware of what we individually need at the time. Might it be a more stable grounding, a deeper stretch or a higher reach? More quiet, more purposefulness, more joy?

If we are in a group, there will be a formal invocation to the worship, a two-line call and response referred to as the *Bar'khu*, "Give praise," when it seems to the leader that there is a *minyan* or quorum. How that is determined (whether for instance women are counted) depends on the nature of the congregation. Everything up to this point has been either preparation intended to get us in the right mood and frame of mind or else the sort of prayer that we could also do alone, in a family or in a very small group. The *minyan* stands for the community as a whole. At times we pray as individuals but there are circumstances when we speak as a people. There are times when we need to hear the voices of others in prayer, to see them and recall that the words we are saying have meanings not only for us personally. We stand up for this brief passage. In doing so we are in a sense called to attention; we also make clear the presence of the requisite number of people. Otherwise, we are simply present for prayer, with whatever we have brought with us.

Start with joy. Not cheerfulness but the wondering delight that Abraham Joshua Heschel perhaps meant by the religious experience he called "radical amazement." That sort of joy should leap from the prayers that begin the evening and morning services by celebrating first the glories of the time of the day and next the constancy of divine love. The principal reason for even noticing the time is that the Torah teaches that we should say the *Sh'ma* twice a day, when you lie down and when you arise (*Deut. 6:7*). Therefore, we mark the time. That in itself, however, cannot begin to account for the sublime grandeur evoked as we thank the creative power "whose word draws down the evening, with wisdom opening heavenly gates, and with understanding regulating time and the changing seasons, arraying the stars in their proper places" and "sends forth the light from the east, rolling away the darkness." The physical universe, of course, is available to be experienced by everyone willing and able to open their senses and understanding to its manifestation of divine love toward creation. We also experience our religious teachings as expressions of God's love for us. These we celebrate in the evening in the prayer *Ahavat olam*, "eternal love," and in the morning with the analogous *Ahavah rabbah*, "bountiful love," differing in specifics but not in theme.

Gratitude for God's loving concern toward the people Israel not only seems but is particularist, and some would reply, Yes, and what of that? Are not all religions and even denominations within religions particularistic? If they aren't, what is the point of the difference? Those less persuaded by that argument might find a different sort of approach helpful. Teaching is a major expression of parental love because we understand teaching embraces far more than transmitting how to zip a jacket and count to ten. Whatever our religion, or even if we have none, we teach (in the words of *Ahavat olam*) our foundational truths and history of the world ("*Torah*"), commandments ("*mitzvot*") including the positive and negative ones such as "Pat the kitty gently" and "Don't talk like that to your mother;" sound advice (*chukim*) like "Look both ways before crossing the street" and laws (*mishpatim*), like "Clean up your own mess," with apt rewards and consequences. Parental love includes providing guidance and boundaries, not despite doing that. While it is certainly appropriate for us to express appreciation for what we have been taught by our parents and tradition, and for us to interpret those teachings as manifestations of love, we need not pray that everybody else will be taught alike.

Instead, having given voice to our gratitude for what we have received, we declare *Sh'ma yisrael adonai eloheinu adonai echad* (*Deuteronomy 6:4*) Problems of interpretation abound, therefore this succinct statement has been the subject of entire books. I prefer to translate in a way that does not pretend that the verse is simple in meaning or even grammatically clear in Hebrew: "Understand, Israel—The Source and Sustenance of all life: One!"

This is as close as Judaism has come to a widely accepted statement of faith. The convert says it upon becoming a Jew; it should be on our lips as we die. All the more remarkable that it is so brief, nonrestrictive and ambiguous. There is an imperative verb (*sh'ma*); a noun naming the collective addressee of the statement (*yisrael*); two names for God, one of them repeated, and standing in uncertain syntactic and grammatical relationship with one another in the absence of verbs pertaining to them; and finally a predicate (*echad*) the point of which is open to dispute. Its haziness of meaning notwithstanding, *Sh'ma* has become so important that—well, here is an oft-repeated story, probably apocryphal but nonetheless believable. A rabbi retires and a new one takes over the congregation. At the first service, when the congregation reaches the *Sh'ma,* half rise for it while the others sit. The ones standing yell at the others, "Don't be ignorant! It's the *Sh'ma,* we stand up." The ones sitting yell back, "Sit down! We don't stand up to say the *Sh'ma.*" At the next service, the brawl is repeated. And at the next. The rabbi can't stand it anymore, phones the retired rabbi and asks what the congregation's *minchag* is.

"That's the *minchag.*"

Those who stand take the text as the Jewish equivalent to the Pledge of Allegiance. They may well sing it out robustly to a popular triumphant melody that Salomon Sulzer composed in Vienna in the first half of the nineteenth century and which many Jews assume is the sole authentic tune. Those who sit follow the principle that the *Sh'ma* is not a prayer to God but a statement that we make in essence to ourselves and are expected to pore over, study, and contemplate in order to teach. What is the right way? That's the right way. Remaining seated seems preferable but goes against the grain for many congregants. One Solomonic strategy offered by some prayer books is to have the congregation remain standing after *Bar'khu* and then sit after *Sh'ma* but before the remainder of the biblical passages that accompany it, known from the incipit as *V'ahavtah,* "And you shall love," which all authorities agree is said while seated.

"And you shall love the Boundless, your God, with your whole heart and soul and substance. And all the lessons I impart to you today shall be upon your heart." The more we consider our religious language, the more it should be clear how Judaism is distorted when it is characterized as a religion of laws and commandments. Those are certainly significant aspects; yet consider how often we encounter the words <u>love</u> and <u>heart</u>. A beautiful teaching from the 19th century Hassidic rabbi Menachem Mendel of Kotzk offers an insight about the preposition "upon" in the second sentence. We would expect the Torah to say, Place these lessons <u>in</u> your heart. However, our teacher reminds us that our heart is not always open to receive the lesson. Consequently, we place the words on our heart so that when the heart opens, the words will sink in.

Less universally accepted than this paragraph are the others that became traditional parts of this rubric. Even when they are included in the *siddur*, non-traditionalist congregations are likely to skip over them. The notion that weather and harvests depend on our maintaining the good will of a stern, watchful deity by obediently following orders seemed too primitive for enlightened generations of the past couple of centuries to stomach. Ironically, our contemporary ecological perspectives open this text for us in a new way. The older mythology does not have to work for us; instead, we understand that climatic consequences follow from our good or bad behavior, not because a mythological "God" rewards us by sending sufficient rain and sunshine or punishes us with floods and parching droughts but because our good practices or our self-indulgent ones will affect the entire ecological system of our planet as well as our immediate environs. The water we have will be sufficient to its season if we have been sensible in our usage and planning. Crops will prosper if we have bred, preserved and planted species and varieties wisely. The Y-H-V-H to whom this is relevant is the coordinated wholeness allowing the world to function.

Andrew Vogel Ettin

Similarly, the passage declaring the importance of fringes on our garments seemed antiquated when most modern Jewish men no longer wore the *tallit katan* or fringe-cornered undergarment, nor were all of us content with commandments that paid no attention to women's ritual observances. To be a Jew in the world, however, is surely to be aware of the boundaries of our lives and the fringes at the corners that do not completely separate us from the secular and non-Jewish environments but do not tie us tightly to them either. Our coherence as a people and a religion, this selection tells us, is related to the *tzitzit* even if we interpret them figuratively. Jewish women and men live aware of the borders and peripheries of our identities. We meet them at school and in the grocery store, at work and when we eat, on the television screen and in the daily news.

In addition, we are more conscious today of the sorts of Jews who have been marginalized even in the fabric of our own communities, those who have been perforce on the fringes of Jewish community and synagogue life; and we know that they too are part of the fabric that should not be forgotten because they are essential to making the garment complete. They might be lesbian, gay, bisexual or transgendered. They might be the older Jews or the singles in communities focused on young families; the intermarried or their children who have felt rejected; shut-ins who cannot attend the synagogue or community activities; impoverished Jews who cannot afford dues but do not want to be embarrassed to admit it to a finance committee; Jews with disabilities who do not find a place in the congregation, some of whom find that the building itself is not physically accessible to them. Or they might be Jews whose approach to worship finds no place for expression outside their own home.

194

Claiming and renewing a traditional practice can help us internalize this concept of connecting us with the marginalized as part of our ritual choreography. During *Ahavah rabbah*, just before the morning *Sh'ma*, in the Orthodox *siddur* one prays that God will "speedily bring us blessing and peace from the four corners of the earth, break the oppressive yoke the nations have laid upon us, and gather us to our land." At the beginning of that passage, the four *tzitzit* are gathered into the left hand and held; as we read the paragraph about the wearing of fringes, we hold them in both hands, bringing them to our lips and kissing them at each mention of the word *tzitzit*. Imagine that in doing this we are also gathering, loving and honoring those of our own people who have been marginalized, as well as praying for God's help to end their oppression. We, the oft-marginalized people who have felt the yoke of nations upon us, need to bring closer to us and embrace the marginalized from among our own, in fact, to perceive them as helping us remember who we are.

Who we are actually, the prayerbook reminds us, are people who have been liberated before and still need the divine impulse that sets people free. Some liberation is geopolitical, and that is the main focus of the section called *Ge'ulah*, Freedom. We should not discount the importance of self-determination for an entire people, for an individual, for the human psyche. The liberation that we call the Exodus from Egypt is the paradigmatic experience, the foundational community-building act celebrated in this blessing. We sing of it in the passage quoted here from the Song at the Sea in the biblical book of *Exodus*, "*mi khamokha*, "Who is like You?". Some congregations, taking advantage of the variety of melodies available to turn this brief biblical poem into a modern song, welcome more exuberance at this point in the service than at any other place. Why not play drums and tambourines, recorders and chimes? Why not get up and dance as Miriam and the other women did? And perhaps also the men. It will be the rare circumstance in which a Jewish congregation does this with spontaneous and choreographed expressiveness that characterizes worship in Black churches; among other constraints, we are disinclined to set aside our irony and contrariety. But we do not have to remain seated and singing in lockstep unison, as if recounting an ancient tale of other people's joy instead of feeling our own. Freedom is serious; celebrating it does not have to be solemn.

The historical exodus is not the only "coming out" to be celebrated by this song. Nor is coming out of the closet in which one has hidden one's sexual orientation. Another kind is claiming one's own identity, even naming who one is through one's given or adopted name; or declaring oneself to be Jewish when it is easy and more comfortable to be silent; or taking an unpopular political position. These sorts of public statements are, to quote the title of a Paul Robeson recording, "Songs of Free Men" and free women as well.

If we have true freedom, what we can hopefully request for the evening is the true restfulness of a peaceful night. *Hashkiveinu . . . l'shalom,* "May we enjoy a peaceful sleep this night and awaken as if to life renewed." The beauty of the sentiments is reflected in the aural qualities of Hebrew's music, as we can hear from the opening phrases, which are arranged below as if they were poetry. Even if you do not understand the words, try saying this aloud, listening to the way the text floats on the repeated broad "a" and the long vowels of "-einu," the gentle rhythmic pulse of the long syllables (underlined) that suggest iambic and anapestic meter; and the neatly balanced phrases settling on the three-fold occurrences of "shalom":

Hashkiveinu adonai eloheinu
l'shalom
v' ha'amideinu malkheinu
l'chayyeem tohveem u-l'shalom
u-f'ros aleinu
sukkat shalomekha . . . .

We prayerfully imagine that spread over us—*u-f'ros aleinu*—is the *sukkah*, the shelter, a hut of God's *shalom*. We do not forget to pray for it stretching over all Israel, over Jerusalem, and some will add "over all the world." A *sukkah* is not a house or Temple; it is fragile and temporary, at least when human beings make it. Our wish arises, even so, from appreciating what it will mean to us individually—to you and me—truly to be at peace with God, with the world, and (not so easy or so obvious) with ourselves. On Shabbat this might be followed immediately by the verse of *Exodus 31: 16*, commanding us to observe the sabbath through all generations. Sabbath and peace go hand in hand as soulmates.

※ ※ ※

When Virginia Woolf's novel *To the Lighthouse* was published, some reviewers interpreted the lighthouse as a symbol that represented a specific idea, some lofty ideal or life goal. Woolf herself, however, described it as an image rather than a symbol. It did not "stand for" something else. Rather, the lighthouse was a focal point for the story and the characters' tensions that emerge through conversations about visiting it. It had no more extraneous meaning than a line that a painter like the novel's Lily Briscoe might use to balance the composition. That is similar what Twyla Tharp means in saying that every work she creates has a "spine." Like a dancer's physical spine, it doesn't have

197

to be visible but it needs to be there. As she writes, "It keeps me on message, but it is not the message itself."[9]

Religious liturgies also have a spine. During the Middle Ages we could not erect great cathedrals or castles. Instead, we developed liturgies. The spine of the Jewish prayer service is a sequence of blessings and prayers that has various names. To the sages of the talmudic era, it was simply *ha-tefilah*, "the prayer." Subsequently it has often been known as the Amidah because it is recited while one <u>stands</u>, and is often referred to as *Shemonei Esrei*, "eighteen," because it formerly had eighteen sections of benedictions; that name has persisted even after a nineteenth was added many centuries ago and despite the fact that on Shabbat the number is reduced to seven because giving thanks for the sabbath replaces the weekday series of petitions for divine help.

Before entering this deeply sacred space we might need to take a deep breath and a moment to focus our intention, our *kavvanah*, to keep in mind why we have come and what we need to do. What we need to do in the Amidah is speak; and although we have been doing so already, this series of prayers asks for something at a deeper level from us. Some modern Jews pray with the good intention of returning to extemporaneous forms of expression through personal expression and meditative exercises, especially during the Amidah. In older times, before prayerbooks were available to everyone, these blessings were more personally worded by each worshipper, with the service leader signaling the themes of the prayers and then davvening aloud for the sake of those who could not formulate their own prayers. The difficulty that *siddurim* were crafted to answer is that we are not all eloquent every day; nor do we all reach a deep level of concentration each time we pray through (traditionally) three Amidah services daily.

Therefore, custom has adopted the practice of the talmudic sage R. Yohanan to preface the Amidah with Psalm 51, verse 17, *Adonai s'fatai teeftakh u-fee y'gid t'hilatecha,* "Y-H-V-H [Breath of Life], part my lips, that my mouth may open in praise." Not everyone is comfortable with appealing to divine agency in this way, or for that matter beseeching God to act on our behalf.[10] But this line acknowledges that we need prompting to express ourselves. We might know intellectually that we should be grateful for whatever we have; we might even feel gratitude inside ourselves; but saying it gives it a tangible reality. Most of us do expect someone to say "Thank you" for a favor or gift, even when this is hard to put into words. Some people are able to satisfy us when they express their gratitude non-verbally. A non-verbal or meditative version of the Amidah can be powerfully articulate in another manner. The psalmist's words might not be literally accurate in that circumstance; still, the principle is relevant. We need to be moved to expression.

The Amidah has a logical structure that, if we take time to reflect on it, can teach us a lot about the way that a people learn religious truths, or at least develop religious assumptions. What is true of a whole people is also true of each one of us; "ontogeny recapitulates phylogeny." In essence the Amidah is like a great arch. On one side, the beginning set of three blessings stands like a mighty pillar or pier; it is balanced on the other side by three concluding and matching blessings, the other pier; both receive and transmit energy. These are linked by a middle section. The shabbat and festival Amidah has a steeply curved arch between the pillars, a holiday benediction that is not very long but seems to stretch skyward like a catenary arch. The weekday Amidah's midsection is flatter, more elliptical, with a much longer distance to span between the pillars.

Andrew Vogel Ettin

We are going to explore the Amidah in the spirit of Eadweard Muybridge, the great 19th century pioneer of photography who used sequences of stop-action photos showing us the movements of galloping horses, running men, tennis players, rowers and boxers in detail that we could not see from an individual snapshot or from observing them in live action. Therefore we will use the freeze-frame capability of language to examine individual moments in the moving stream of prayers that comprise the Amidah so we may better understand the parts and the process of the whole sequence of movement.

In life, art and religion, we learn first from what already exists, interpreted for us by the transmitters of knowledge. The prayerbook calls this initial stage, the first section of the Amidah, *avot*, "fathers," to which many of us add *v'imahot*, "and mothers." Our parents are usually our first teachers, and when they are gone from this earth, we memorialize them during Yizkor prayers as *avi mori*, "my father, my teacher," and *imi morati*, "my mother, my teacher," words that are true no matter whether they have been ideal teachers or not. For good or ill, we have learned from them and by their examples, positively and sometimes negatively. The *siddur* actually has in mind the traditional patriarchs and matriarchs of the Jewish people;. thus it addresses the blessing to "God of Abraham, God of Isaac and God of Jacob; God of Sarah, God of Rebecca, God of Rachel and God of Leah." The sages taught that we say "God of . . . " separately for each one, rather than "God of Abraham, Isaac and Jacob," because each experienced God differently, thereby teaching us some different aspect of the divine.

Some are comfortable with the devout acceptance of the trio, or the trio and quartet, patriarchs and matriarchs of the tradition. Others might be as well but occasionally stimulated to reflect on the biblical stories of those people's experiences in life and encounters with divinity. What—I might ask myself—was Isaac's or Rebecca's special true knowledge of God as we grasp it in the Torah, how did that affect their lives and what do I learn from it? Can I put together the many faces of God perceived by these seven figures and recorded in the narratives about their lives so as to expand my comprehension of the ungraspable Unity?

Perhaps for us those names are only that: names in which we retell the stories associated with misty personages or archetypes of history or legends, whose doings have little interest and no compelling truth to me at this moment in my life, absorbed as I am in the particulars of my existence and my own concerns. I might be gratefully aware moreover of recent people who have formed my heart, soul and mind. They are relatives and friends, some living and breathing, some no longer in this world though in their own ways alive in me, perhaps in ways of which I might not even be conscious. They are also creative artists and thinkers, contemporary or ancient, whose achievements have shaped my inner being. The great dancer and choreographer José Limón wrote wittily that "My parents were Isadora Duncan and Harald Kreutzberg. They were not present at my birth; I doubt that they ever saw one another . . . ."[11] We might be sensitive to yet another dimension of *avot v'imahot*. Rabbinic terminology often uses "mother" and "father" in referring to governing principles, stimuli or origins for action; the *avot m'lachot*, "fathers of labor," for instance, are the thirty-nine main categories of labor not to be done on Shabbat, from which numerous other specific excluded activities are derived, like children from their progeniture. In recognizing what values motivate or govern my actions, I acknowledge my "mothers and fathers," my muses. Through this first Amidah blessing we honor the tradition, our past. The teachings that we have received along with illuminations of our understanding and spirit are gifts of divinity in its various manifestations, consciously acknowledged here.

If the first blessing addresses the legacy of the past, the second looks both at the moment at hand and far ahead into the future. A deity should continue reliably throughout time, not just be a god of the past but a god of <u>now</u>. We give thanks for the expressions of divinity that we perceive all around us. At appropriate times of the year we recognize special climatic needs as the Jews of the Middle East experienced them, so from Sh'mini Atzeret at the end of Sukkot until Pesach we insert blessings of gratitude for rain the and wind, and beginning on the first day of Pesach we give thanks instead for the dew providing crucial moisture to save plants from parching summer heat.

This *G'vurot* ("strengths") section of the Amidah also contains one of Judaism's clearest statements of belief in the resurrection of the dead. And thereby hangs a tale. In its conventional wording, it blesses God, *m'khayyeh ha-metim*, "who gives life to the dead." This was a major point of controversy during the days of the Second Temple between Pharisees, who believed in resurrection, and Sadducees, who did not. The victorious Pharisees were able to give their idea doctrinal status through the Amidah in the thrice-daily liturgy. Responding to modern rationalism, leaders of Reform Judaism revised this in its 1973 prayer book *Gates of Prayer / Shaárei Tefilah* to *m'chayeh ha-kol*, "who gives life to all." That sentiment is inoffensive to any theist, though one could also say that it is theologically thin. The 2007 Reform prayerbook, *Mishkan Tefilah*, reflecting a return toward tradition and perhaps a new attitude among contemporary Jews toward non-rationalistic spirituality, provides the earlier wording as an equal option.

But in what sense can God, as some like to say, "overcome anything"? If God can "give life to the dead" and not merely in metaphoric terms, then why does God not preserve us from the anxieties, grief and loss that attend the passage out of this life, not to mention the suffering that often precedes it? Here we must differentiate between curing and healing. A cure is a medical solution. Penicillin is a cure for pneumonia; the cure for appendicitis is removal of the afflicted organ. Healing, however, is a response of the whole system. A person dying of an incurable illness may nevertheless be healed by attaining physical, emotional and spiritual comfort and by reassurance about the wellbeing of those whose future they hold in deepest concern. God who "cures" death could do so by undoing it. Even if there is some profound value that accrues to us in dying, through experiencing that passage out of life as we know it, this God could still reverse the consequence of leaving this realm of the senses. In that case, we get to come back, presumably wiser, but still in need of something more from living. The God acknowledged in the phrase "who gives life to the dead" does that. By contrast, God who "heals" us from death takes away our confusion and fear in contemplating it. A response in the Matins service of the Office for the Dead developed in the early medieval Catholic church and much quoted in later literature says in commenting on *Job* 17, *timor mortis conturbat me,* "fear of death torments me." That fear may undermine plans and hopes; it may sicken, sadden and terrify us. The fear itself may feel like an ailment, and to be healed of that is a cause for blessing. God who does this "gives life to all."

As we move carefully through this *tekhyyiat ha-metim* blessing, we should be alert to the resonances of its inner language. God upholds the living *b'chesed,* in loving-kindness, and quickens the dead *b'rachamim rabbim*, with bountiful compassion. Further, we attest, "You support the falling, heal the sick, free captives, and are faithful with those who sleep in the dust." This language not only promises physical resurrection of the dead. It also speaks of hopefulness for the afflicted. The sick might not be cured but they can be healed. Captives can be freed. When this benediction was composed, freeing of captives (from the Romans or from kidnapping brigands, for instance) was most likely understood literally, for the Talmud refers repeatedly to halakhic concerns primarily involving women or children who were held captive and discusses what might be the proper response to kidnappers' exorbitant ransom demands. Now the danger comes from terrorist and guerrilla groups, or tyrannical governments. For the unfortunate victim, hope in God may be of greater comfort than hope in human agencies. Inasmuch as it recalls *Daniel* 12: 2, it also promises that justice ultimately will be satisfied: "And the many who sleep in the dust of the earth [*mi-yishney admat-afar*] shall awake, some to everlasting life [*l'khayyey olam*], and some to shame and everlasting contempt." Demands of theodicy will eventually be satisfied as people receive the reward or punishment that they deserved but did not get in their previous time above ground earth.

More deeply, we recollect that the deepest gloom may lighten. How often has it occurred that someone broken in heart, spirit or body recovers strength, joy or confidence as time passes and life changes? So the Amidah begins by recognizing links with the past from which we derive knowledge, with the present from which we derive life-giving sustenance, and with the future that gives us hope that we will not be overwhelmed by that which makes us fall, sickens or enchains us, drives us down into the dust.

The third section is known as *Kedushah*, holiness. In the morning and afternoon services when a minyan is present it is filled out with dramatic biblical dialogue recording the vision of the celestial celebration of divine majesty; the evening service more succinctly and less visually honors the divine name: "You and Your name are holy, and holy ones praise you each day, Selah!"

The first two blessings in their different ways honor God's immanence. They acknowledge holiness present in our genetic and biographical history and personal development, and in the way that we experience our hopes and dreams. *Kedushah* recognizes God as also transcendent. This is the awesome God. Not God to be "feared," although the biblical command *yirah et-adonai elohecha* (*Deut.* 10: 12, for instance) is usually translated as "you shall fear the Lord your God," just as the rabbinic term *yirat shamayim* is usually translated as "fear of Heaven." That word "fear" is pernicious, though lexically it is partly accurate. Our ancestors, for whom human kings were often as fearsome and arbitrary as deities, needed their own god to be powerful beyond all else. They sensed that the protective might of the divine sovereign demanded obedience and allegiance. Woe to anyone who cheated or disobeyed because the consequence of their misdeed would surely be divine punishment or abandonment not solely of the offender but of the whole community. The deity was not only an individual's god but the god of a people. Woe to a people who treated divine law lightly, for they would be left defenseless before their foes or a pitiless nature; if not the onslaughts of Assyrians and Babylonians, then torrential rains or earthquakes or a plague or a parching copper sun would bring them ruin.

Today, the notion of God as the ultimate judge, knower and seer of all, constant and incorruptible, still answers a need, rather as the Freudian concept of the super-ego does. But often it pushes itself forward as the only or at least the dominant notion about God: the demanding disciplinarian who accepts no excuses and overlooks no fault. "He" is a genius but also the ballet-master, orchestra conductor, theater director, coach who drives fear into every performer's heart with a word or look—the *maestro*, the master who is accustomed to assume that his authority is absolute. This is the unquestionable and unquestioned image of God for many people. Some find it a false image, others an oppressive, terrifying one. To many, it is the image of God that drives them from houses of worship and organized religion.

This blessing recognizes the gap between the human and the divine. That gap is what the word *kadosh* {*kuf-dalet-shin*), "holy," is about, and approaching it could indeed be fearsome. When Moses asks to see God, his answer is that "You cannot see my face because no mortal being can see me and live" (*Exodus 33:20*). But there, God provides an alternative, a safe place to be and a way of perceiving God's work in the world. You can see my back as I pass by, God says; in other words, you can see what I have done when it is accomplished. Moses and God are set apart from one another. The Hebrew root *k-d-sh* refers to something <u>set apart</u>, removed from the ordinary because it is sacred or consecrated to God. The innermost section of the Temple is not only the "Holy of Holies," the place of most intense sanctity set apart by a curtain even from the holy area of the tabernacle, but also the most restricted of the restricted areas, the enclosure which only the High Priest could enter and only on Yom Kippur. Indeed, the Talmud goes further in defining the nuances of sanctity, claiming for instance (*Pesachim 86a*) that the upper chamber of the *kodesh kodashim* was yet more restricted, more *kodesh*, not because it was more sacred but because it was entered more rarely to check for needed repairs.

The verb *yirah* (*yud-resh-aleph*) has another connotation that many of us today find more apt: being moved to <u>awe</u>. The Romantics sensed this element in divinity when contemplating the looming eminence of Mont Blanc, the thunderous precipice of Niagara Falls or the whiteness of Moby Dick, and evoked in massive symphonies and vocal works or grand edifices. We may feel it ourselves at the edge of the Grand Canyon or the base of Mt. Everest, on the shore of a seemingly endless ocean or on a small ship bobbing before the great Antarctic ice wall; in contemplating the dizzying perspectives on the outer universe from the Voyager's cameras or the inner universe from an electron microscope, our heads spinning and insides thrilling in response to the scale and detail. Or we listen to Mendelssohn's Octet and peer at a Vermeer and feel ourselves moved not by the brilliance of the individual but by the capacity of a human imagination so joined with perfect technique that the word "miraculous" seems inevitable. And perhaps we look intensely at our beloved and feel out there and inside us "a kosmos" (as Whitman called himself). In short, this is the blessing for life's "Oh—Wow!"

The longer *Kedushah* used in the morning and afternoon services is virtually a miniature oratorio or baroque *sacra rappresentazione*. Unfortunately, not even on major holidays is this passage's magnificent drama likely to be fully expressed during the service; the potential awaits the skills of artists with the resources of Mark Morris and Steve Reich, and perhaps Dreamworks. We can come close in our minds, or if we are truly fortunate with the right sort of congregation, to engaging in the dialogic exchange of celestial forces uniting in praise. Quotations from visionary passages in *Isaiah, Ezekiel* and *Psalms* explicitly put into our mouths the words of fiery angels (*seraphim*) celebrating God's all-encompassing, everlasting grandeur. Standing in a group, we might turn to one another as the text suggests, sensing ourselves in the divine presence so that we and the space in which we stand are vessels inhabited by the Shekhinah, and like the spirit-beings whose words we repeat, we sing out, conscious of being surrounded by the divine presence suffusing all that is, as if the synagogue's walls themselves were transparent, or we were transported to another world of consciousness. "Holy, holy, holy All the earth is filled with God's glory." *Kadosh kadosh kadosh adonai tzeva'ot:* holy in the realm of assiyah / action; holy in the realm of yetsirah / feeling and relating; holy in the realm of b'riyah / forming; transcendent holiness itself / adonai of multiplicity.

Some trace of choreography persists in the custom that many have of raising their heels at each *"kadosh."* Others press their heels downward to sense being rooted in the sanctified earth. We know from derisive comments and halakhic rulings as early as the 16th century that some worshippers jumped off the ground when they said *kadosh*, as if striving to take off like flying angels, a reminder that not every ecstatic practice is a good one. Followers of the late 18th century hassidic rabbi Levi Yitzhak of Berditchev transmitted the teaching that we should recite the *Kedushah* quietly but proclaim the "Kadosh" line aloud, eyes closed but turned upward, while during the leader's repetition of the Kedushah we shut our eyes.[12] Through such techniques that heighten *kavvanah*, which is our full and purposeful engagement with the meaning of the prayer, we internalize the experience as we engage our imaginations with the visual and aural splendor evoked by the text's poetry.

The previous blessings have connected us with the past, the present, the future, and this one lifts us into the transformation of this moment into a moment of sacred awareness. We experience, as if transformed from our frail mortality, the higher level of conscious in which we become aware of divinity suffusing all of time and space.

If it is a holiday, like Shabbat, we can linger in sanctified quasi-timelessness to celebrate sanctity embedded in human ceremony, our observance of the festival or the special sacred time of the sabbath day. The blessing for the holiday, the earthly day that is distinguished by its *kedushah*—by holiness and by separateness—is the fourth and central blessing. This one extended segment replaces the thirteen requests that we make on the normal days. When we are in the realm of continuing daily needs, we have agendas to address; our desires and wants are particular. On holidays, all is one; the only specificity that we need is to designate the day and its honorific title; Pesach is honored as *zeman cheruteinu,* "the season of our freedom," Shavuot as *zeman matan torateinu,* "the season of the giving of our Torah," Sukkot as *zeman simchateinu,* "the season of our joy," and Shabbat is among its other attributes *yom menuchah,* "a day of rest."

Much as the first two blessings complement one another but also lead naturally to the third, so the third and fourth blessings complement one another. The third, the *Kedushah,* raises our mortal consciousness to a semblance of the Otherworldly consciousness, as though we could project our minds into the *olam ha-bah,* a phrase generally translated as The World to Come but which we might also think of as The Beyond. The fourth blessing, known as *Kedushat ha-yom,* the Holiness of the Day, expresses our awareness of sanctity flowing into human time to bestow on us a time-outside-of-time. For on this day, whether it be Shabbat or another holiday, from one sundown to the next, ordinary time no longer counts. Work ceases. Extended periods are given to praying and learning, as if the clock and the normal daily schedule were irrelevant. We speak here of the theory, of course, for any leader of services knows that in fact people do care about how long the service runs, and when they can leave for lunch. Significantly, the refreshments customarily following the Friday night service have become widely known as "the *oneg*," the Hebrew word meaning "delight," notwithstanding the clergy's wish that the delight come from the substance of the holiday, and of course the sermon.

If we think of the Amidah as an arch, the Shabbat or festival *Kedushat ha-yom*, being the fourth of seven sections, is the keystone. In some formulations of Jewish mystical teachings, we speak of four "worlds" or dimensions, the fourth (known as *Atzilut*) being the highest and most transcendent level, closest to the realm of pure spirituality. As we have noted, the Torah says that God on the seventh day *shavat v'yinafash*, which can be translated to mean, Ceased from working in physicality and returned to spirituality. In a way, this blessing for the day's *kedushah*, its separateness in sanctity, takes us out of time's realm into the sphere of holiness, as close as we mortal beings can get to timelessness.

✳ ✳ ✳

If, however, this is a weekday, we must then descend from this supreme height, returning to practicalities of living, expressed in a series of petitionary prayers and blessings through which we both ask for what we need and give thanks to the bountiful source from which needs are met. Consider the themes of these petitions (*bakhashot*) as an insightful traversal of the resources we want, from the most sublime to the most practical. The Hebrew rubrics below are traditional ones going back to Second Temple times, though the English paraphrases are intended as guides to stimulate and inspire personal prayer, especially but not solely for those who might be unfamiliar or uncomfortable with the conventional prayerbook texts that translate the wording more literally. I have separated them into groups to clarify some unifying principles within this section. This outline should make the logical order clear.

Binah—gratitude for knowledge, understanding and good sense
Teshuvah—for correction of our faults
S'lichah—for receiving forgiveness

Ge'ulah—for deliverance from oppression, sorrows and anxieties
Refu'ah—for healing those ailing
Shanim—for a fruitful earth and a prosperous year

Kibbutz galuyot—for rescuing all who are exiled
Mishpat—for true justice
Ha-minim—for suppressing evil and violence
Tzaddikim—for the wellbeing of the good

Binyan yerushalayim—for Jerusalem and Israel renewed and transformed
Malchut—for progress toward fulfilling our best (messianic) hopes for the world

Tefilah—for knowing when and how our prayers are accepted

The initial group of three blessings focuses on our inner needs as members of the community. Each one can be applicable to each of us, albeit that is not the direction of the original wording. Typically, we express pleas and confessions alike in the first person plural rather than singular. Aware of our personal and familial needs, we know that they are not unique; others have needs, anxieties and suffering as great or greater. An acute understanding of how we behave undergirds the process instilled in this way. Some of us may think most immediately of our own need while forgetting or minimizing that of other people. The traditional language guides us differently, to speak on behalf of the community. And some may find it easier to speak of ourselves under the cover of the collective, voicing our personal failings or desires as those of "Your people Israel."

We first pray and give thanks for enlightenment, the mental processes by which we gain knowledge and develop our understanding. We cannot pray for faith or belief; and anyway, these are implied or taken for granted by the previous benedictions. A major result of growth in understanding is to recognize first our collective imperfections and errors and next to recognize as well those of others, for we must look first to our own failings and than beg forgiveness once those faults have been recognized and addressed. John Milton insightfully evokes the moral wisdom of that process in Book 10 of *Paradise Lost*. Eve begins the repentance and repair—in Jewish terms, *t'shuvah*, "return"—by recognizing and admitting her own fault first, thereby prompting the more stubborn Adam to his own *t'shuvah* that has to take place before they mutually ("unanimous" is Milton's word) can confess and seek pardon from God. Many Jews as well as Christians are familiar with the way the sequence was formulated by a Jew of the 1ˢᵗ century C.E. in the so-called Sermon on the Mount: "And forgive us our transgressions as we forgive those who transgress against us."

The next series of petitions broadens our concerns for wellbeing in the world. The *Ge'ulah* text addresses God as "the redeemer of Israel." That is God's redemptive role in Jewish theology, not being our personal, individual redeemer. Not our perfection but our flawed yet penitent nature dares to ask that oppressive burdens be lifted from all of our people. Similarly, the requests for healing and prosperity ask that "we" be healed and that the year and its harvest be good *aleinu*, for us. Naturally, "us" may include "I" and the blessing of God as the healer is one of the traditional spots where a personally pertinent silent prayer for oneself or someone else is particularly apt.

One deep insight conveyed through this perspective is that our individual wellbeing, spiritual as much as material, ought not be isolated from the web of our social being. If I am only concerned with my personal redemption from spiritual bondage and oppression, regardless of the condition of my community (understood here as "Israel," those bound together by some commonalities of history, culture or confession), then I am deeply maimed in spirit. If only my health matters to me, or it matters so much that I cannot pray first for the relief of others' dire circumstances, then I am sick indeed. If I think that my own prosperity, my year's harvest, comes regardless of the conditions of the planet and the society and my neighbors, then I am impoverished in ways that I do not even perceive.

Community concerns, especially political ones, are the focus of the third set of benedictions, although it has been pointed out that the section directed against *minim*—whether we understand that term as "heretics" or "slanderers"—and *zedim*, "villains," is in truth a malediction. That is counterbalanced by the blessing following it, which is for the righteous (the *tzaddikim*), as well as the pious, the elders of the people Israel, the sages, the righteous converts, "and us," *aleinu*, a wonderfully bold yet modest conclusion inasmuch as it assumes that we who speak the blessing fall outside of these honored categories, but nevertheless hope that the grace intended for them will extend to us as well.

It is a strategy similar to that of the Amidah's first section, *Avot*, in which we invoke the names of the patriarchs, and now the matriarchs, to our own benefit, not so much for reflected glory as reflected merit. Please favor us, we plead, because we are the descendents of those who loved and were loved by God, even if we ourselves are unworthy. A bit of humility sometimes helps.

Paired with these is the desire for Jewish exiles to return to the land of Israel and for Jewish courts of justice to be re-established. These benedictions date of course to the time of oppressive Roman occupation of the land of Israel. Forced expulsion of Jews following uprisings, slavery, and loss of any citizenship lasted for centuries. In exile Jewish courts could sometimes operate within specific communities but unpredictably so, certainly not everywhere, with limited scope and only on sufferance of the local or regional non-Jewish government. The blessing for courts of law refers to alleviating our "sorrow and moaning," noting that only God rules in loving-kindness and mercy, judging righteously. To our ancestors the connection between these two blessings presumably was that the return of the exiles could allow one system of law to govern all the Jewish people, and presumably clarifying the distinction between *minim* or *zedim* and *tzaddikim*. Actions of rabbinic courts in modern Israel reveals the naïve optimism of such a wish.

From our contemporary perspective we recognize that everything about these ideas is politically problematic. However, we bring to them a different vantage-point on exile and justice. The ability and willingness of Jews to settle in *ha-aretz*, the Land, as the land of Israel is known, is but one dimension of the ingathering of exiles. Making our synagogues and community organizations hospitable to all women, lesbians and gays, interfaith families, singles, the physically impaired, indeed all the kinds of people who were marginalized, excluded or overlooked is another form of bringing home the exiles among the Jewish people.

Nor are we alone in having populations in exile or in coerced diaspora. True, there is a significant distinction between *galut*, an exile commanded and enforced by dictate, and *diaspora*, which is a dispersal of population regardless of reason and not necessarily coerced. One may "choose" to go into "voluntary" exile. However, some diasporas are rather like "elective surgery" for a condition so painful and debilitating that survival without the surgery seems unbearable. In desperate circumstances, when leaving one's homeland seems the only way to survive and perhaps prosper, what do "choose" and "voluntary" really mean? The biblical stories of Joseph and Ruth, to name just two, certainly invite us to broaden our sensibilities toward those who cross national boundaries because of famines, adventures and misadventures, slave-trading, and longings for a home of the heart and a family of one's choice.

The prayer for restoring the legal system, which many prayerbooks universalize (at least in translation) perceptively concludes with praise of God as the lover of *tz'dakah u-mishpat*, "righteousness and justice." We have come to recognize the distinction between law and justice. As Dr. Martin Luther King, Jr., reminded his clergy critics in the open letter he wrote from jail in Birmingham, Alabama after being arrested in a civil rights demonstration, "everything Adolf Hitler did in Germany was 'legal' . . . It was 'illegal' to aid and comfort a Jew in Hitler's Germany." There are unjust laws, in other words, and even when the law itself is just, innocent people may spend years wrongly imprisoned because the legal system may work unjustly or unrighteously. In this petition we call on a higher inspiration, a motivating power beyond human prejudice, ignorance or self-interest to resolve the division between the process of legal systems and righteous justice.

Who were the *minim* and *zedim* and why do we denounce them? We think we know the origin of this passage, although scholars differ about its intended target. It was composed by the sage Rabbi Shmuel bar Nakhmani in response to a request from the great Mishnaic leader Rabban Gamliel the Second near the end of the 1st century C.E. and added to the original eighteen blessings. Were *minim* Jews who collaborated with the Roman occupiers, or "slanderers" providing the government with dangerous reports about Jews and their activities? Were they Jews, perhaps including but not limited to followers of Jesus, who opposed and defied the dominant Jewish religious authorities and thereby were labeled heretics? The arguments, while more or less interesting in themselves, are revealing about the ways in which "heresy" is defined and the relationship that develops between a powerful ruling force and individuals among the subject people who gain advantages by siding with the dominant power. These are certainly as pertinent to our sociopolitical reality today as they were over 1900 years ago, regardless of where we live.

Let us change the question's tense, therefore. Who are the *minim* and *zedim* and why do we denounce them? By reframing this, we move from merely repeating a historically mandated formula to considering our own values. Whom do we see as "the enemy" and are we prepared to call out for divine punishment of them? Some ultra-Orthodox rabbis in Israel and elsewhere have denounced Reform and Conservative Judaism explicitly as heretical for teaching flexible approaches toward halakhah. Jewish critics of Israeli political decisions have been labeled "self-hating" and accused of encouraging anti-semitism and terrorism. From the progressives, one can hear rhetoric as intense against hard-line opponents. Knowing that "anything you say can be used against you," against whom are you or I ready to utter the *chatimah*, the concluding "seal" of the benediction, "Blessed are you, Adonai, the shatterer of Your enemies and humbler of the arrogant"?

Understandably, some modern prayerbooks, notably those from Reform, have omitted this section, while others have revised the wording at least in the translation to invoke God's might for subjugating evil, rather than obliterating evildoers. That assumes that we really can effectively imagine a concept of "evil" without giving it (to adopt Shakespeare's phrase) "a local habitation and a name." Presumably this is why the impetus toward evil-doing became displaced onto a contrarian figure, *ha-satan*, "the adversary," who in turn became personified into a personage called Satan, and why the emotional or psychological difficulties that afflict people are often called their demons. Another approach is to recognize how the Amidah expresses each one's personal prayer. In her *Weekday Amidah in Guided Imagery* Rabbi Marcia Prager treats the *minim* as "evil forces" of negativity within the individual, "the voice . . .that is unrelentingly critical, negative, or judgmental." The enemy here is that which wars against the best in us and in our deeds, arrogantly threatening the semblance of the divine by maligning and deprecating who we are and what we do.

Whether we perceive our most pressing contention as being with external or internal hostility, this section impels us to confront the contentions in our view of the world. We may wish for the contentiousness to end; we may wish for the hostility directed against us personally or us as a community to be obliterated. Transcending such desires can be nobly virtuous. Yet to do that we need not to repress them but to recognize them. Articulating them so as to consign them verbally to God can be a way of liberating ourselves from their toxic effect on us, personally or collectively.

And let us candidly admit that some of us may even want our enemy crushed by divine power not only because we feel righteous ourselves but we also know that we cannot effectively act against our foe. That may be true on the personal level (struggling to subdue our private "demons") as well as on the political (endlessly contending against terrorism and brutality) or planetary (overwhelmed by the difficulties in preventing climatic disasters). Our capabilities are limited and we know that. Some struggles we have at least a chance of winning. In others, we recognize that we are overmatched and maybe even helpless. If *zedim* are not only "malicious ones," purposefully antagonistic, but "evildoers" whose nature is to cause harm, indeed we may usefully extend our understanding of the blessing. In our contest with the rampantly destructive virus or cancer, dividing and multiplying its own cells while consuming healthy ones, we certainly need good medicine but in some way we might know that we and our physicians are limited. Nature, the individual's body, good genes, happenstance or luck—all of these might be said to be "in God's hands." When human resources become exhausted, we are likely to "hope and pray for a miracle."

Against *zedim* we counterbalance the *tzaddikim*, the righteous. This blessing specifically calls for God's compassion as well as a good reward for all who are recognized under this category. Although it is seemingly innocuous in itself, the passage implicitly admits a problem in theodicy, namely, the gap between what is right and what is. The righteous—let alone the rest of us—do not always seem to enjoy divine compassion or get their good reward; every one of us can think of good people who have suffered or apparently gone unrewarded in their lives. The *minim* and *zedim* often seem not to get what they deserve, either. Verdi's *Rigoletto* will always end with the virtuous, innocent Gilda dead in her devastated father's arms while the smug, sybaritic Duke who raped the kidnapped girl returns blithely to his palace, cynically singing about women's fickleness. War criminals live safely notwithstanding their brutalized victims' nightmares and the unnamed bodies disintegrating in unmarked graves. While we do not have the power to transform this imbalance in cosmic justice by ourselves, we can at least admit it and wish that it were otherwise by extending our hopes for goodness to flourish. One consequence of that, of course, is that goodness would be seen as rewarded, thereby eliminating one of the impediments to good behavior, the perception that one prospers through selfishness and dishonesty, not through goodness and righteousness. Like other blessings in the weekday petitionary *bakhashot*, this one expresses the best for which we hope, rather than giving thanks for the way life is. It acknowledges that if we must ask, then all is not perfect. Among our tasks as caring human beings, we should perceive the imperfections and envision the perfecting of them.

The next group of blessings looks ahead to history coming to full fruition. It joins what is known in theological terms as soteriology (a teaching concerning salvation) and eschatology (a teaching concerning the end of time). The prayer for the holy presence to return to Jerusalem and rebuild it for eternity, and the related prayer for salvation through the blossoming of a restored Davidic monarchy have been uncomfortable for many Jews since the beginning of the 19th century for various reasons, including the particularist emphasis on Jerusalem and Israel, salvation for the Jewish people rather than the whole world, the plea for a restored monarchy in general along with the special focus on the line of David. More than any other component in the Amidah, this section has been creatively reworded and translated in various *siddurim* as we continually recast its concepts in the light of contemporary needs as well as experiences. Especially since 1948 we have felt the need for rethinking what we ought to say about these hopes. After all, since that time Jews have been in only voluntary diaspora, otherwise free, more or less, to emigrate to Israel and live in Jerusalem.

But wait. Israel's rabbinic establishment does not make *aliyah* quite so easy or pleasant for everybody who considers themselves Jewish. Jerusalem is an expensive place to live. Life in Israel is challenging. There are wars; there are terrorists; there's a frustrating civil bureaucracy and a Kafkaesque religious one. There are Israelis to deal with. Not to mention Palestinians. And what would I do there?

This makes light of a serious situation. Still, the simple expression of longing for something inaccessible becomes much more problematic when we take a large step closer to making that long-expressed desire become real. It is especially so when we find in taking that step that we seem to be rediscovering the truth of Zeno's paradoxes. The pre-Socratic philosopher Zeno of Elea, who did not know anything about messianism, proposed in a series of mental puzzles that even physical progress was illusory: logically the goal toward which we strove would always remain out of reach because at each <u>instant</u> there is no movement at all (since movement occurs during time as well as through space) and all apparent forward progress requires that we traverse half of the necessary distance first, ad infinitum, such that there will always be half of the remaining distance left to travel. In other words, striving to realize our collective desire for the sacred city and the messianic kingdom, the closer we appear to get, the more impossible it seems ever to reach our destination.

That is why the benediction is a behest for God to "return with compassion to your city, Jerusalem, dwell in it and rebuild it soon in our day . . . Blessed are you, Y-H-V-H, who rebuilds Jerusalem." It does not say, "Help us to return to Jerusalem so that we can dwell in it and rebuild it." The rebuilt Jerusalem for which we pray can only be the one inspired by the presence of God, not the one in which we buy a condominium with a view. The Davidic monarchy, or the more general hope for the reign of righteousness and justice or for the glory of the people Israel spoken of instead at this point in some modern *siddurim*, represents hope for a commonly accepted, stable and just government that will last—a truly messianic political dream. These two blessings bear our hopes for the world. We ask that those who have been long exiled, vulnerable and marginalized, often subjugated and terrorized wherever they have lived—quintessentially the Jewish story of so many centuries—have a secure home place to dwell, a place that they desire. We ask that this home place exemplify safety and glory, a sanctuary for those in need and the *keren*, "horn," of Israel. It is God's work to achieve when we cannot through our own efforts or good will.

If we read these texts in spiritual terms, we recognize that the ingathering of exiles is something more than a political act or even a socially welcoming gesture. The Lurianic kabbalists say that disorder and dislocation in the world can be traced back to an early stage in the creative process when the divine energy that poured into the universe to give it life and form was too powerful for the less than divine vessels meant to contain it. The vessels shattered, dispersing bits of the sacred sparks of light that one day, with our cooperation, will be gathered up. Returning those in exile, like returning the *afikomen* during the Passover *seder*, enacts on the human plane the essential process we hope for on the spiritual plane. Similar to the return of the *afikomen* but on a much grander scale, the return of the exiles is a dramatization of the essential sacred task of reuniting the shattered shards of the divinely made vessel of humanity.

The last layer of this inner filling of the *T'filah* is a petition that is itself known confusingly though aptly as *T'filah*. This passage asks God, for the sake of divine faithfulness and mercy, to hear and fulfill these prayers. We have just offered a series of requests and now appeal to "our king" (*malkhenu*) not to turn us away empty. *Sh'ma koleynu*, "hear our voice," we cry out. Since God is the repository and source of everything, the sovereign of all worlds, there is perfect logic here in so presenting our needy selves to the monarch and prevailing upon the compassionate side of divinity to be good to us. Most versions of this say that God hears "the prayer of Your people Israel," reflecting a traditional perspective on our relationship with God. Many, however, including some older Sephardic *siddurim* as well as modern texts expressing a universalist outlook and more congenial relationship with people who are not Jewish, say instead that God hears the prayer of *kol peh*, "every mouth."

There is more in this blessing than meets the eye, for we do not plead for what we expect will be ours without asking. Speaking this petition implies anxiety about whether or not our prayers will be answered favorably or indeed even heard attentively. Why else do we need to assure ourselves and remind God that "You are the God who hears our prayers and entreaties"? This is not simply a postmodern worry. The same talmudic passages promising that the gates of heartfelt pleas (the gates of tears) are always open also claim that since the fall of the Second Temple the gates of prayer are closed. Marc Brettler points out conflicting passages in the psalms about whether or not God has to be summoned to heed us.[13] For instance, in 4:2 the psalmist implores, "Hear me when I call . . . Have mercy on me and hear my prayer" (*sh'ma t'filati*). In 65:3, however, God is simply called *shome'a t'filah*, "the hearer of prayer."

The language of gates is of course a way of speaking about what "gets through" to whatever makes a difference in what happens. Is it *t'filah* alone, prayer either articulated according to prescriptive forms or formulated silently in our heads, or is it passion strong enough for tears? Our talmudic passages beautifully claim that it is the latter. Citing *1 Samuel* 16: 7, in which God differentiates between appearances that human beings value and the inner nature that God cares about, the talmudic sage Raba says, *Rakhmana libi b'eh*, "The Merciful One requires the heart" (*Sanhedrin 106b*). The *siddur* coalesces the outer words of prayer with the inner urgings of the heart in this culminating plea, the thirteenth and last of the petitions, which speaks with particular and rhythmic urgency that is hard to represent in English translation. The following transliteration of the first half of the blessing is arranged as if it were verse to help us hear that by emphasizing its rhymes, assonance and phrasing.

> *Sh'ma koleynu*
> *Adonai eloheynu.*
> *Khus v'rakheym aleynu*
> *v'kabeyl b'rakhamim*
> *u'v'ratzon et-t'filateynu*
> *ki eyl shomeya t'filot*
> *v'takhanunim atah.*

Hear our voice,
Y-H-V-H our God.
Have mercy and compassion toward us

and accept with mercy
and understanding our prayer,
for You are God who hears prayers
and supplications to You.

In such a passage, printed as a prose paragraph in *siddurim*, we perceive how biblical and rabbinic Hebrew prose takes on qualities we usually associate with poetry; the prose is artfully crafted for sonority as well as meaning. For the services of the Yomim Nora'im these words are often set with a powerfully urgent, pleading melody that responds to the tonal beauty of the words. It is a prayer but one that carries tears inside it.

There are times when we hope, but are not sure, that God is listening, or cares about us. The impulse to cry out, to shout louder, to plead ("Hello! Is Anybody out there? Is Anybody listening? I know you can hear me! You know that you really do care!") may seem futile, rationally preposterous, even infantile. This is not a moment in our conversation to focus on rational explanations or sophisticated theology, the *logos* or reasoning about God, *theos*. It is instead one of those times when we give in to the urge to say, "I need you to listen because this is important to me." The God who hears prayers is the conversational partner who cares enough to listen to what we need. That does not mean that the response will always be exactly what we have requested, or even that the response will be clear to us. In that moment, and for the moment, we feel compelled to speak as if, and this speech-act carries with it the as if of faith. Earlier I wrote about my grandmother's spontaneous addresses to God. I never asked whether she really "believed in" God or, if she did, what her God was like. It was enough to know her "as if."

In order to give the thirteen *bakhashot* (requests) enough attention so that we can appreciate what they allow us to say, we have slowed down time. We have considered these passages as if we could pray them leisurely, giving ourselves the opportunity not only to speak the words but also to think of how they relate to us and even beyond that to contemplate their deeper spiritual significance. Little of that is likely to happen frequently, let alone regularly, especially not on a weekday. One approach that some of us find to be successful at least occasionally is for the leader to call out the theme, not just the name, of each of these prayers, allowing a moment for the congregants to formulate an appropriate request in silence or *sotto voce* themselves, perhaps followed by the leader's public offering of an appropriate prayer. It is an ironic fact that on the days when we have time for thoughtful contemplation of wants and needs, these passages are not recited because on shabbat and festivals we are honoring the day's sanctity by not making personal requests of these sorts, or asking for God more to work on behalf of humankind.

How can we understand the notion of God the Omnipotent resting? Is it possible to reconcile it with the idea that from moment to moment it is God who keeps the world from disintegrating, an idea that seems to preclude rest? A midrash on one of the more mysterious Hebrew terms for God, *el shaddai*, which is often understood as God the Almighty, associates it with the word *dai* (*dalet-yud*) meaning, "sufficient, enough," with which many people are familiar from the rollicking *seder* song "*Dayyenu*," that is, "It would have been enough for us." The midrash explains that *el shaddai* teaches us that God's power is known not only in pouring forth created things but also in knowing when to decide "Enough!," setting limits that will prevent chaos or entropy (*Bereishit Rabbah* 5:8). *El shaddai* is the *el*, the God, *she'omer dai*, who says "Enough!" Without those limits, the process of creating spins ahead with no boundaries. Surely it is not good for cells or atoms to multiply and divide out of control, ceaselessly. We need rain, which might descend for forty days and forty nights and the world will still recover, but it must not go on forever. The builders of the Tower of Babel failed by not knowing when to stop. Moreover, as students of the martial arts must learn, withholding force is also a form of power. An actor will not excel by "chewing the scenery." Controlling the energy, using it in proper measure when appropriate but otherwise holding it in reserve, is artistry, for the contained force has great power. Diastole is essential to providing the atria and ventricles with the blood they require. In the rhythmic pulse of creation, God's resting is the diastole following the systole that pours forth in the making of things. No contraction, no life.

While we recognize that the pace of weekday living does not permit us to immerse ourselves in the *bakhashot* one by one, if we comprehend that we can engage them on a more than superficial level, not just literally offering "lip service," they are available to us when we most need them. As something happens in our life or in the world beyond us, these prayers are like our medicine cabinet. It is good to have one available, but it does us no good unless we know what is in it. We also need to open it from time to time even if we take no medicines regularly to remind ourselves of what resources we have and whether anything has expired. Unless we do so, we cannot know what needs to be refreshed or replenished.

✳ ✳ ✳

From this extended series of petitions or from the benedictions for the Holiness of the Day that replaces them on Shabbat and holidays we turn to the Amidah's concluding set of three blessings. They parallel the opening set of three, completing the Amidah's grand structure. The first of those, *Avot*, recalling the faithfulness of the patriarchs and matriarchs, finds its counterpart in the first of the latter series, recalling the Temple service. The middle blessing of the first group gives thanks for our daily experiences of divine gifts to the world, much as the middle blessing of the last group expresses gratitude for all that we receive; the last of the opening blessings honors the revelation of transcendent holiness, while the last of all these benedictions prays that we all have the blessing of the *or panekha*, the light of the divine countenance revealed through the immanent holiness of the *torat chayyim* (which we can understand as either the <u>living</u> <u>torah</u> or the <u>teaching</u> about <u>life</u>).

The first of these, called *Avodah*, which in this context means "service of worship," may seem strange in a weekday liturgy as it approximates thematically what just preceded it, the *T'filah* blessing entreating that our prayer be heard and answered favorably. The need for it is clearer on Shabbat and festivals because we have not yet expressed this appeal, the formal religious equivalent of the petitioner's closing statement, "Hoping for a favorable reply." Looked at carefully, however, it differs subtly from the *Birkat T'filah*. While the previous one primarily rests its claim on divine compassion and forbearance, the *Avodah* concerns itself mostly with the appropriateness of our service.

> May You graciously and lovingly find us and our prayers acceptable, now and ever. May the service of Your people Israel always seem worthy. Blessed are You, Y-H-V-H, restoring to Zion Your divine Presence.

Caught up as we are in the post-Romantic spirit of individual dignity, many of us find such importunate language difficult to stomach, even if we dutifully recite it. This sort of reaction might distract us from peering through the formal language to recognize what this blessing is really about: the implicit perception that our prayers and worship service might not be exactly what appeal to God. In the years following the Temple's destruction, this prayer perhaps acknowledged a problem of authenticity:, for the liturgy was our surrogate for the Temple-based and sacrificial services instituted through the Torah. Was God disappointedly awaiting the rising smoke from the burnt offerings? Were our substitutions of prayers acceptable?

A substitute is what the liturgy was, insofar as we can take the talmudic sages at their word. When the people Israel were worthy to be reunited with the land Israel, the divine presence would be restored to Zion. One day, the Temple, the House of God, would be rebuilt in the holy city of Jerusalem so that it could become again the dwelling-place of the Shekhinah and therefore the meeting point between earth and heaven, the secular and sacred. Consequently, this *Avodah* blessing in its full traditional wording prays for that reconstruction and along with it the reinstating of the biblically mandated rites, specifically those involving "fire" as Orthodox *siddurim* still say.

Over the course of recent centuries, as the liturgy itself became as institutionalized as the Temple once had been, the nature of the problem has shifted. Now, we are probably more concerned about our attitudes and the substance of our prayers than about whether it is proper for us to practice this form of worship rather than that of our biblical ancestors. We might *davven* regularly, but how often with fire, with burning passion? In truth, the modern concerns were also apprehensions of the ancient sages. The early hassidic rebbe Chaim (Halberstam) of Zanz was asked, "What do you pray for?" He responded, "I pray that I will be able to pray." Often, our state of mind, our purposefulness, our *kavvanah*, is not sufficiently focused for the text we recite to turn into a prayer.

Therefore, the particularity of this prayer need not be a stumbling-block for those who do not respond favorably to its references to the historical city and Temple or the dynastic descendents of King David. In the *Avodah* we pray that our prayers will be "acceptable" because they are the right prayers and offered in the right spirit, ignited and illuminated with the fire of devotion. In longing that the divine presence, the Shekhinah, return to Zion, we hope that the prayers of our people, "Zion" being understood as the whole community of Jews, are suffused with the spirit of true worship.

The second of the concluding three blessings, the *Hoda'ah*, "Gratitude," is so significantly different in structure and phrasing from all the others that it might have been composed separately and inserted here, or else intended as the conclusion to the entire series.[14] While broadly expounding on the theme of God's generous gifts to the world, it also expresses along with our consciousness of them our awareness of our own fragility, a theme that differentiates this from the second blessing, the *Gevurot*.

> Gratefully we give our thanks, Divine Spirit that sustains past, present and future. You are our strength, the shield of our people, generation after generation. Rock of life, our lives are in Your hand, our souls under Your command; Your miracles appear before our eyes wherever we turn; Your wonders and goodness apparent to us morning, noon and night. We thank and praise You, the Source of Compassion, for Your unfailing kindnesses. Praise to You, the gracious One, the Good—may Your Name always be lauded.

Andrew Vogel Ettin

Anyone who has contended with a serious illness, or knows someone who has, anybody who has been to a funeral or even read of a sudden death, is probably aware of having sensed their heart beating and had the disturbing flicker of realization that their life could end in an instant—indeed, at that very instant— and that neither we nor anyone else might be capable of preventing it. Life will be irretrievable, and for that we have no physical remedy. It is out of our hands. Perhaps the sense of mortal vulnerability prompts the accompanying outpouring of gratitude that attests our bountiful awareness of living amid quotidian miracles. On the two post-biblical holidays when we are most conscious of being grateful for God effecting our miraculous deliverance from annihilation, Hanukkah and Purim, this is the point in the daily service when we insert special readings and prayers of gratitude for divine protection of our ancestors and us. That sense is so profound that traditionally we bow in reciting the opening words, *modim anakhnu lakh*.

A bridge between the last two sections of the Amidah is formed by one of the best known biblical formulaic benedictions, *Birkat kohanim*, the Priestly Blessing. A modern translation of *Numbers* 6:24-26 might be,

> May the source of life's goodness bless you and protect you.
> May holiness shine on you and enrich your lives.
> May the sacred ever be before you and bring you peace.

In its fully developed traditional form the giving of the blessing seems highly theatrical. In fact it is known as *dukh'nen*, the *dukh'n* being the platform on which the kohanim stand, as if on stage. A designated congregant calls for the kohanim, who come forth shoeless, ascend the platform, drape their prayershawls to cover their heads and hands as they raise their arms and spread the fingers of both hands in the three-branched pattern resembling the Hebrew letter "*shin*" that viewers of "Star Trek" will remember Mr. Spock using. (That was a contribution from the actor Leonard Nimoy, who recalled it as a powerful symbol from the synagogue he attended as a boy.) They solemnly chant the blessing that is called out for them, word for word, one word at a time, lest they mar the benediction by forgetting something.

Each element has a particular meaning. The fingers form a *shin* because that is the initial letter of the divine name *shaddai* (understood to mean "almighty") as well as the letter placed the outside of a mezuzah and on the sides of the tefillin worn on the head; the *shin* carved into the tablets of the Ten Commandments was also the subject of commentary and wonderment. The head is covered because the priests were required to give their blessing wholeheartedly (*Bemidbar Rabbah 9:4*); and there was concern that they might be distracted by seeing someone to whom they did not extend such generous feelings. Similarly, the people were not to look at the priests, whose hands are covered according to the teaching (*T. Chagigah 16a*) that during the blessing the Shekhina, the holy presence that we dare not gaze upon, became manifest there. The prohibition against looking at the priests during the *dukhanen* has been so strong that some people do not merely avert their eyes but absurdly turn their backs, an unwarranted gesture that vitiates the blessing.

This ceremony is somewhat of a bricolage. The ascent of the *kohenim* onto the platform recalls the historical setting of the Temple, when their blessing concluded the daily morning sacrificial service; the chant *nusach* (melody) is ritualistically solemn and formal. The fingers are configured symbolically to represent an initial letter and recall religious artifacts. The shielding of the priest's head has an ethical purpose, while the hands are cloaked for what is essentially a supernatural reason.

Even while the blessing is being chanted, the non-verbal communication taking place resonates with meanings. The *kohen* who transmits the blessing does not look at the recipients; instead, the blessing flows out to the community with the intention that the generosity is open and unrestricted. Those who receive do not see the faces of the *kohenim* but are conscious of the *tallitot* spread open like the *kanfei ha-sh'khina*, "the wings of the Shekhina" (*T. Shabbat 31a* for instance), emanating the blessing that is not given by the individuals cloaked by the shawls; instead, the *kohenim* are the conduits for channeling it. Ideally, this ritual exemplifies a tacit re-balancing in the asymmetry of the ancient priest-Israelite relationship. The high-status *kohen* performing an exalted function negates himself to be the selfless, ego-less transmitter of generous divine love. The Israelite beneficiary also carries out a necessary function by accepting the blessing, taking a gift without qualm, obligation or embarrassment. Giver and recipient not seeing one another, their relationship is one of mutual reliance and trust; not looking, they implicitly express mutual openness to the other along with modesty toward both the other and toward the sacred conversation taking place between them. They model the exchange that also occurs when *tzedakah* (a charitable contribution) is provided for individuals: in Jewish practice the giver is not to know who the recipient is, and the recipient is not to know who gave. For in this way we guard the privacy of both for the modesty of the giver and the dignity of the receiver.

But what do the words of the blessing really mean? The Hebrew verb forms can denote either a future tense or a desire for something to occur, in other words, either (to stick to familiar wording) "The Lord will bless you" or "May the Lord bless you." The latter seems better grounded theologically: the *kohenim* of old who recited this following the sacrificial services may express the wish that the people will be blessed in return for bringing their gifts and offerings but they cannot make promises on God's behalf.

We can imagine what being blessed means. But what of "keep you"? The second verb, *v'yish-m'recha*, in the King James version "keep," comes from the root *shin-mem-resh* meaning "protect." We meet it in other permutations on Shabbat, for instance in the mystical song *L'kha dodi* ("*shamor v'zakhor*") recalling the fourth of the Ten Commandments in Deuteronomy, and in *V'sham'ru* ("The Israelites shall shield Shabbat"). Wishing that we be protected as well as blessed is a wish that we be fortunate to enjoy our blessings. Like the protective incantation cast over the human couples at the end of *A Midsummer Night's Dream* by Oberon, Titania and their fairies, this benediction (literally, "good saying") asks that we not only receive good things but also that no misfortune befall us, and perhaps that we be shielded from the effects of others' envy. These distinctions appear as well as others in the midrash on Numbers, *Bemidbar Rabbah* already cited, which also suggests that it means we should be "kept" faithful, and kept in God's care in both this and the next world.

Ya-eyr adonai panav eylekha vichunekha, the *kohen* prays. "May you be illuminated by God's face and treated generously." The phrase "Adonai's [the Lord's] face" appears numerous times in the *Tanakh* as an idiom for familiarity with the divine nature. The Hebrew Bible does this longingly, with its fine indifference to systematic theology and the impossibility of imaging God properly in anthropomorphic terms, and regardless of Exodus 33:20 wherein God tells Moses, "No mortal can see my face and

233

live." One especially relevant moment is in the exclamation of Psalm 27, lines 8 and 9,

> *My heart pleads to You, seeks for You, face to face.*
> *Hide not Your face from me, nor angrily push Your servant away.*

The *Birkat kohanim* speaks not of intimate familiarity face to face (*panim al panim*) with God but rather of enjoying radiant illumination and the experience of divine grace, like Moses' radiant face when he descends from Mount Sinai or emerges from the tabernacle: the Hebrew *y'eyr* beginning the second line derives from *or,* "light," and the English "graciously" from Latin *gratias,* thanks. The wish, in other words, is that one gratefully knows oneself beloved of the highest and deepest power, that which we call God. This need to be loved and know that one is loved is the profound human desire expressed in other contexts in the poem "Dreams" by Anne Brontë, "To know myself beloved at last." Raymond Carver similarly writes in his "Late Fragment" of the satisfying gift "To feel myself beloved on the earth." Such knowledge prepares us for the blessing's conclusion, wishing that we be confident of secure acceptance by the goodness of the sacred, and therefore be at peace.

One Amidah blessing remains, a multisection blessing for peace. I suggested that this parallels the third opening blessing, the *Kedushah,* albeit on a more worldly plane; for the one celebrates the sublime holiness of the divine itself, the source of all life and spirit, while the second longingly yearns for the divine gift of peace on earth equivalent to the transcendent peace divinely established in the cosmos. It may be that our sense of the universe is less harmoniously tranquil than our ancestors' was, for we know about exploding comets, dying stars, supernovas

234

and black holes. Yet the planets and constellations we have observed for centuries nevertheless remain in more orderly relation to their neighbors than nations generally manage to do for more than a few years or decades, and intergalactic wars are as far as we can tell the product of science fiction writers projecting onto the cosmos-scape the violent competitions with which we human beings are too familiar.

It is on this blessing for peace that the entire Amidah not merely closes but comes to rest, for this anchors the entire series. We can even say that it reveals the spine of the prayers. The word *shalom* (*shin-lamed-vav-mem*) designates peace that is more than the absence of hostility; it is also the presence of tranquility. Its near neighbor *shaleym* (*shin-lamed-mem*) means whole, undamaged, complete. Everything for which we have given blessings, both the petitions for what we desire and the gratefulness for what we have received, points toward these qualities of peacefulness and wholeness.

We want to be at one with our past, the world around us, the transcendent glory and majesty of creative energy, time and timelessness. We want all of our various needs met, the spiritual as well as the physical, aware that dissatisfactions with our life and lot are disruptive in themselves and the stimulus to conflict with others. We want to sense that we and our lives matter to something deep within our universe. We want to feel that we have cause for boundless gratitude and that we can express our gratefulness authentically, generously, unconstrained and without doubts, resentments or misgivings, sensing ourselves as whole, complete, and at peace. That is why we reach this prayer only after we have opened ourselves to the expansive gratitude of the preceding *Hoda'ah*, knowing that there is nothing left to want other than that profound, harmonious *shalom*.

Andrew Vogel Ettin

In redacting the prayerbook, the rabbis of earlier times had two prayers for peace available to them that were each so beautiful that the sages could not choose one over the other. Faced with this embarrassment of riches, they included both, apparently arbitrarily assigning *Shalom rav,* "abundant peace," to the evening service and *Sim shalom,* "give peace," to the morning, though nothing inherent in the texts would make one or the other more appropriate to its time of day.

A silent prayer for personal peace follows in many editions of the liturgy. Originally formulated for his own use by Mar bar Ravina in the 5th century C.E., *Elohai n'tzor,* is intended to be private (though it has been set to music for public use) and it may be replaced by your own meditation or prayer. The personal character reveals itself in the first word: not "our God," *eloheynu,* but "my God," *elohai.* There is much psychological insight behind this prayer, in which we ostensibly talk to God but are truly counseling ourselves. We recognize that we lack tranquility when we feel tense, hostile, anxious or defensive in our relations with other people. This negativity is something that we can strive to alleviate, unlike many other problems that, being more global or systemic, are beyond our control. In calling for God's help, we admit that we need to have a higher standard of emotional equilibrium than we usually set for ourselves in normal daily practice. Again, "God" need not be "the old man in the sky" but, better, our highest version of who we would like to be.

> My God, restrain my tongue from trouble-making and
> my lips from speaking falsely. May my soul be calm
> when others malign me; may I be unassuming toward
> all. Open my heart to Your Torah; inspire my spirit to
> pursue your *mitzvot;* and thwart the designs of any who

intend my harm. For Your own glory, answer my behest; protect and save those who revere and trust in You.

The word translated here as "trouble-making" is *ra* (*resh-ayin*), which is usually translated as "evil," as in "the evil eye" or "the evil impulse." To rabbinic tradition, however, the *yetzer ha-ra* is more complex than suggested by a term like "the evil spirit," which is likely to bring to mind a malignant figure from a horror movie or the little red pitchfork-wielding devil perched on the left shoulder while the good angel encourages us on the right. Were it not for that instinct of *yetzer ha-ra*, they say, hens wouldn't lay an egg (*Yoma 69b*). It is the *yetzer ha-ra* that inspires us to build a house, marry, have children, and compete in business (*Kohelet Rabbah 3:15*). We might say that more generally this *yetzer* is the stimulus to make changes, stir things up, not be complacent. Therefore the negative expression of this inclination is not deeply malevolent as is usually believed; rather, it is to stir things up in a way that causes trouble. We need to be reminded, at least by saying it to ourselves, that the same mouth that has spoken in praise can also speak to cause harm, and it can speak lies. We cannot keep others from maligning us, even in a litigious society in which people are quick to sue one another; but we can hope that their attempts to damage us will not work; more practically, we can also govern how we react to this in our social contacts and within our souls.

As a coda to this part of the Amidah the redactors of the liturgy placed the text that Rabbi Yohanan used after praying, Psalm 19, verse 15, *Yi-h'yu l'ratzon imrey fee v'hegyon libee l'fanekha adonai tzuree v'go-alee*, "May the words from my mouth and the thoughts in my heart be acceptable before You, Y-H-V-H, my Rock and my Deliverance." There is surely a valid point to the

Andrew Vogel Ettin

question raised in the Talmud (*T Ber. 9b*): since this text works just as well prior to our prayers, why save it for afterward? One sage replies cleverly there that David first wrote eighteen other psalms, therefore it makes sense to recite this passage from Psalm 19 after the eighteen blessings of the Amidah. His almost flip-pant-sounding response indicates that there is no better answer. In other words, it was basically a matter of taste; Rabbi Yohanan loved both texts and found them suitable in this order as door-ways in and out of the Amidah. Obviously the early liturgists felt that a meditative prayer was needed to signal the ending of the Amidah; since the optative character of this verse makes it well suited as an envoy to accompany our prayer offering, and it ends with affirmations of our surety about God's constancy and saving grace, it serves as an apt penultimate wish.

The finale to the entire Amidah is provided by a much-loved statement that has been set to various singable melodies. Our version of the text includes a universalizing wish for every-thing that dwells on Earth (*v'al kol yoshvey teyveyl*).

> *Oh-seh shalom bi-m'ro-mav*
> *hu ya'asey shalom*
> *aleynu v'al kol yisrael*
> *v'al kol yoshvey teyveyl,*
> *v'im'ru ameyn.*
> Maker of peace in the firmament, work peace among us, among all of Israel and all that inhabit the earth, and we say, Amen.

The lesson to be learned from uttering these sentiments at this point in the sequence of prayer is that our personal comfort or spiritual harmony is not the last word. We remember to pray on behalf of the needs of those who share our religion and tradi-

238

tion; yet our prayers should also acknowledge that we are not, as the villainous Haman implies in the Purim story of *Esther*, a people separate from the rest of the society or even the rest of the world. When nations are not at peace, when human beings are not at peace with nature, neither can *kol yisrael*, "all of Israel," know genuine peace. That is one of the inescapable lessons that has ironically accompanied the development of the modern state of Israel, though we should not forget that it was at least as true of the biblical one, so often caught between warring empires, torn by internal antagonisms and ambitions, and susceptible to plagues, droughts and famines, as the *Tanakh* and talmudic literature repeatedly attest.

❋ ❋ ❋

One major prayer follows the Amidah, or two when we have a minyan. Either or both of them can function for us as a meditative conclusion to prayer even if we follow halakhah by not reciting the second, the Kaddish, aloud when we pray without a minyan. As one of them is potentially controversial and the other often misunderstood, we will give them some attention in order to approach them with better appreciation.

The first of these declares, *Aleynu l'shabeyakh l'adon ha-kol*, "It is up to us to praise the sovereign of everything." Its antiquity along with its foundational meaning is attested by the traditions that ascribe its origin to the biblical Joshua or the talmudic-era redactor of the Rosh Hashanah service, Rava. The grand arc of this prayer takes us from the opening section extolling the divine majesty that from the beginning stretched forth the heavens and brought the Earth into being to its concluding words taken from the prophet Zechariah (*14:9*) promising a time when God's oneness will be universally accepted. Set in the last half of the twentieth century to easily sung melodies that have proven infectious

239

even when not always appropriate to the sentiments of the text, *Aleynu* lends itself to enthusiastic congregational singing of the Hebrew words that overrides the meaning, about which many attendees at the service are not aware until the passage is read in English rather than sung in the original.

We will return to the motifs described above after considering the sections most difficult for many modern Jews. These passages not only emphasize the uniqueness of Jews but ascribe exclusive and triumphal purpose to that. "You [God] have not made us like the other peoples of the earth or given us a place in life like theirs, or a destiny like theirs, for which we bow in thanks." We pray to Y-H-V-H [Adonai] in the traditional text that "idols" will be removed and "false gods" obliterated, that everyone will know that "to You every knee must bend and every tongue swear loyalty" so that "all will accept the yoke of your kingdom." Such sentiments were understandable enough at a time when monotheistic Judaism struggled to survive amid polytheistic yet nonetheless nationalistic and tribal deities, and even during the subsequent centuries as Christianity attempted to delineate a concept of a triune God. They have since seemed disturbing enough that most non-Orthodox prayerbooks over the past two centuries (and even some traditional earlier ones) have edited the original or shaped the translation to make the ideas in *Aleynu* more palatable to modern and diaspora sensibilities. A version in the Reform *Gates of Prayer* offers, "Then will false gods vanish from our hearts," suggesting that the problems does not reside in other peoples' objects of worship but in our own inclination to devote ourselves to something other God, perhaps wealth, prestige, knowledge, pleasure or fame. An insightful, simple approach has been offered by R. Zalman Schachter-Shalomi who substitutes at two crucial places in the first paragraph the Hebrew

240

homophone *lamed-vav cholem* for *lamed-aleph*, both pronounced "loh," thereby turning the phrase "has <u>not</u> made us" into "has made us <u>His</u>" along with all the other nations and peoples.

Much of our difficulty in these passages comes from the earlier generations (whether that of Joshua at the fall of Jericho or Rava in post-Second Temple times or a composite of anonymous sources) interpreting an ideal vision of the future in the sociopolitical terms that were shaped by their immediate contexts. For our understandings of the world have been colored by our experiences of many other other nations, cultures, ideologies and religions so certain of their transcendent truths that they would wipe out everyone else's "idols" and "false gods" in the name of their Truth or the purity of the race. To the rabbis and sages, effectively the community leaders, who shaped this text and brought into the standing structure of daily prayers, the most relevant frame of reference was politics. God, who (or which) cannot be really understood totally and therefore could be partially understood and misunderstood in many ways, was most conveniently imagined as king of kings because they lived and frequently were oppressed under the reign of human monarchs. To kings, one bends the knee, swears loyalty, and accepts the ox's yoke of burdens. That was their frame of reference; it need not be ours. Shifting the paradigm (as R. Schachter-Shalomi has said) may help us do something more than re-tune the disquieting language; it may help us re-imagine what this prayer really offers to our hopes for the future but in terms closer to our contemporary vision.

Perhaps the opening lines of *Bereishit* (Genesis) have become so familiar that we do not recognize the great leap of understanding contained in them. As we experience our world, it is very easy to see everything in it as discreet, separate. Here are birds, here are fish, here a mountain, there an ocean; here is a leopard, there a stone, here a human being, there a tree. Perceiving them as separate, we can imagine their own gods: the thunder god, the river god, the mountain god, the underworld god and so on. Each might go his or her own way; they might have competing agendas; they might coexist in tension rather than cooperation with one another. Regardless of how or when or where it came about, the imaginative grasp of an essential oneness at the core of everything and a coherent process of cosmic development is extraordinarily exciting. We today understand these at least partly in terms of concepts such as the "Big Bang" theory, molecular structure, DNA and other discoveries of science which lead us to perceive commonalities in the universe. We human beings indeed share primal matter with all other living creatures, with the dust of the earth and with the stars. We came about late in the developmental process (biblically, on the "sixth day" or stage) because the logic of the physical universe required so many preconditions for vegetable and animal life, each of those starting from the initial expanding pulse of light. We are just beginning to grasp as a species what it means to live with the interconnectedness of whales and rain forests, icecaps and agriculture on our own planet, not to mention the significance of volcanoes and water channels on other planets. We have yet to learn how to live well and wholly, or holy, with these and with our human neighbors of other tongues and customs.

A beautiful quotation in *Aleynu* from *Deut. 4:39* hints at this deep meaning, "Know today, and take it to your heart, that Y-H-V-H is God in heaven above and on the earth beneath; there is none other." The last clause is simply two words in Hebrew, *eyn ohd*. In context, the translation just given is the probable one. However, grammatically *eyn ohd* can have a different, far more radical meaning: There is nothing else. That is the way that it is understood in (for instance) Hassidism, by the Jewish mystics, and in Jewish Renewal, as a panentheistic insight: There is nothing other than God.

This comprehension is what is meant by understanding the oneness of God. *Y'hye Adonai echad,* "Y-H-V-H will be one," that is, the separable dimensions of physicality and spirituality, thinking and feeling, intention and actuality, timelessness and the moment, that comprise the eternal divine—"God" that we call Yud-Hey-Vav-Hey to express the coalescence of all these dimensions and more—will be understood as unified. *U-sh'mo echad,* "And God's [His] name shall be one" acknowledges that so long as God is known by different names, human understanding will misperceive the unity. It also implies that when we come to the ultimate stage of comprehension, even "Adonai" or the mysterious Y H V H formulation will dissolve, for the only name that will seem suitable in speaking of God will be *Echad,* "One." That is the lesson of *Aleynu.*

The second of the concluding prayers is the best-known prayer in our liturgy (the *Sh'ma* not really being a prayer so much as an affirmation of belief). This is the *Kaddish.* Five forms of the Kaddish have been transmitted; the one at the end of the service which is the most familiar version is the *Kaddish yatom* or "Orphan's Kaddish," which is usually called "Mourner's Kaddish" because it is recited on behalf of one's sibling, spouse, child, or either parent, regardless of whether or not they were Jewish, and not exclusively by orphans. This is what most people think of when they mention "the Kaddish" and assume that it is a prayer for the dead. The other versions differ according to phrases or paragraphs that are shuttled in or out of the basic text. The *Kaddish de-rabbanan* or Scholars' Kaddish which might be the original form, concludes a session of study; the *Kaddish Shaleym* ("Full") and *Hatzi* ("Partial") *Kaddish* end sections of worship services; the fifth version, the Burial Kaddish, which we are unlikely to experience outside of Orthodox funerals, adds to the opening paragraph phrases anticipating the resurrection of the dead.

Sometimes referred to as a doxology (a theological teaching) and traditionally requiring a minyan, the Kaddish in its various forms attests verbally to the supreme magnificence of God, which is to say the awesome greatness of the unfathomable source- and-coherence of the cosmos that seems to dwell at the core of existence. Knowing that we cannot express this in words, we nonetheless accumulate words that attempt to say it all by accumulating predicates in praise of God's incomparable grandeur. That purpose and the strong rhythmic pulse of the Aramaic set by the opening words probably account for the text taking on so many uses in the worship service, being inserted in its *Hatzi* and *Shaleym* versions for the congregation to recite at the ends of liturgical segments in the way that symphonic composers use rhythmic orchestral *tutti* passages at the ends of movements. The more traditional the liturgy used in a congregation, the more often we are likely to encounter each of the four synagogal versions in one service.

It is customary that only people observing a year of mourning or a *yahrzeit* (anniversary of a death) stand and recite the Mourner's Kaddish, but this custom has become subject to many congregational variations. Particularly in the wake of the Shoah, which so devastated entire families that none of the siblings, parents, children or spouses survived to say Kaddish for the deceased, some congregations have adopted the practice of everyone standing and reciting it. Another variant is to have all say Kaddish but only the mourners stand. As the list of deaths that occurred during the year and the yahrzeits currently observed may be read before Mourner's Kaddish, some of us welcome those observing a mourning period to rise when their relative's name is read; we may ask for any other names that should be mentioned that are not on the congregation's list before welcoming others who customarily stand for Kaddish to do so as we begin the recitation, which may be chanted though it is more often simply read. Most prayerbooks, even Orthodox, supply transliterations of the Kaddish, for we know that some who never otherwise attend the synagogue may do so for this purpose alone.

More than most parts of the service, the Mourner's Kaddish entails considerable sensitivity about other people's feelings. After leading a service in a Reform synagogue where the custom (*minchag*) was for everyone to rise and recite this prayer, I stopped to speak to a young woman whose father had died recently in another part of the country. She told me how much she valued having been in her father's more liturgically conservative synagogue where only she and other mourners rose and recited Kaddish, thereby having their time of personal loss noticed by the congregation and accorded particular respect during the week following his burial. Seeing that she had stood, people in that synagogue who did not know her approached to offer condolences. In our community she was relatively new and not well known, and as she had changed her surname at marriage, the family name read from the list was not the same as hers. Few people were aware that this person standing near to them had recently suffered a great loss because everyone was standing for kaddish. Here, in her own congregation, she felt that her fresh grief had become invisible in the practice followed by everyone as a matter of form simply because "Please rise" was a standing order before the Kaddish.

The requirement that Kaddish be recited in the presence of a *minyan* ought to have protected her from just that feeling of being alone and unnoticed in her sorrow. Yet this community's custom had arisen with the best of intentions during World War II, when just as members were gathering to welcome Shabbat, news arrived that a young member had been killed in military service. At the Kaddish, the grieving congregation rose and recited it together with his family and continued the practice of standing when the obligatory year of mourning ended but the war did not. Thus it became their custom, all the more meaningful when details of the Shoah emerged, and it was preserved after the original reason was remembered by almost no-one. Ironically, the generously caring practice worked in the opposite way for the person who lamented that her individual bereavement went unrecognized. However, in some congregations the invitation for those observing a mourning period to rise is totally ignored even when they are obviously present. Asked why, they are likely to say that they don't like to call attention to themselves, don't want people "looking at them." The offer is nevertheless worth making even when people do not want (or do not yet want) to accept it. It is easier for someone to decline an invitation than to apologize to the person who wanted to be invited and was not.

Moving from the Mourner's Kaddish to anything else tends to be an awkward, often jarring transition, for the congregation expects familiar signals that the service is over. Is there a closing song? The congregational president's announcements of news and activities? A request for everyone to move into the social hall for refreshments? A reminder of the starting time of the next service? All are anticlimactic.

Because of this, and despite halakhah, there is deep value to continuing in a private, personal kaddish. This might actually work best regarding the people for whom we are not obligated to recite the prayer: perhaps a more distant relative, a friend or teacher, someone who was not central in our life but who does hold a significant place in our memory. We might take a moment after praying to allow such a figure to appear to us, or to hear their name or voice in our inner ear. In that memorial moment, consider what you recall, what their legacy is in your life. Remember them into the world that they no longer inhabit in their body. This might be the opportunity to say thanks that we feel we never properly communicated when they walked with us.

If this is a service in which a portion (*parashah*) of the Torah has been read, and perhaps also the haftarah (the associated passage from the Prophets), maybe they have been not merely declaimed in Hebrew but *leyned*, chanted according to traditional *trop* or pneum markings found in some printed texts, and using particular melodic patterns that developed decades or centuries ago in various communities. Such cantillation, which laypeople along with rabbis may learn as a special skill, has intrinsic value as an authentic, ancient Jewish art form, along with being mnemonically helpful, as most people find that it is easier to remember a song than a speech. Moreover, it moves the reading of the biblical text from mundane speech, from mere narrative and instruction, to musical poetry, more accurately reflecting its nature. As musical poetry it is also more evidently open to multiple levels of understanding and more varied techniques of interpretation. If the reader has sufficient spiritual authority along with imagination, the method of leyning itself can become a form of interpretation. Perhaps the reader can vocally suggest the different voices in the passage so that it comes dramatically clear. Maybe a section can be chanted *sotto voce* to evoke our own reticence in transmitting that particular text, for instance the passage in *Deuteronomy* 20: 12-18 mandating the destruction of the indigenous Canaanites. Leyning that passage myself, I have done so in *Eicha* trop, the melodic mode used for chanting Lamentations on Tisha b'Av, connecting that memory of Jewish suffering with the biblical commandment dictating and presaging the suffering of others. We can, in short, combine the artistry of reading the text with the ethics of interpreting it.

✳ ✳ ✳

The Talmud, commenting on the mishnaic passage we cited earlier claiming that the earlier pietists would prepare for an hour before prayer to focus their attention on God, adds that they would "pray for an hour and then wait again for an hour" (*Berakhot 32b*). The sages also claim that these exemplars would therefore spend nine hours in prayer. Cited in this way, these figures not only arouse wonderment from the modern reader; they clearly did so even in mishnaic times. Perhaps this is an instance, familiar enough, of romanticizing some previous generation, usually two steps removed from our own, that embodied all that we find lacking in ours. There were spiritual giants walking the earth in those days, we imagine. Perhaps so; or perhaps we project onto their lives the deep snows and vast journeys of yesteryear. Certainly we overlook all that was difficult and unpleasant for them and perhaps also in them.

Still, the passage is less remarkable for what it says about the piety of the earlier generation than for the balance of time that it propounds. We would assume that prayer itself would be most important and therefore take the greatest amount of time. Here we find instead that it is only one-third of what is ideal. <u>The preparation and the sequel are each equally important.</u> That is not at all what we would expect; it is certainly not the experience of most modern synagogue attendees. Prayer itself, in other words, is only part of what we might call the process of prayer. We take an hour to make the journey, an hour to linger at our destination (maybe it is a hilltop, wooded grove, cave or island), and then an hour to return; the trip is the entire event, the going and coming as well as being there.

What seems most unexpected is the last item in the talmudic reference, the hour after prayer. We easily fathom why it takes an hour of preparation to clear and focus our mind and move us to a state of concentrated devotion before prayer. That also slows our pace of thought and speech. It does not stretch probability to speculate that perhaps the *hassidim ha-rishonim*, "early pietists," had developed meditative techniques to prepare them for prayer, in which case the preliminary period might also have slowed their heart rates and breathing. An hour at prayer would therefore not seem excessive. However, we might not expect to take an hour as well at the latter end. The Talmud says nothing about what happened during that third hour. Maybe, given that they were reporting the practices of an admired generation long gone, they no longer knew. Was it a period for reflection and "processing," a time to mull what they had prayed for, what the prayers meant to them in that moment, how to bring them into the day's living? Was it a period of what an athlete or dancer might call "cooling down," letting the "muscles" of the praying mind and body return to a normal state of mind for the work to follow?

As the Talmud has not handed us a detailed agenda, we should trust our own experiences to help us here, albeit guided by this insight that what happens after prayer is as important, as necessary, as the prayer itself and what precedes it. As we go to work or school or start the chores for the day, we prepare ourselves. What is on the schedule today? What requires the greatest attention and time? What is the order of the day? What do I need, materially and emotionally? When we journey home and sit down at the end of the day, sometimes we are drained. What we most need is to be quiet and allow our exhausted bodies to recuperate or let the swirling emotions settle. Other times, we want to review, analyze, remember. We not only spend time preparing for a vacation trip and have the time away; we then take time afterward to sort through the memories and the photos, as well as tell others about it.

This stage is forgotten in prayer life today, though traditional *siddurim* contain so many concluding prayers and meditations that we might suspect they reflect a reluctance to leave prayer to begin the day's tasks. Having taken some minutes, let alone an hour, for a morning prayer, we must rush at once to do what else is required of us. If we have prayed at the synagogue on shabbat, we hasten to the *oneg* table for pastry and conversation. In normal circumstances, someone lingering to sit alone in the sanctuary reflecting after a service might be deemed in urgent need of pastoral intervention along with being an impediment to closing the place on time. True, some *siddurim* designed for Orthodox or other traditionalist worship have texts available for individual use after prayer, such as Maimonides' Thirteen Principles of Faith. However, reading another time-honored rabbinic passage appointed for us to study from the prayerbook does not seem to be what could most benefit us at this moment. *Psalm 46:11* tells us, "Be still, and know that I am God" (*har'pu u-d'u kee-anokhee eloheem*). Will our synagogue allow us simply to sit and be still?

What do you need? Each in our ways, we should guard against closing our hearts and souls too quickly. We need that time to reflect, recapitulate, descend, unwind. If we are so inclined, we could use a journal to record our insights, impulses and impressions, not a diary of our busy-ness but a journal of our inner travels. The journal might take form not through words but as a sketchbook, a collage, a sculpture or canvas, a dance or musical composition. That "book" each of us makes ourselves.

✳ ✳ ✳

Bereishit / To begin with

At the start, I wrote that "This is not THE book on Jewish worship." It seems fitting that the end should really be the beginning of another chapter, which you will write for yourself. You might do it in words, but it is more important that you do it through practice. This book will be successful if it stimulates your discoveries, insights, moments of illumination, especially when you are able to transmit and share them.

Remember, even when it is difficult to do so, that a problem can be an opportunity. George Balanchine's adventures in choreographing his wonderful *Serenade* are inspirational. One of the unforgettable images in *Serenade* is an opening tableau of seventeen ballerinas arranged diagonally in five rows, the middle one of five ranks and, on either side of it, two rows with three dancers each. Asked how he came up with this strange, striking pattern, Balanchine pragmatically answered, "I had seventeen dancers, not sixteen." If he had one more or one fewer, he explained, he would have arranged them in two equal rows. The odd number presented an opportunity that he did not miss. In rehearsal, a dancer slipped and fell; Balanchine kept the fall as part of his choreography. The congregation I wrote about in Chapter Two did not preserve the "ritual" by which the Torah crown repeatedly knocked the cover off of the thermostat but, stimulated by these accidents, it invented a better one.

We don't always have exactly what we anticipated or planned for, but we do have opportunities unlooked for. I filled in for a vacationing rabbi during the full intensity of a Southern summer, the air so palpable and weighty that to go outside meant to feel the humidity drape across your shoulders like a woolen tallit, so the attendance at a particular Friday night service was awkwardly scanty. Scattered about the sanctuary were two widows sitting together, an unmarried older woman, two other women whose husbands were traveling on business, a widower in his eighties, an unmarried middle-aged man, three families with their young children, two female members of my family, and six visiting high school students, one of whom turned out to be Jewish. The reading for that shabbat happened to be—though Isaac Bashevis Singer claimed that "coincidence" is not a Jewish word, so it did not just happen but it was *bashert*, destined, that the reading should be—*Numbers 26-29*, a section including the story of Zeloph'chad's daughters, extraordinarily all of them named in the Torah (27: 1). Machlah, Noah, Hoglah, Milkhah and Tirzah stand before Moses, before Eleazar the priest, before the whole assembly to request that their father's inheritance be shared amongst them despite the law saying nothing about women inheriting, as he had no sons. This night they are also before me, asking something simpler but much the same: Notice us; let us present our story, our plea before this assembly; deal justly with us. I try. Because of the mix of people attending, I set aside my prepared d'rash to teach less formally.

Unexpectedly, I recall a midrash on the two verses right before their tale begins, *Numbers 26: 64-5*, which say that "not a man" (*lo haya ish*) had survived from the generation that Moses enumerated at Sinai other than Joshua and Kaleb. The men died, but according to the commentary, the women lived because they preserved law and virtue. When I first saw that interpretation, it seemed only to express the conventional attitude that women embody piety; but that night in that congregation, another reading took shape. Zeloph'chad's daughters strove for justice through a way of peace. The five sisters, not fighting one another for individual gain but united for their common good, turned the establishment's tools against it, wedging a place for themselves in a tightly constructed edifice of male-centered wealth, privilege and dynasty, and thereby making a place for other women. Moses, stumped, communes with God and returns to announce that yes, indeed, in the absence of sons, daughters inherit from their father. These women used (here I adopt Audre Lorde's terms) the master's tools and therefore cannot dismantle the master's house. But instead, they can claim for themselves what God lets Moses know they deserve, the equivalent of Virginia Woolf's "room of one's own, and five hundred pounds a year." They will survive. Something of this gets said. My daughter smiles and raises her eyebrows in approval. Two of the older women turn to one another, nodding.

May it be your blessing to find what you need when you need it, to use your opportunities and to have a community that welcomes them. May you and they find ethical meaning within long-established rituals and language. May you be inspired by new rituals and language. May you celebrate with joy and spirituality in the service of beauty.

For Further Discoveries

Availability of books, recordings and internet resources gives us unprecedented access today to Jewish resources worldwide. Here are just a few suggestions for expanding on what you have found in this book. Most of the authors are rabbis active as teachers, liturgists and spiritual leaders.

The teachings of Zalman Schachter-Shalomi, familiarly known as Reb Zalman, have inspired many innovations and innovators of contemporary Judaism seeking to connect modern practice with traditional resources. His publications retain the oral sensibilities of a learned guide who is also a raconteur, adding special value to his recordings and DVDs. *Jewish With Feeling: A Guide to Meaningful Jewish Practice* (New York, 2005) is a fine introduction to renewing one's own Judaism and to the movement known as Jewish Renewal, based on his idea that we are developing a new paradigm of Jewish observance for the modern era. *Wrapped in Holy Flame* (San Francisco, 2003) transmits a packed treasury of Hassidic wisdom transformed by Reb Zalman's contemporary outlook on spirituality and practice.

Reb Zalman and many of those taught and inspired by him are associated with Aleph: Alliance for Jewish Renewal. The organization's website, www.aleph.org, is an excellent starting place for further discovery. Especially notable are the training courses and retreats available through Aleph at many locations. The Reb Zalman Legacy Project, www.rzlp.org, offers a portal to his works in various media.

Andrew Vogel Ettin

The Path of Blessing (Woodstock, VT, 2003) by Marcia Prager is an ideal work for developing an understanding of Jewish prayer, the practice of blessing and our relation to God, based on six little words, those Hebrew words that begin most benedictions. Engagingly written, it is accessible to a novice yet thought-provoking for experienced practitioners. Those with more detailed interest in liturgy will be stimulated by the series *My People's Prayer Book* (Woodstock, VT, 1997-2007), whose principal editor is Lawrence Hoffman, a major authority on liturgical history and practice. Jack Kessler's recordings include an excellent series demonstrating the appropriate *nusach* for all services and holidays.

Arthur Waskow's *Seasons of Our Joy* (Boston, 1982) remains the text I consult most often for information and inspiration on Jewish holidays, as it offers in one compact volume everything from historical and biblical contexts to suggestions for creative celebrations, and recipes as well. His Shalom Center (www.shalomcenter.org) is devoted to social justice across a broad spectrum of concerns; he is also the editor of a two-volume anthology *Torah of the Earth* containing thematically arranged traditional and contemporary texts on ecology and the environment.

Shefa Gold's *Torah Journeys* (Teaneck, NJ, 2006), part of a sequence of her stimulating works, opens an inner dimension of each week's Torah reading for individual spiritual exploration. In addition, her recordings of original songs and chants (the latter based on biblical texts) are among the more inspiring expressions of Jewish music for worship and meditation.

The rich contemporary soundscape of Jewish music includes klezmer, Hassidic, Sephardic and Mizrachi influences, among others, including hiphop and classical minimalism, often in creative fusion. The span is suggested in recordings of traditional songs by groups like Voice of the Turtle, Altramar and The Klezmer Conservatory Band or original compositions by cantors such as Richard Kaplan and Jack Kessler and classically trained composers or performers including Steve Reich, John Zorn and David Krakauer.

Those who want a good understanding of the history and theory of kabbalah are faced with a bewildering array of books, not all of them reliable. Two that are especially worthwhile and complementary in their approaches are Byron L. Sherwin's *Kabbalah: An Introduction to Jewish Mysticism* and David Ariel's *Kabbalah: The Mystic Quest in Judaism* (both, Lanham, Md., 2006). Arthur Green's compact study *A Guide to the Zohar* (Stanford, 2004) is focused on that text and associated with Daniel Matt's superb ongoing translation of the *Zohar*. Any of Green's books are self-recommending; his *Ehyeh: A Kabbalah for Tomorrow* relates kabbalah to contemporary issues. As an intellectual historian, Byron Sherwin is also concerned with connecting traditional texts to contemporary concerns; among his many books, *Jewish Ethics for the Twenty-First Century: Living in the Image of God* (Syracuse, NY, 2000) is especially stimulating. The Spertus Institute of Jewish Studies (www.spertus.edu) in Chicago, at which Sherwin is a vice-president and professor, offers both onsite and distance-learning programs, including graduate degree courses, of high quality.

Notes

1   See "True Colors," Matthew Gurewitch, *Smithsonian Magazine*, July 2008.

2   Till Janczukowicz , "Richter the Master," vol. 3, Decca 4758130.

3   *Dynamic Judaism* (New York: 1985), 197.

4   Dramatists Play Service, New York, 1992, 49

5   James Oestreich, NYTimes, Oct. 21, 2007, "Grown-Up Enough for Beethoven," http://www.nytimes.com/2007/10/21/arts/music/21oest.html

6   *The Creative Habit* (New York: 2003), 78.

7   As we recall from *Tu b'shevat*, "15" would not be written this way; but *yud* normally equals 10 and *hey* 5.

8   Gian-Carlo Menotti, *The Consul* (G. Schirmer, New York: 1950), 41.

9   *The Creative Habit*, 146.

10   See for instance Ellenson and Falk in Lawrence J. Hoffman, ed. *My People's Prayerbook* (Woodstock, VT: 1998), *vol. 2,*, 52.

11   José Limón, *An Unfinished Memoir* (Middletown, CT: 1998), 1.

12   *My People's Prayerbook,vol. 2,* 85

13   *My People's Prayer Book, vol. 2,* 146

14   Brettler in *My People's Prayer Book, 2,* 164

Raymond Carver's "Late Fragment" appears in his *All of Us: The Collected Poems* (New York: 2000), 294.

CPSIA information can be obtained
at www.ICGtesting.com
Printed in the USA
LVHW021336150722
723529LV00004B/202